CW01082127

CONTINUUM ADVANCES IN RELIGIOUS STUDIES

Series Editors:

GREG ALLES, JAMES COX, PEGGY MORGAN

Continuum Advances in Religious Studies:

Contemporary Western Ethnography and the Definition of Religion, M.D. Stringer
A New Paradigm of Spirituality and Religion, MaryCatherine Burgess
Religion and the Discourse on Modernity, Paul-François Tremlett

Contents

Acknowledgements

No words can adequately express my gratitude to the many people who have helped and supported me in this process. However, I still want to say thank you to Professor James Cox for his guidance and encouragement and to Professor William Gillies, who reminded me in 2001 that I was on an adventure. I am grateful to Peter Bell, my Chaplaincy colleagues and friends, the Church of the Holy Girlfriends in Omaha and Edinburgh, Richard Roberts, Joyce Rupp, Dale Stover, Mike Lawler and Robin Russel for their steady support and encouragement.

Particular thanks go to Kate Langton and Fiona MacAulay for their wonderful support and outstanding skills in helping me put this book into final form and to Ashley Theunissen and Rónán Daly for their help with the index. You were lifesavers! In addition, I give thanks to friends Sue and Ernest Haffke for letting me stay in their home and write while they were away. Heartfelt thanks also goes to Ramona Hunt, another dear friend who welcomed me into her home, baked my birthday cake, and enabled another 'cave' experience while I worked steadily to complete all my writing. Friends and family on both sides of the pond served as caring midwives for me in completing this book.

I am grateful for the generosity of all who participated in my field research. Thank you for trusting me with your life stories.

Finally, I honour my parents, grandparents and other ancestors who made it possible for me to experience the world as I do. They and the Board of Directors for White Buffalo Associates have both inspired me and given me the strength, vision and joy needed to travel this amazing life path.

Dedicated to my son Sean and the next Seven Generations

Chapter One

Religion, Spirituality and Contemporary Shamanic Practice in Scotland – Exploring the Relationships

The Religion/Spirituality Dilemma

Religion, spirituality, and their relationship to each other are centre-stage in a transformational shift in consciousness occurring globally and serving as a primary catalyst for a new paradigm of spirituality and religion currently emerging in the West. It is urgent that this process be understood because tension caused by this shift has erupted into waves of violence sweeping across the Western world in the name of religion and belief. How do these phenomena relate to *shamanism*, especially contemporary shamanic practice in Scotland? What difference does it make, and why would shamanism be clustered with religion and spirituality when the issue of a paradigm shift is addressed?

These are some of the questions explored in this book. This exploration starts by acknowledging the massive changes that occurred in exponential proportions during the twentieth century. By looking at technology as only one area of change, we see how it has helped create global communication systems, develop widespread transportation opportunities, establish world-wide economic ties and, in the process, expose world cultures and religions to each other in ways not previously experienced. Furthermore, by enabling development of the atomic bomb, technology has given human beings the ability to destroy all life on the planet.

That leap into a global perspective has occurred in many areas and prompted a variety of reactions. For some, the idea of being part of a 'planetary community' brings an expanded sense of unity and interdependence. For others, it raises concerns that making a place for different religions, especially for those from different cultures, marks the 'beginning of the end' for their own religious beliefs and ways of life. For all of us, the underlying awareness of our new capacity for mass destruction prompts significant emotional involvement, not just passing cognitive interest. What do we believe and value? How will we survive? Are war, violence and destructive behaviours inherent in our human nature? Where do love and compassion fit in? What is right action? How have our religious institutions – originally considered sources for guidance in these matters – helped their members to meet these challenges of modern life?

A quantum leap is transformational, which raises even more questions. What is transformation, and how is it different from any other kind of change? Normal change is fairly limited and can be reversed, if desired. We can try a new style of clothing or a new type of work, but then discover it does not suit us. Nothing permanent has happened. Transformational change involves a qualitative shift that cannot be reversed. Like a caterpillar becoming a butterfly, its essence remains the same, but its form changes to something else. Returning to life as a caterpillar is not an option.

When transformational changes in human beings occur, the process involves a shift in consciousness. What is consciousness, and how does it relate to the way we see and understand the world? Though there are higher education programmes devoted entirely to consciousness studies, in the context of this book we rely on its essential meaning as *awareness* – awareness of self, other, and the world around us. To the extent that we pay attention, we grow more aware of what is happening within us and in the relationships and life we share with others. For healthy ego development, two-year-olds naturally focus on themselves as the centre of the universe. However, as their sense of self develops, they learn that others exist too, and that growing up involves relating to those others. Over time, that awareness begins to extend to life outside the family and neighbourhood into the community, nation and world.

At this time in history, our awareness of life beyond the narrow confines of community and nation has been shifting into an awareness of life on the planet and in the universe. That shift is transformational, because once we have perceived the 'bigger picture' we cannot go back and pretend life is as it used to be. Furthermore, our perceptions about meaning and belief are being tested by having to face different perceptions held by people from a variety of different cultures and religions throughout the world. We are left with the challenge and responsibility for developing a perspective of common ground and common good that is large enough to build unity while, at the same time, containing and respecting diversity. This is no small task, but the survival of the planet may depend upon our ability to do it.

How does transformational change constitute a paradigm shift? More to the point, what are the transformational changes occurring in religion and spirituality that have prompted a paradigm shift in their relationship?

Finally, how can learning about contemporary shamanic practice in Scotland help us better understand and address these issues and questions about religion, spirituality, their relationship to each other, and the impact they have on a global society?

The purpose of this book is to describe the new paradigm of spirituality and religion, show how it is reflected in the lives and work of a limited number of contemporary shamanic practitioners in Scotland, and discuss the implications and their relevance to the larger questions raised above. In order to do that, the chapters in this volume build on each other. This chapter continues by providing a review of selected definitions and/or descriptions of the terms *paradigm*, *paradigm shift*, *religion* and *spirituality*; a narrative describing aspects of my own background and perspectives, which influenced my choice of topic, research design, and interpretation of results; an explanation of how choosing contemporary shamanism as a research focus actually opened a doorway for me to understand the religion/spirituality dilemma; and a summary of the format and flow of the remaining chapters.

Definitions

When considering the following definitions, please see summaries of 'common threads', which I provide for each presentation of religion and spirituality, as flexible guideposts that can withstand varying degrees of change. They are much like tall buildings designed to survive the shock of earthquakes without sustaining too much damage.

Paradigm and Paradigm Shift

Fundamentally, a *paradigm* is like a pair of spectacles. It provides a frame for the embedded assumptions an individual and/or group has about what the world is like (Kuhn: 5). In that way, a paradigm also sets boundaries enabling individuals and communities to create areas of enquiry, formulate questions, identify priorities and focus on what is relevant. Without a paradigm, all facts within a given area would be random and hold equal weight (Kuhn: 14–15). In her paper 'The Nature of a Paradigm', Margaret Masterman of the Cambridge Language Research Unit addresses a number of paradigm definitions provided by Thomas S. Kuhn in his book *The Structure of Scientific Revolutions*. Those with particular application to our study of religion and spirituality include 'paradigm as organizing principle' – as the way in which one approach to organizing and explaining a set of facts is suddenly replaced by a new approach to organizing and explaining the same set of facts; 'paradigm as gestalt figure' – in which perception changes to interpret that same image differently (e.g. duck and rabbit within the same figure); and 'paradigm as a new way of seeing' – an experience of 'scales falling from the eyes', thus providing a new way of approaching what had been a rather obscure puzzle (Masterman: 65).

Paradigms are not ideological sets of beliefs one must accept or reject in order to be included or excluded from a community, though they do assist communities in formulating theories, habits and behaviours that make sense and help solve problems or puzzles in life and work. However, anomalies and/or novelties do periodically appear in contradiction to an accepted paradigm. From a scientific perspective, these anomalies emerge naturally within 'normal science', which does not aim for novelty. When they occur with increased frequency across a growing spectrum, consistently defying the existing paradigm's ability to explain or solve a dilemma, and meeting with considerable resistance from 'guardians of what has been', it is likely, according to Kuhn, that a paradigm shift is imminent or in progress.

For those undergoing a *paradigm shift*, the old paradigm no longer makes sense, provides meaning, or has the capacity to solve the puzzles that the new paradigm can solve. Their shift in consciousness is not into relativism, but into a framework they perceive as *better* than the former one. When the transition is complete, they still see the same information, but from a completely different perspective. Drawing again upon Kuhn, they 'do not see something *as* something else; instead, they simply see it' (Kuhn: 85). Furthermore, Kuhn says this change occurs not in a mystical way, but through a natural process of recognizing what stands outside the norm, working through the crisis caused by that occurrence, and emerging with an altered perception of what works better. This is not an 'ideological choice', but a 'gestalt shift' that just 'is' ... until the next set of anomalies prompts another crisis.

Religion

There are scholarly differences regarding the need to define the term 'religion'. Furthermore, current materials are already so extensive that any review of definitions must be prioritized and limited. What follows is a sampling of perspectives from religious studies, sociology, anthropology, counselling and social work. Its 'common threads' summary precedes a brief introduction to a new model of religion I used extensively in this research.

We find two basic orientations to this: a non-essentialist approach, which contends that a clear definition of religion is not possible, and an essentialist approach, which claims that it is possible to define religion. Of interest to this study is the recognition that use of the term 'religion', as we attempt to understand it today, is a relatively recent phenomenon. During Luther's time, religion was generally seen as the source of truth, but the deists of the Enlightenment subsequently transformed that meaning into an abstraction more familiar to twentieth-century thinking. According to Gavin Flood,

> The abstraction 'religion' – along with the abstractions 'culture', 'mysticism' and 'spirituality' – originated in the context of the critique of Christianity in the Enlightenment and the rise of the modern individual, which has since become an *etic* category in being applied outside of Christianity. (Flood: 45)

In similar fashion, scholar John Hick referred to the pioneering work of North American scholar of religion Wilfred Cantwell Smith, noting that Cantwell Smith's research has shown that

> the notion of a religion as a particular system of belief embodied in a bounded community was unknown (apart from early adumbrations which he notes at the beginning of the Christian era) prior to the modern period. . . . It was later, after the red-hot volcanic experience and thought of the great reformers had cooled into the abstract theological disputes of the seventeenth century, that the notion of a religion as a system of doctrines was effectively formed. (Smith, 1991: vii)

Among the scholars who have thought that defining religion was a worthwhile endeavour is Emile Durkheim, who described religion as

> a unified system of beliefs and practices relative to sacred things, that is to say, things set apart and surrounded by prohibitions – beliefs and practices that unite its adherents in a single moral community called a church. (Durkheim: 46)

For him it also had a social function – a system of collective activities that includes rituals, which support and express beliefs shared by people united in their common conception of the sacred. Perceived in this way, the sacred then confers an ideal and transcendent quality to the physical universe (Durkheim: 38), and it is this perspective that religion contributes to society.

Flowing from that, Durkheim contended that the fundamental categories of human thought and science have religious origins, and therefore religion has given birth to all great social institutions. He concluded that 'If religion generated everything that is essential in society, this is because the idea of society is the soul of religion. Religious forces, then, are human forces,

moral forces' (Durkheim: 314). In line with this, the notion of 'god' for
Durkheim was more related to the highest aspirations and potential of
society itself – to the 'god of society' – than to a separate or distant supreme
being. He further held that believing in a supernatural power fosters a sense
of dependence on that 'god', which for him was society; thus, believing in this way engenders loyalty and unity within society. According to
Robert Segal,

> Durkheim never claims that religion alone unifies society. Indeed, society
> must be sufficiently united for its members to assemble and thereby to
> create religion in the first place. Religion is, however, the best means of
> preserving and, more, intensifying that unity. (Segal: 8)

For Max Weber, who along with Durkheim was a founding father of the
sociology of religion, individuals, not society, were the prime movers in
shaping both religion and society, though society plays an important role
in creating both. Weber's focus was on 'the relations between religious
ideas and commitments and other aspects of human conduct, especially the
economic characteristics of human conduct within a society' (Weber: xx).

He was concerned with the subjective motives of individuals, in order to
discover typical patterns, and with systems of meaning, or cultural com-
plexes, that might link societal perspectives with individual interests. Like
Durkheim, Weber thought in evolutionary terms and contended that belief
in the supernatural was a universal phenomenon. He used the process of
rationalization to clarify and systematize his ideas, especially those related
to how human beings conceive of their place in the universe and in doing so,
legitimize the ways in which they go about achieving goals that express and
fulfil a sense of meaning and purpose in their lives (Weber: xxxii–xxxiii).

Weber saw religion as originating and functioning initially through societal interaction with a magician who could use specific techniques to help
secure immediate physical ends such as food, clothing, shelter and health.
The next stage of religion for him was the development of a priesthood in
response to the existence of a cult, or congregation; out of that emerged a
metaphysics providing a comprehensive explanation of the world and an
accompanying code of ethics that replaced magic (Segal: 11). This new
kind of rationalized religious social organization actually highlighted for
Weber the seeming paradox of how a transcendent god may be reconciled
with the imperfect reality of suffering. It followed for him that religions
of salvation then emerged as ways to 'save' those oppressed with suffering
and to provide a 'theodicy of good fortune for those who are fortunate'
(Gerth: 271).

Concerned with undeserved suffering, Weber pointed out that one's worldview, closely related to one's social class, directly affects one's understanding of salvation or redemption. He said that underlying all the possible worldviews is a desire to be 'saved' from something senseless in order to live in a world order that reflects a meaningful 'cosmos'. Furthermore, he claimed that one result of this thorough rationalizing of the world and of life was the shifting of religion into the realm of the irrational – to a dimension of 'mystery' that became the only possible 'beyond' in a world robbed of gods (Gerth: 281–2). Another result he observed was the continued presence of those who want to monopolize administration of religious values and goods by gaining and maintaining power and control, especially over those irrational dimensions.

One potential threat to those in power has typically been the 'irrational' prophet – one who breaks through established societal and religious norms and declares another order to be legitimate by invoking a source of moral authority. Prophetic charisma, according to Weber, belongs not only to that individual, but also to the new normative order itself, thus leading to a lineage of charisma or a charisma of office. Talcott Parsons says that Weber's concept of charisma is identical to Durkheim's concept of the collective sacred (Weber: xxxiv). Weber further describes two types of prophets, each one implying different ways of relating to a source of legitimation: an *exemplary prophet*, who is a model for others to follow in their own immanent relationship with the divine principle; and an *ethical prophet*, who demands that others follow in compliance with a transcendent, externally legislated call from outside the self (Weber: xxxv–xxxvi). Related to this, Weber wrote:

> The sacred values that have been most cherished, the ecstatic and visionary capacities of shamans, sorcerers, ascetics, and pneumatics of all sorts, could not be attained by everyone. The possession of such faculties is a 'charisma', which, to be sure, might be awakened in some but not in all. It follows from this that all intensive religiosity has a tendency towards a sort of *status stratification*, in accordance with differences in the charismatic qualifications. 'Heroic' or 'virtuoso' religiosity is opposed to mass religiosity. (Gerth: 288)

Because fully developed 'church' institutions, which organize 'mass religiosity', claim corporate authority to bestow or deny sacred values, Weber acknowledged that they naturally struggle with the presence of prophets and virtuosos who often ally themselves with another authority.

With Durkheim and Weber providing a context for modern sociology of religion scholarship, we turn to social anthropologist Clifford Geertz, who has urged researchers not to abandon the valuable contributions of Durkheim and Weber, but to widen them and place them in a broader context of contemporary thought. Committed to a cultural dimension of religious analysis, Geertz is known for his use of the term 'paradigm' in order to conceptualize the worldview of a culture. He has defined religion as

> a system of symbols which acts to establish powerful, persuasive, and long-lasting moods and motivations in men by formulating conceptions of a general order of existence and clothing these conceptions with such an aura of factuality that the moods and motivations seem uniquely realistic. (Geertz, 1973: 90)

Like Weber, Geertz sees religion as fulfilling an individual need for meaning, which includes the challenge of explaining the inexplicable. For him the inexplicable falls into three categories: experiences like death and dreams, which cannot be explained, but only accounted for, though they need not be justified; experiences like suffering, which are unendurable, but must be borne and accounted for, though they are still not justified; and experiences like the Holocaust, which are unendurable and must be justified, not merely accounted for and borne (Geertz, 1973: 100–8; Segal: 15). Along with Durkheim and Weber, Geertz's perspective is that the nature of society can shape the nature of religion, though in areas beyond just social organization. He has described how a society's conception of reality, as seen in its worldview, and its way of life or ethos, as expressed in its attitude, character and mood, must fuse; in other words, ethos must be a living reflection of a society's view of reality – embodying its most comprehensive ideas of order (Geertz, 1973: 127).

Reflecting on Durkheim, Geertz wrote the following:

> If Durkheim's famous statement that God is the symbol of society is incorrect, as I think it is, it remains true that particular kinds of faith (as well as particular kinds of doubt) flourish in particular kinds of societies, and the contribution of the comparative sociology of religion to the general understanding of the spiritual dimensions of human existence both begins and ends in an uncovering of the nature of these empirical, that is to say lawful, interconnections. (Geertz, 1968: 20)

To Geertz, a religious perspective involves a vital link between the values that guide how one ought to live and the way one's life is actually lived. It is made up of religious patterns, or frames of perception, through which one interprets experience and accepts guidance for action or conduct;

and its main context for creating and sustaining belief is ritual (Geertz, 1968: 99–100). For him, loss of power on the part of classical religious symbols was caused by the secularization of thought and the ideologization of religion. Elaborating, Geertz said that

> the brute empirical fact is that the growth of science has made almost all religious beliefs harder to maintain and a great many virtually impossible to maintain. Even if they are not direct antitheses, there is a natural tension between the scientific and religious ways of attempting to render the world comprehensible, a tension which need not, in my opinion probably will not, perhaps even cannot, eventuate in the destruction of either of them, but which is nonetheless real, chronic, and increasingly intense. (Geertz, 1968: 103–4)

Similar to Geertz in his attention to the collective nature of religious endeavours, Peter Berger wrote in his 1973 edition of *The Social Reality of Religion* that human society is a dialectical phenomenon in which people form and are formed by society itself; in that process, they engage in the collective enterprise of world-building, also known as the creation of culture (Berger, 1973: 13–16). In addition, the experience of living within a society takes people to marginal situations, the most precarious and terrifying being that of death, all of which threaten social order, assumptions, and established meaning. For Berger, efforts to face these threats, restore stability, and re-inforce meaning call for aligning with sources more powerful and comprehensive than local societal efforts – sources that are perceived to be cosmic or inherently universal. In that context he defined religion as 'the human enterprise by which a sacred cosmos is established' (Berger, 1973: 34). Sacred for him was a 'quality of mysterious and awesome power, other than man and yet related to him, which is believed to reside in certain objects of experience' (Berger, 1973: 34). Berger explained that an orderly sacred cosmos emerges from and transcends its own opposite, which is chaos; as such, living in right relationship with the sacred cosmos is an important way people protect themselves against the threats of chaos and its resultant meaninglessness.

How does one know how to live in right relationship with a sacred cosmos? In response, Berger addressed the issue of legitimation, which he called a socially objectified 'knowledge' that explains and justifies a social order by establishing symmetry between objective and subjective definitions of reality. He continued by saying that 'All legitimation maintains socially defined reality. Religion legitimates so effectively because it relates the precarious reality constructions of empirical societies with ultimate reality' (Berger, 1973: 41).

In that process, religion represents an alignment of a society's deepest aspirations with what is perceived as the fundamental order of the universe, thereby reinforcing the understanding of 'as above, so below', and reflecting an image of a world family of all beings. Furthermore, religious ritual is then seen as a 'reminder' of the legitimate story of ultimate meaning that has been accepted by a society. The action of ritual, together with the telling of religious legitimation and mythology, restore continuity between past and present and between the individual and the collective in a way that transcends them all. As Berger said, 'society, in its essence, is a memory', and 'through most of human history, this memory has been a religious one' (Berger, 1973: 49).

Another important perspective active in contemporary religious studies is exemplified in the work of James Cox. Utilizing a phenomenological approach when trying to understand religion, Cox defined 'religion', but incorporated the concept of 'prior intuition' into that definition. For him, intuition meant

> a seeing into meaning that largely originates from the creative interplay of the mind with the data of the external world. Intuitive insight is at the core of almost all advances in human knowledge. (Cox, 1999: 267–8)

Referring to a 'scientist's creative genius' – to what might also include the maxim 'to sleep on it' as a way of freeing up creativity when approaching a challenge, Cox contended that religious scholars should personally reflect on and clarify their own intuited sense of religion prior to interpreting the data they gather about the religion of another, thus improving their ability to analyse and interpret results. Influenced by anthropologist Felicitas Goodman and her use of the term 'alternative reality', and confident in his own understanding of how important a shared reality is to a religious community, he has defined religion as

> comprised of an identifiable community's beliefs about and postulated experiences of a non-falsifiable alternate reality; such opinions and experiences are influenced by and expressed through varied, symbolic and observable phenomena such as rituals, oral and written traditions, ritual specialists, morality and art. (Cox, 1999: 271–2)

As part of his phenomenological method, Cox uses *epoché*, which is the 'holding back of judgements' when investigating or gathering data. He contends that by performing *epoche* and including 'prior intuition', students of religion may be able to better 'appreciate the perspectives of the people they are observing' (Cox, 1998: 5). Through his inclusion of both *epoché* and 'prior intuition', Cox has attempted to address a concern raised by some scholars who question whether even a phenomenological approach can sufficiently identify the biases of the researcher and the research programme.

One of those is Gavin Flood, who wrote about the relevance of a scholar's personal biography, the importance of recognizing that 'the researcher is a social actor in a socially legitimated activity, as are the people or community who are the object of research', and the critical need for bringing to light and evaluating the values held by that researcher (Flood: 38–9). He has placed religion within the context of a cultural worldview and identified language as a critical constraint affecting any religion. With that as a context, he has broadly defined religions as 'value-laden narratives and behaviours that bind people to their objectives, to each other, and to non-empirical claims and beings'. As narratives, religions are then 'less about truth claims and more about identity, less about structures and more about texts, less about abstraction and more about tradition or that which is passed on' (Flood: 47).

Another scholar, Graham Ward, reflected in his recent collection of essays on a post-modern god the opinions of those whose current perspectives on religion include the following interpretation of key developments occurring after the Reformation and the Enlightenment:

> The reorganization of spatiality, temporality, corporeality, and language reflects a change in social relations and the practices which inscribe them: the secularization of those relations in which religious associations were expunged from the public realm (where they had been the source of far too much contention and internecine warfare). The privatization of the religious led to the erasure of God-talk from the public arena – privately one could believe what one wished, but these beliefs had no 'street value'. Secular ethics and politics flourished in the wake of a flagrant humanism. I wish to argue that with post-modernism God emerges from the white-out nihilism of modern atheism and from behind the patriarchal masks imposed by modernity's secular theology. (Ward, 1997: xxi–xxii)

Ward has contended that with modernity, god-talk became privatized, and the metaphorical and literal interpretations of religious language, which originally had been coextensive, became decontextualized. However, with the emerging understanding from Nietzsche that 'there is no foundation, no ground, no origin that ultimately is not governed by a perspective', modernity actually brought the death of its own 'god', and in so doing, restored freedom to irrationality and metaphor (Ward, 1997: xxix).

Scholar Martin Prozesky has called for 'a radically new understanding of religion, because the ones we have inherited cannot do justice to the global phenomenon of faith in all its basic forms and characteristics' (Prozesky 1984: 1). Not unlike Geertz in his recognition of the interactive role between religion and cultural worldviews, Prozesky has contended that over time both have been challenged to expand their parameters based on new discoveries about the world and their role in it. In light of that, he has described religion in its various cross-cultural forms as fundamentally 'a quest for ultimate well-being' (Prozesky, 1984: 234).

Rather than creating definitions, two other religious studies scholars have designed models for the study of religion. Frank Whaling's model 'stresses eight elements of religion: religious communities, rituals, ethics, social and political involvement of religions in wider society, scripture/myth, concepts, aesthetics and spirituality' (Whaling, 35). Similarly, Ninian Smart's model has six dimension of religion: doctrines, myths, ethics, rituals, social institutions and religious experience (Smart: 8–11).

Identifying flexible working definitions of religion is particularly useful for those whose professions call for helping people to cope with life issues that often overlap with religion. To assist mental health counsellors in their work with clients who raise concerns about religion and spirituality, the Association for Spiritual, Ethical, and Religious Values in Counseling (ASERVIC), a subgroup of the American Counseling Association (ACA), has published a white paper stating that 'Religion is "an integrated system of belief, lifestyle, ritual activities, and institutions by which individuals give meaning to (or find meaning in) their lives by orienting them to what is taken to be sacred, holy, or the highest value"' (Corbett: 2; ASERVIC: 3). The title of the paper was 'Spirituality', but an expanded definition of religion was included in order to differentiate the two terms.

In a similar vein, the Spring 2007 issue of the *Journal of Religion and Spirituality in Social Work*, a United States publication, printed an article describing and summarizing an academic research project conducted to discover whether the 'personal spiritual characteristics' of social workers affects 'their conceptualizations of spirituality and religion' (Hodge and Boddie: 53). Research participants listed 'organized beliefs or doctrines', 'practice of spirituality/faith', 'personally constructed', and 'belief in/experience of God' as the top aspects in their definition of religion.

Summary of Common Threads

Common threads running through most of these definitions of religion. include: an organized and codified set of beliefs; identification of 'legitimate' authority; institutionalization in some form; a reference to God, a higher power, the sacred, or some transcendent sense of meaning; and ritualized expressions of commonly held beliefs and experiences. Because of this configuration, many academic researchers who use definitions like these often find themselves back at the doorstep of institutional religions without having discovered a tool or model to help them constructively study newly emerging religious movements and/or the religious perspectives of those standing on the edge of or outside religious institutions. Their definitions have unintentionally excluded those not fitting the 'institutional' profile.

Hervieu-Léger

One exception is sociologist of religion Danièle Hervieu-Léger, who has proposed 'an analytical method which, while enabling the circle to be broken, might also enable religion in modernity to be considered the subject matter of sociology' (Hervieu-Léger, 2000: 4). In her book, *Religion as a Chain of Memory*, Hervieu-Léger not only provides the background and theoretical concerns of critical importance to consider when studying new forms of religious expression, but she also describes how her proposed method addresses the consequences of religion when it is deprived of memory and continuity. She employs a working definition of religion as a chain of memory embodying a chain of belief from one or more traditions, or parts of traditions, invoked by a community of people who experience themselves joining in a core lineage with others who have gone before them in the process of choosing that lineage and set of beliefs as the legitimizing authority for the way they believe individually and collectively. Hervieu-Léger's definition of religion appears to open up options for learning about those on the fringes or outside institutional religious traditions. Because of this, her model is described more fully in Chapter Two and then systematically applied in the analysis of shamanic fieldwork presented in Chapter Seven.

Spirituality

Like religion, attempts to define spirituality come from a variety of perspectives. Spirituality as a subject of academic research in non-religious institutions of higher education is a relatively new phenomenon. Until recently, spirituality appeared to be a 'tool' used by religion. For example, religious studies scholars Paul Heelas and Linda Woodhead say that religions like Christianity have used the term *spirituality* to refer to devotional practices designed to help their believers enter 'into an intense relationship (involving self-surrender) with the divine' (Heelas *et al*, 2005: 5).

Growing out of their Kendal Project results, Heelas and Woodhead claim that religion is giving way to spirituality in Britain. Their research project set out to discover whether a spiritual revolution was underway, and if so, whether spiritualities in the holistic milieu were overtaking traditional theistic religions. As anticipated, the study showed that there were two primary worlds – a congregational domain that promotes what Heelas and Woodhead call a 'life as' form of the sacred by emphasizing 'a transcendent source of significance and authority to which individuals must conform at the expense of the cultivation of their unique subjective-lives', and a 'subjective life' form of the sacred, which emphasizes 'inner sources of significance and authority and the cultivation or sacralization of unique subjective lives' (Heelas *et al*, 2005: 6).

Furthermore, the study revealed that 7.9% of the population of Kendal participated in 'life as' congregations, and 1.6% participated in the 'subjective life' holistic milieu – though the congregational domain was in a decline, and the holistic milieu was increasing (Heelas, 2005: 45).

Heelas and Woodhead discovered that personal beliefs were tending towards spirituality and the highly relational 'unique you', also known as 'the we of me'. In other words, paying attention to the uniqueness of the self is beginning to involve seeing the unique self being fully expressed in relationship with others. They have started asking whether Christianity can cater to those involved in this massive subjective turn of culture and still remain theistic. They have also noted that the proportion of women involved in congregational church life has begun to fall – due in part to overall changes in women's roles and also to the way church life reflects the changing relationship between society and religion. Finally, the issue of power and control has emerged. Woodhead has explained how power in religion often takes the form of 'power over' another, whereas power in spirituality is imagined differently. It is seen as an 'energy' acting from within to unblock one's natural energy and release it to tap into the wider life-force energy (Woodhead, 2005). According to her, when faced with a rigid 'power over' leadership in a given religion, those interested in spirituality tend to move away from religion and towards practices and/or groups that they perceive will help them grow spiritually.

Religious studies scholar Ursula King has written about spirituality in the new millennium as being something urgently needed 'for the cross-cultural, mutually interdependent context of our new global society' (King, 2001: 2–3). Convinced that spirituality has become a universal code word for the crisis of meaning and commitment in contemporary society, King has written about how important, in her view, is the task of humanity addressing what she calls a 'spiritual well-being, of a balanced and wholesome spirituality which relates to our political, economic, scientific, educational and cultural activities as well as to our deep personal needs and our sense of embodiment' (King, 2001: 3).

Acknowledging that much traditional spirituality has been bound up in dualistic patterns of thinking, she has pointed to post-modern thinkers who 'champion a more integral, naturalistic and pantheistic spirituality which is in rhythm with the energy of the universe and that of our own inner life force'. Furthermore, because the spiritual in contemporary society is more diffuse and less tied to religious institutions, she contends that 'it can be given a more focused meaning when it is understood as the core dimension of the human as well as the centre and heart of all religion' (King, 2001: 4). Drawing upon the work of David Ray Griffin, King has come to support a view of spirituality that refers to 'the ultimate values and meanings' by which people live – whether or not they are 'otherworldly', and regardless of their content. She claims that spirituality can now also refer to an academic field of study, and she affirms Ewert Cousins, editor of a twenty-five volume cross-cultural series on world spirituality, who has described the emerging new discipline of 'global spirituality', which goes beyond merely retrieving 'an ancient discipline in a modern academic mode' (King, 2001: 5–7).

Another religious studies scholar, Richard Roberts, says that 'spirituality affords human renewal, peak experiences and an enhanced sense of reality' (Roberts: 63). In his book *Religion, Theology and the Human Sciences*, he also reflects on his experience at the 1993 Parliament of the World's Religions as a 'remarkable expression of global spirituality' and 'a significant step on the path towards the recovery of both the use and intrinsic values of religion in a threatened world' (Roberts: 268–9).

According to former Dominican priest and theologian Matthew Fox, 'When religion is true to itself and is itself healthy, it is about spirituality, for spirituality is meant to be the core of religion.' He quickly adds, however, 'it is evident that one can also be spiritual without religion' (Fox, 2001: 2). Author of numerous books related to spirituality, Fox's primary definition of spirituality is probably best summarized by the book he wrote describing spirituality as *compassion* (Fox, 1999). At the same time, the broader context for him is 'creation spirituality' which, while studying in Paris, was the focus of his doctoral work on the history and theology of spirituality. In his book *Original Blessing: A Primer in Creation Spirituality*, Fox describes this tradition as feminist, wisdom-centred, prophetic, and focused on social justice, eco-justice and gender justice issues (Fox, 2000).

Another perspective on spirituality comes from sociologist Gordon Lynch, who has written about progressive spirituality. He defines progressive spirituality as an ideology – a 'cultural tool-kit' with a 'set of conceptual, social and material resources that can be drawn on for different purposes' (Lynch: 41). His writing gives voice to an emerging religious movement among progressive religious thinkers and organizations on the 'religious left'.

Moving to the field of transpersonal psychology, Michael Daniels, transpersonal psychologist at John Moores University in Liverpool, defines spirituality as 'a belief in spirit or a commitment to a spiritual perspective on life – often used in a nonreligious sense' (Daniels: 310). In the related field of mental health, the ASERVIC white paper mentioned earlier describes spirituality

> as a capacity and tendency that is innate and unique to all persons. This spiritual tendency moves the individual towards knowledge, love, meaning, peace, hope, transcendence, connectedness, compassion, wellness, and wholeness. Spirituality includes one's capacity for creativity, growth, and the development of a value system. (ASERVIC: 1)

It also says spirituality comes from the Latin word *spiritus*, which means *breath*, and that it reflects a deep sense of belonging, wholeness, connectedness and openness to the infinite (ASERVIC: 2). From the social work research study cited in the last section, the top descriptors in their search for a definition of spirituality included: something that is personally constructed – with no reference to the transcendent; a belief in or experience of a higher power or of God; something beyond the individual; and a connection to others, the world, and the universe (Hodge and Boddie: 60).

Finally, we turn to Richard Potter, an academic who heads the social work department at a liberal arts college in the US and has addressed what he calls 'understanding the core of spirituality'. His perspective is that 'there are central processes relevant to all forms of spirituality, regardless of the cultures in which they are embedded' and that understanding those processes is crucial. Potter has identified those processes as opening the heart; mastery; creating personality; spiritual teaching and transmission; and spiritual freedom. He has further claimed that they are 'beyond culture because they are necessary for the expansion of consciousness under all cultural circumstances' (Potter, 2004: 67).

Summary of Common Threads

In summary, common threads found within many of these definitions and descriptions of spirituality are more personal and subjective, yet they are relational and outward-looking as well. They reflect an embodied, personal experience of meaning and ultimate value that expands into circles of compassionate relationships with most life on the planet and in the universe. These threads include an openness to 'the more' that is not limited to a theist god, an appreciation of the contributions women bring to an understanding of spirituality, a different perspective on the issue of 'legitimate authority', and a questioning of the ways in which spirituality and religion may or may not function together in the future.

Self-Reflexive Narrative

Religion, spirituality and shamanism have been elements of my life for many years. Though my father's family were Protestant, I was raised Catholic in Carroll, Iowa – a small town in the USA, and was a young teen when Pope John XXIII convened the Vatican II Council. His call to open the doors and windows of the church and let the breath of creativity and spirituality shape contemporary ways of expressing fundamental values had a profound effect on me. I began to look beyond external rules, practices and rituals that may have lost their relevance. That helped me start to see underlying meanings and values that had become hidden and perhaps needed to be retrieved, understood, and re-created in light of modern life circumstances. One of those areas was social justice, and that motivated me to become involved in civil and human rights work in the late 1960s. This was in addition to what I had been taught since I was a child about the mystical tradition that the church had continued to uphold, however begrudgingly at times, over the centuries. All of these propelled me into a dialectical exchange between mystical experiences and critical analyses of my own religious beliefs; this process formed a regular part of my thinking. It was supported and encouraged by priests, nuns, and a variety of religious figures around me.

I joined with others in informal small communities that creatively explored religious and spiritual matters cognitively and experientially. It was an exciting time – one in which facing and addressing the transformational changes occurring in society and church were seen as important contemporary expressions of religious belief and spiritual practice. Part of that paradigm included an understanding that one's perception and experience of 'God' would evolve and mature throughout life. I expected no road map for how that would look – only that it was likely to happen, and that aspects of it would relate to individual and societal interpretations of cultural reality.

In 1977 I completed a postgraduate degree in religious education at Creighton University in Omaha, Nebraska – focusing heavily on the cognitive, moral, and faith development research on adult men and women that had been conducted and was being published at that time. Those studies expanded and deepened a developmental perspective that for me had begun to grow in importance not only through the experiences described above, but also during my undergraduate teacher training in human development among children and teens. That theoretical perspective of development continues to influence how I understand the world.

During my years as a secondary education teacher, I taught in a public school and later chaired the Religion Department in a Catholic high school. From 1980 until 1992 I worked for the Omaha-based Union Pacific Railroad in the areas of personal injury management, programme development, organizational change, and leadership. I also began training in psychodrama and sociometry, which is the use of quantitative and qualitative methods to study interpersonal choice-making within groups, and earned a postgraduate degree in human relations.

The human relations work increased my ability and commitment to goal setting, planning, programme implementation, communication, and the desire to create and foster a context that values human relationships, diversity, problem solving, conflict resolution and collaboration. That and the psychodrama/sociometry training helped deepen my ability and commitment to see and understand another person's perspective through encounter, role reversal, and related techniques designed to facilitate understanding of one's self, the perspective of another, and the impact social issues have on all of us. One result of that training and experience has been my consistent focus on how an individual worldview might be connected with perspectives common to larger groups, societies and cultures.

My exposure to shamanism and shamanic training arose inductively in response to experiences that had occurred during prayer, meditation, Jungian active imagination, and guided imagery sessions. Native American friends who knew about shamanism recognized shamanic aspects in my experiences and suggested I learn more about what was happening to me. In 1986 I began studying core shamanism with anthropologist Michael Harner, founder of the Foundation for Shamanic Studies. Eventually I started teaching and facilitating basic shamanic workshops, in addition to providing shamanic healing sessions for those who sought my help in that way.

In 1994, shortly after leaving the Union Pacific and starting my own business, I became licensed as a mental health practitioner and a certified professional counsellor – primarily as a way of helping me maintain a grounded, ethical perspective for my human relations consulting and my shamanic practice. Seeing the connection between mental and spiritual health, I also wanted to build bridges with the mental health community. One way I did this was through regular supervision sessions with a senior mental health professional, and by presenting workshops at various professional mental health conferences.

Though people in my local Catholic parish remained supportive of my continued spiritual explorations, including shamanic learning and practice, leadership in the larger Catholic Church had become increasingly focused on limiting or reversing numerous Vatican II initiatives. I found myself on the edges of an institution that had helped form me. However, that formation was beyond institutional boundaries, and it has not prevented me from maintaining relationships with the gamut of people who stay within, negotiate the borders of, step outside, or have never entered, the parameters of institutional religion. Since the early 1990s many from that broad spectrum have come to me for spiritual counselling, group spiritual retreats, and shamanic teaching and/or healing.

Though I have worked with groups of only women, since 1998 I have also co-facilitated numerous retreats and/or experiential workshops for both women and men in the United States and in the UK. Since September 2004 I have worked as a spirituality and multi-faith chaplain serving 'all faiths and none' at the University of Edinburgh. As with mental health practitioners, in that chaplaincy role I have tried to build bridges and develop good relationships with the University's Honorary Chaplains, the student religious societies, and a few religious communities in and around Edinburgh – all of whom represent a variety of faith bodies. To that end, the Edinburgh International Centre for World Spiritualities (EICWS) has often invited me to contribute to many of the spirituality events they have sponsored in recent years. Those events have included the divine feminine, spiritual practice, ritual, shamanism, Celtic spirituality, and music for peace. I am no stranger to facing conflict and diversity, and my experience and training have led me to value the affirmation of both commonalities and differences.

Evolution of my Research Focus

Intrigued and personally drawn to the notion that shamanism may contain a cluster of core elements that are found in shamanic cultures throughout the world, but expressed differently depending upon those cultures, in 2000 I decided to initiate a scholarly study to determine whether evidence of core shamanic elements could be found in a broad base of academic literature and in the shamanic work of practitioners in a culture other than my own.

Having been exposed to several Native American, or First Nations, forms of shamanism and to the issue of outsiders appropriating indigenous spiritualities in a kind of 'spiritual imperialism', or cultural theft (Geertz, 1996; 1992), I chose to study at the University of Edinburgh because most of my ancestors had lived in the UK prior to emigrating to the USA, and I knew that research facilities there were excellent.

My MSc year in Celtic and Scottish Studies began a month after the attacks of September 11, 2001, heightening my awareness that if shamanism truly possessed a cross-cultural core, it might provide insight into how divergent cultures, with conflicting worldviews about religion and/or spirituality, might find a global common ground that also respects differences. During that year, I discovered scholarly evidence for a model of shamanism that does indeed include a core of cross-cultural elements. I also applied that model to three folk tales, gathered in Scotland by ethnologists and stored in the archives of the School of Scottish Studies (Burgess, 2002). To my surprise, I discovered in those tales more shamanic elements than I had originally anticipated finding. Later on in the PhD process, I tested further my shamanic model by expanding and deepening my theoretical shamanic research into what is presented in Chapter Four.

During that MSc year, I attended one shamanic journey drumming group, learned about shamanic offerings at The Salisbury Centre in Edinburgh, and eventually started meeting people who knew of shamanic practitioners or were part of an informal network of shamanic practitioners living in Scotland. Because I had just completed a literary analysis, discovered the existence of a shamanic network, and realized my own shamanic experience would probably help me develop trust with potential research participants, after I transferred to Religious Studies, I decided to direct my PhD research towards current shamanic practice in Scotland.

Being in Religious Studies gave me exposure to Hervieu-Léger's definition of religion. I read her book and checked other scholarly sources commenting on and critiquing her work. They portrayed a picture of someone with academic credibility in her field, and they helped me decide that her model of 'religion as a chain of memory' would serve as a useful tool for looking at religious phenomena, including contemporary forms of shamanism, which function on the edges of or outside historical faith communities and institutional churches.

Finally, I began to understand how important it would be to set a broader cultural context for my research. Both contemporary shamanic practice and Hervieu-Léger's new model have emerged in the midst of a massive transformation of religion and spirituality. I knew I needed to address that reality.

Opening the Door

As described above, the focus of my research evolved from a simple literary analysis of cross-cultural shamanic elements in Scottish folklore to an exploration of contemporary shamanic practice in Scotland. I then decided to apply Hervieu-Léger's definition of religion – not because it made a major difference to me whether shamanism is considered a religion, but because using her model might reveal information and insight previously inaccessible or not understood about religious phenomena occurring on the edges of and outside institutional religions. Finding a tool to do that very thing had been a key motivator for Hervieu-Léger, and I was happy to use that tool in research that might bring greater understanding about shamanism and religion.

It did not take long for me to realize I could not study contemporary shamanism or religion without addressing the transformational cultural context in which they were operating. When I began my research into that context, I started to see more clearly that the shamanic practitioners and their clients were operating out of a paradigm that reflected a new perspective on religion, spirituality and the religion/spirituality relationship. Suddenly I knew my research had taken a quantum leap into a realm most intriguing to me, but one I had not consciously anticipated visiting. The multi-layered approach I was using, coupled with fieldwork stories and observations I was gathering, had led me to an opening or doorway into a fuller understanding of the religion/spirituality dilemma. I was delighted.

Though my previous life experience should have made it easy for me to predict that discovery, I had not been looking for it. Instead, I had embarked upon my research with a desire to learn what I could, do my analysis, and draw my conclusions about the relationship between contemporary shamanic practice and my three 'models'. Of course, I knew that neoshamanic practices reflected changes in religion and spirituality, but I had not fully appreciated how a multi-layered approach to studying shamanism would reveal a 'bigger picture' that could be of interest to a variety of people anxious to understand more about religion, spirituality, how they interact with each other and, finally, the impact both have on individuals and societies currently experiencing massive transformational change on a global level.

Why Shamanism?

To understand how shamanic practice relates to religion, spirituality, and social change, it makes sense to look briefly at an overview of shamanic development, its place in the world, and its emergence in contemporary societies. A more detailed study of shamanism and its cross-cultural elements can be found in Chapter Four. However, the following introduction begins the process of establishing shamanism's relationship to religion and spirituality and identifying its role in social change.

Shamanism, like many religious movements, is a religious phenomenon with ancient roots and modern forms. It is not included or acknowledged as a world religion; in fact, scholars debate whether it qualifies as a religion at all. However, most indigenous systems of shamanism have fragmented under many of the same pressures that have threatened traditional religions. That fragmentation, along with the unexpected survival of various traditional shamanic cultures and the emergence of new shamanic forms, provides a parallel to what has been happening with traditional religions and other new religious or spiritual phenomena.

> From the Stone Age to the New Age, the figure of the shaman has continued to grip the human imagination. Being chosen by the spirits, taught by them to enter a trance and fly with one's soul to other worlds in the sky or clamber through dangerous crevasses into terrifying subterranean worlds; being stripped of one's flesh, reduced to a skeleton and then reassembled and reborn; gaining the power to combat spiritual enemies and heal their victims, to kill enemies and save one's own people from disease and starvation – these are features of shamanic religions in many parts of the world. And yet they are regarded by the communities in which they occur, not as part of some extraordinary sort of mystical practice, but as a specialized development of the relationship which every person has with the world around them. (Vitebsky, 2000: 55)

In this amazing description of the shamanic figure within a shamanic community, Vitebsky captures the essence of this ancient spiritual system of shamanism that has existed for millennia as an integral part of many world cultures. He builds on the work of Mircea Eliade, a historian of religions and comparative religions scholar, who through his 1951 French version of *Shamanism: Archaic Techniques of Ecstasy*, 'documented the striking correspondences in shamanic practices, worldviews, and symbolic behaviours in hundreds of societies around the world' (Narby and Huxley: 4). Underlying those correspondences Eliade found basic commonalities in understanding the concept of soul, believing that a non-physical reality filled with spirits exists, recognizing that many humans experience themselves communicating with beings in the spiritual realms, and honouring shamans as ones in their midst who through soul journeys specialize in working with those spirits for the health and well-being of individuals and their communities.

Because shamanism is a rather complex system that stretches across several disciplines, scholars studying it have come from various backgrounds that include anthropology, ethnology, and religion. Understandably, the history of shamanic research reflects the values and cultural perspectives of those scholars as they have attempted to learn about shamanism and its function in society. As Narby and Huxley state in their book:

> Even after five hundred years of reports on shamanism, its core remains a mystery. One thing that has changed over the last five centuries, however, is the gaze of the observers. It has opened up. And understanding is starting to flower. (Narby and Huxley: 8)

That understanding, which flowered significantly after the publication of studies by Eliade and other scholars of shamanism, began to blossom into fullness in the West during the second half of the twentieth century with descriptions of contemporary forms of shamanism – sometimes called 'modern shamanism', 'new shamanism', 'urban shamanism', 'contemporary shamanism', or 'neo-shamanism' (Wallis: 30). According to Merete Jakobsen, these new forms are designed to 're-establish a link for modern man to his spiritual roots, to reintroduce shamanic behaviour into the lives of Westerners in search of spirituality and, thereby, renew contact with Nature' (Jakobsen: xi). Because these shamanic forms often operate within the context of a 'global village', scholar Robert Wallis has approached his research in this area by using a 'multi-sited ethnography' that requires 'multiple-positioning' on the part of the researcher (Wallis, 22). He contends that despite the tendency for observers to categorize neo-shamanic forms with 'New Agers' in a derogatory manner, their impact on society has primarily been ignored. Because of that, Wallis has written a book aimed at providing a more 'balanced' examination of contemporary shamanism – one that recognizes both positive and negative aspects by addressing 'the diversity of practices and practitioners rather than catch-all stereotypes' (Wallis: xv).

Carlos Castaneda, through his series of books which were based on what he described as an apprenticeship with shaman Don Juan, has come to be considered the one who first exposed contemporary cultures on a large scale to a shamanic perspective. However, it is anthropologist Michael Harner who in his studies of various shamanic cultures built on the work of Eliade, communicated with Castaneda, and by establishing his Foundation for Shamanic Studies began actively to develop contemporary shamanic forms that are often considered central in the 'neo-shamanic movement'. As a scholar whose research gave him the opportunity to become a participant-observer within the Jivaro Indian tribe in Ecuador and the Conibo Indian tribe in Peru, Harner learned first-hand many of the indigenous shamanic ways (Harner: 1). Based on that experience and his understanding of other scholars like Eliade, Harner coined the term *core shamanism* to refer to those universal core shamanic elements that are found within most shamanic cultures, though they are often expressed differently depending on each specific culture and its particular worldview. According to Wallis, the techniques that emerged from Harner's paradigm of core shamanism have been 'highly influential' and 'are probably the most widely known and practised in the West' (Wallis: 46).

If this is so, how has this happened, and how have contemporary shamans come to draw upon these techniques? Is their apparent similarity to indigenous shamanism, with its ancient roots, merely a romantic fantasy of days gone by, another form of spiritual oppression perpetuated yet again on indigenous peoples, or a transformation of ancient traditions to meet contemporary circumstances and needs? How might modern scholars approach their research of this phenomenon in ways that shed light on the religious and spiritual implications for our modern society? According to Wallis, who uses the term 'shamanisms' to reflect the diversity of shamanic expressions,

> Despite numerous studies on shamanisms, the political and ethical sensitivities of neo-Shamanisms have gone largely unrecognized. Academia consistently marginalizes neo-Shamans, yet ironically there is more literature on shamanisms written by, or aimed at, neo-shamans than there are academic publications. (Wallis: 2)

Why has this happened? What blocks modern scholarly attempts to understand contemporary shamanism or other new religious movements that, like shamanism, have developed what many practitioners of these phenomena experience as modern expressions of ancient beliefs about the religious and spiritual quality of life? How is it that academic disciplines such as sociology, anthropology, ethnology and religious studies have encountered so many challenges in their efforts to design analytical tools authoritative enough to assist in research?

Cultural Change

Introduced earlier, and described more fully in Chapter Two, part of the answer lies in the massive cultural and intellectual changes that continue to transform our modes of thought radically, societal patterns, structures of consciousness, and perceptions about the unconscious and unseen dimensions of life. These fundamental changes in both individuals and society at large have challenged attempts to define religion and spirituality – in great part because the desire for any definition generally reflects a desire for stability in thought, not for fluid parameters that become prevalent during times of change.

Perhaps this dilemma can be further understood by looking at similar transformations of great magnitude that were experienced centuries ago, but from a somewhat different perspective. For example, starting with the Reformation but flowering with the Enlightenment, forward-looking thinkers sought to liberate individuals and cultures from 'their embeddedness in superstition and unexamined traditions' and from 'docile obedience to unaccountable forms of governance' (Fowler, 1996: 149). A time of radical change, the Enlightenment made an impact in all areas of life through new theories of government and politics, empirical and analytical approaches to science and technology, new approaches to education, rigorous analyses of religion and religious traditions, the separation of cosmology and theology, and scientific methodology that resulted in the development of psychology and sociology. It was a revolution in consciousness that had a parallel only with our own today, and its primary instrument and model for change was the use of reason.

This is expanded upon in Chapter Two: during the modernization of society that developed from the Enlightenment era up to the present, facets of religion were systematically analysed, explained away in the light of newly formed disciplines of study, and demythologized to the extent that in the middle of the twentieth century, many historians and social scientists believed religion itself would disappear by the end of the millennium (Berger, 1973: 130; 1999: 2). This modern process of separating the activities of daily living from a sense of the sacred, something traditionally associated with religion, resulted in both individual and societal loss of memory regarding collective traditions of meaning, and thus a loss of continuity. In the words of Hervieu-Léger:

> The process of rationalization which informed the advance of modernity went hand in hand with the process of 'dismantling the gods', and the triumph of autonomy – both of the individual and of society – implied the ineluctable disintegration of the religion-bound societies of the past. (Hervieu-Léger, 2000: 1)

However, we now know that while participation in traditional religions was generally diminishing, religious activity *per se* had begun to increase. Rather than leading to the decline of religion in society and individuals, the 'secularizing effects' of modernization have actually 'provoked powerful movements of counter-secularization' (Berger, 1999: 2–3). These movements have often taken new forms both within and outside traditional religions, further challenging scholars to determine whether or not they can actually be considered religions. Shamanism reveals similar characteristics. In addition to the question about its status as a religion, it has survived fragmentation and continues to find various expressions in contemporary societies.

Summary

Shamanism, religion and spirituality have much in common. This has been an introduction to shamanism and its role as a doorway into understanding a new way of looking at all three phenomena. What follows in Chapter Four is a more comprehensive study of shamanism and its cross-cultural elements, which are incorporated into the fieldwork. Chapter Five then introduces the shamanic practitioners and their clients, the contexts in which they work, and the methodology used to conduct the field research.

Format and Flow of the Remaining Chapters

Building on our understanding of the new paradigm that is emerging, what follows in Chapter Two is an in-depth review of critical factors from sociology, anthropology, psychology, gender studies and religious studies in a way that helps us understand the impact of transformational cultural change on religion and spirituality. Hervieu-Léger's search for a new definition of religion, resulting in her model of 'religion as a chain of memory', forms the basis for Chapter Three. Chapter Four includes a comprehensive look at indigenous roots, cross-cultural elements, contemporary expressions and current challenges found in the study of shamanism. Setting the context, choosing shamanic participants for the three case studies, clarifying the research purpose, and selecting the methodology are processes presented in Chapter Five. This is followed in Chapter Six by presentation of the field research I conducted, and the methods used to explore connections between indigenous cross-cultural shamanic elements and neo-shamanic expressions in Scotland. Chapter Seven describes how I applied Hervieu-Léger's model to that field data in order to determine differences between religion and spirituality in the lives and experiences of the shamanic practitioners – discovering in the process a lineage of spirituality, not belief. A shamanic worldview, global consciousness, patriarchal paradigm, developmental theories, and the role of community form some of the patterns, conclusions and resulting issues emerging from this research, and presented in Chapter Eight. Finally, the book culminates in Chapter Nine with a clear look at the new paradigm of spirituality and religion, and how it can provide a framework for understanding contemporary responses to institutional religions, emerging global spiritualities, and changes in the spirituality/religion relationship; and how this perspective may assist people wanting to explore and effectively address some of the critical issues facing our world.

Chapter Two

The Impact of Transformational Cultural Change on Religion and Spirituality

Introduction and Context

If transformational cultural change highly influences religion and spirituality, then identifying relevant cultural and religious change factors becomes particularly important. Furthermore, attempts to understand transformational processes are best served through a 'systems' approach. My hope is that this chapter offers a unique lens that sharpens our understanding of the current religion/spirituality dilemma, and in doing so opens new avenues for collaborative problem solving.

Though there are many factors with a transformational impact on religion and spirituality, the significant ones I have chosen to address include: social and cultural change; secularization; changing religious forms; personal and collective memory; consciousness; faith and belief; developmental theory; and the patriarchal paradigm. They are presented here with enough information to show how they fit into a larger pattern. Though explained more fully as part of presenting Hervieu-Léger's model of religion in Chapter Three, issues such as tradition, legitimizing authority, and believing are integrated into several of the above critical factors. The chapter ends with a chart listing these eight critical factors and the relevant points contained within each of them.

Social and Cultural Change

Sociological Theories

According to US sociologist Charles Harper, there are currently three established sociological theories of society and change. Because they each reflect a different image of society, they also provide differing approaches to change within society. Though each one perceives and explains change in a different way, what they hold in common is that 'All three perspectives argue that at some point cultural and symbolic factors are critical in understanding change' (Harper, 1989: 96).

Modernity

The modernization of society over the last several hundred years is one major example of how social and cultural change has dramatically affected religion. For a great number of people, this process set religion and science against each other, rationally explained why religion would eventually be discarded, and distributed to various societal disciplines many responsibilities and areas of control that had previously been held by Christian churches. Modernity has brought severe fragmentation in many contemporary manifestations of belief, and the disappearance of numerous links between society and religion. At the same time, Richard Roberts has noted that religions are often 'victims of their own conceptions of modernity' and they 'frequently believe that "religion" is dying or dead'. He says, however, that 'in reality, religion and forms of religiosity, especially spiritualities, are very much alive and answering human needs in a global and local marketplace from which many established churches have explicitly or tacitly retreated' (Roberts: 184).

Global Interdependence, Identity and Change

This new religiosity has occurred on individual and small group levels, but it has also happened at the same time as another, much larger, phenomenon has come into focus – namely, the development of an emerging world system marked not just by economic interdependence, but by 'interpenetrating dimensions' that 'affect the future quality of life (if not the survival) of individuals and nations' (Harper: 1989, 257). As this global awareness increases, the question of identity on many levels comes to the forefront for societies in general and for religions and spiritualities in particular. According to UK sociology of religion scholar Kieran Flanagan,

> Personal identity, that which is the responsibility of the actor to craft, is intermingled with collective identities, thus making efforts to reconcile levels of analyses of both highly problematic. In these many shapes and sizes of identities, there is a property of searching, of insecurity and distrust. (Flanagan, 2004: ix)

He goes on to describe how, as familiar societal structures are uprooted in this era of post-modern relativity, people tend to seek ways of securing a stable identity. An example he gives is of fundamentalism, which he says 'expresses a form of resistance to the indefiniteness of a culture of post-modernity' and highlights the importance of looking at the relationship between religion and identity (Flanagan, 2004: x–xi).

There are other ways in which identity and religion come together, too. Scholars Simon Coleman and Peter Collins, who edited the book *Religion, Identity and Change*, have pointed out that religion and identity merge in areas of ambiguity that can prompt considerable creativity as localized boundaries expand to include a global field. Indeed, they describe how the process of globalization has brought a growing self-consciousness among increasing numbers of people whose individual levels of identity include that of self, a national society, a world system of societies, and all human-kind (Coleman and Collins: 15). What remains is discerning whether those in the West who adopt views and practices from around the world reflect a truly 'global' perspective and not just a Western understanding of the global.

Post-modernism/Post-modernity

Post-modernism and post-modernity are terms that need some explanation. According to Ursula King, the dissolution of long-established societal 'certainties' – even those ushered in by events described in the above section on modernity – has created a crisis of fragmentation in Western culture in which everything is called into question, including meaning and the traditional values of faith. She describes 'post-modernism' as that ongoing process of change which results in the condition of post-modernity, though the terms are often used synonymously (King, 1998a: 6). In her opinion, the negative aspects of post-modern fragmentation are matched by a number of positive influences. Furthermore, King contends that the deconstruction of post-modernism 'is not necessarily destructive of all certainties and meanings, but can provide new threads for weaving dynamic patterns of new significance and promise' (King, 1998a: 13).

Agreeing that post-modernity is 'less indifferent to religious belief than it might seem' is Kieran Flanagan, mentioned above, who has suggested that post-modernity has actually given rise to the seemingly contradictory movements of New Age spirituality and to the rehabilitation of tradition found in fundamentalism (Flanagan, 1996: 6). However, Paul Heelas argues that New Age spirituality is not post-modern. He says that by 'promising that it is possible to experience this spiritually-informed sense of humanity', New Age spirituality 'is associated with a major, perennializing, shift within modernity (Heelas: 76).

Referring to globalized religion and the 'condition of post-modernity', Roberts has said that 'global and globalized religion confronts deconstruct-ive fragmentation because it does not itself seek to avoid juxtaposition of the extremes of universality and particularity'; instead, it manages the tension by celebrating diversity 'whilst honouring and seeking to articulate univer-sal exigencies' (Roberts: 263).

Whole-Systems Change

Holding this kind of 'both/and' perspective is a step towards understanding the much more complex concept of 'whole-systems change'. Beyond just acknowledging the need for multidisciplinary or multifaceted approaches to complex issues, or even to individual systems or organizations, the ability to address whole-systems change requires a shift in paradigm. That paradig-matic shift enables one to see entire systems relating to other systems in an interdependent web that is itself transforming. According to Richard Bar-rett, who has pioneered a whole-systems approach to cultural transforma-tion within organizations, 'The methodology and techniques used in a whole-systems change process need to reflect what is acceptable and appro-priate for the levels of consciousness, worldviews, and motivational drivers of the people involved' (Barrett, 2006: 7).

Another pioneer in approaching transformational change from a 'whole-systems' perspective is one of the founders and leading figures of the human-potential movement, Jean Houston. She writes, 'I believe that the world is set for the radical transformation that I call Jump Time. In this time of accelerating change, all cultures, regardless of their social or economic level, have something of supreme value to offer the whole.' For her, 'Jump Time is a whole system transition, a condition of interactive change that affects every aspect of life as we know it.' Though she remains 'generally optimistic' about this, she does say that this radical change involves a 'breakdown and breakthrough of every old way of being, knowing, relating, governing, and believing' – something that 'shakes the foundations of all and everything' (Houston: 10–11).

For scholar Ken Wilber, who is best known for his work on consciousness and integral philosophy, a whole-systems approach must utilize what he calls AQAL – all quadrants, all levels. AQAL is a model with four dimen-sions that contain and share a variety of eight 'paradigms for gaining repro-ducible knowledge'. Wilber thinks 'that any approach that leaves out any of these eight paradigms is a less-than-adequate approach according to avail-able and reliable human knowledge at this time'. Furthermore, he says using that model to approach any complex situation 'gives us the inside and the outside of the individual and the collective' (Wilber, 2005: 4). Wilber, Barrett and Houston are among a growing number of people who refer to the importance of addressing 'consciousness' when dealing with change.

Secularization

The concept of secularization has been described by Bruce as a social condition in which religion has declined in several areas: its importance for the operation of non-religious roles it used to play; the social standing of its roles and institutions; and the extent to which people participate in religious practices, express beliefs of a religious nature, or live their lives in ways that reflect religious beliefs (Bruce: 3). According to Bruce, 'the most potent and the most neglected part of the secularization paradigm' is relativism, which he considers more of an 'operating principle' or 'cognitive style' that represents the move from the authoritarian and exclusive claim to a single truth held by the Christian church to a 'social and cultural diversity' that has combined 'with egalitarianism to undermine all claims to authoritative knowledge'. In his opinion, a natural outcome of this is that the tolerance needed to maintain harmony in diverse egalitarian societies weakens not only religion, but also codes of behaviour and most forms of knowledge (Bruce: 29).

Another voice is that of Callum Brown, who brings a social historical perspective to the sociology of religion and to an understanding of religious change. Brown has said that the secularization Bruce and others describe is actually 'de-Christianization', not just the decline of religion. In addition, he has noted that the decline in participation on the part of women has had a significant impact on the decline of Christianity, especially in Britain. In his preference for analysing this issue more in terms of cultural history and forms, rather than from an organizational and social empirical perspective, he has indicated that he is more interested in what people are thinking than in what they are doing. He wants to know their motivation – what is in their head (Brown, 2005).

Challenging Bruce's secularization theory and Brown's 'de-Christianization' theory is Steven Sutcliffe, who wrote about the devolution of the Scottish Parliament as a case study showing the emergence of a post-Christian culture. Sutcliffe argues that the diffusion of Christian culture and values during a time of growing cultural pluralism in Scotland has actually signalled the 'laicization and domestication of religious discourse and action in culture at large: literally, in "profane" culture' (Sutcliffe, 2004: 88). For

Sutcliffe, this shift has relocated, rather than erased, religion; in effect, it has become an appropriation of religion from professional church leaders and ministers by non-clerical people who are interested in and enthusiastic about it.

Roberts and Berger also disagree with Bruce regarding secularization. Roberts contends that 'the intimate interface between religion, culture and society is best explored not by the measurement of declining religiosity but by fresh investigation of key zones of affinity and interconnection' (Roberts: 10). Berger has made the point that

> the assumption that we live in a secularized world is false. The world today, with some exceptions to which I will come presently, is as furiously religious as it ever was, and in some places more so than ever. This means that a whole body of literature by historians and social scientists loosely labeled 'secularization theory' is essentially mistaken. (Berger, 1999: 2)

Recent research into the patterns of religion in Europe, especially in the North, being conducted by sociologist Grace Davie from the University of Exeter, has shown that in Britain since 1945, increasing numbers of people have tended to retain dimensions of religiousness, but not belong to institutional religions. She has said that 'believing without belonging is a pervasive dimension of modern European societies, it is not confined to the religious lives of European people' (Davie, 2002: 2). Looking for ways to understand this situation, she uses the term 'vicarious religion' to describe how a minority of people actively participate in religion on behalf of a larger number who understand and approve of what the minority is doing, but choose not to participate themselves.

Is the apparent demise of traditional religion, especially Christianity, truly heralding the end of religion, or the emergence of new forms of religiousness that can and will survive the major cultural upheavals occurring in contemporary societies? That question takes us to some of the research that has been conducted about changing religious forms.

Changing Religious Forms

Another sociologist who wrote in the early 1970s, Henri Desroche from France, approached religion from the standpoint of spiritual forms. His perspective was that forms of spirituality are social; therefore,

> where social structures are relatively fixed, their spiritual content is regularized. Where history moves again, spirituality is heightened, seeks new forms. (Desroche: xi)

He also conceptualized two sociologies of religion – one addressing the non-religious factors of religious phenomena, and the other analysing the religious factors of non-religious phenomena (Desroche: xiii–xiv). By doing this, Desroche was contributing to the expansion of perspectives from which religion could be studied.

Michel de Certeau addressed the issue of religion in modernity by asking the question of whether Christianity is even viable today. Of particular relevance is the way de Certeau described how Christian experience repeats the experience of Jesus, but in different ways. He wrote that just as any significant event 'makes possible or in a very real sense permits another type of relationship to the world', the early Christian church's experience of the life, death and resurrection of Jesus left traces, or effects, that led to more than the events themselves. He continued:

> It is, in historical research, one more trace of the relationship which from the beginning believers have fashioned when what they heard and learned became for them an event by 'opening their hearts' to new possibilities. And the writings of those believers express not the event itself, but that which the event made possible in the first believers. (de Certeau: 144)

As the end of the twentieth century approached, Thomas Luckmann and James Beckford described the changing face of religion when they wrote:

> For some, religion was expected to continue to contribute towards the stability of the new type of society even if it had to assume heavily modified or disguised forms. For others, religion in all forms would have to be swept away if the potential benefits of the new social order were ever to be realized. Still others refrained from such a long-term speculation, preferring instead to examine in detail the shifting and possibly unpredictable relationships between religion and political forces, economic affairs, moral values, education, and the practical affairs of everyday life. (Beckford and Luckmann: 1)

Beckford and Luckmann also addressed their concern that sociologists need to think about religion in contexts and categories much broader than the nation state. Following this, both acknowledged the tension between the globalization of religion and Luckmann's concept of invisible, privatized religions.

Many people have bridged their 'privatized' religions by joining what have come to be known as new religious movements (NRMs). One scholar who has specialized in researching NRMs is Eileen Barker, a sociologist of religion from the UK. She has explained that most of these movements began after the Second World War and offered their members either 'a religious or philosophical worldview' or a 'means by which some higher goal such as transcendent knowledge, spiritual enlightenment, self-realization or "true" development may be obtained' (Barker: 145). Though she has urged against applying generalizations about NRMs to all the movements, some typical characteristics she has attributed to them include variety and generalization in their beliefs; a cadre of converts, or first-generation believers; charismatic leaders, rather than 'committees'; a socio-economic status that is generally 'from the more privileged sections of society'; and a primary appeal to young adults in their early twenties (Barker: 9–15).

Related to Barker's work, Marion Bowman and Steven Sutcliffe have directed much of their research and writing towards alternative spirituality that is often labelled New Age or folk religion. Though there is not space for an in-depth exploration here, some of their work is contained in the publication they edited jointly, *Beyond New Age* (Sutcliffe, 2000b) and in Sutcliffe's *Children of the New Age – A History of Spiritual Practices* (Sutcliffe, 2003).

Memory is one of the important issues prompting the question of whether these new spiritualities will survive during this time of fragmentation and relativity. The next section explores how memory affects religion and its transmission, especially in cultures of change.

Personal and Collective Memory

In 1992, French sociologist Maurice Halbwachs's pioneering work on collective memory was translated into English. Its relevance to the transformation of religion in modernity is Halbwachs' insight into how important memory is in the process of passing on cultural, especially religious, traditions from one generation to another. Influenced by Durkheim in his understanding of the collective aspects of society and by process philosopher Henri Bergson in his appreciation for the psychological aspects of individuals, Halbwachs believed 'that collective memory is essentially a reconstruction of the past in the light of the present', that 'it needs continuous feeding from collective sources', and that it is 'sustained by social and moral props' (Halbwachs: 34).

To him, a society in the process of transforming its religion is essentially moving into unknown territory by asserting new principles that shake the societal centre of gravity and eventually require re-establishment of equilibrium. Because that society knows the new religion is not a complete beginning, it strives not only to adopt larger and deeper belief systems without losing the collective framework that had developed over time, but also to incorporate into that framework elements from older traditions (Halbwachs: 86). As the religious society stabilizes, it begins to articulate what it considers legitimate and what is heretical.

Halbwachs explained that the distinguishing feature in both orthodoxy and heresy is the way in which each perspective 'recalls and understands the same period of the past which is still close enough for there to exist a great variety of remembrances and of witnesses' (Halbwachs: 94). This, in turn, leads to the presence of two religious currents that each speak for the legitimacy of new traditions: the dogmatics, who claim 'to possess and to preserve the meaning and understanding' of doctrine, and the mystics, who claim 'to recover the meaning of texts and ceremonies' by means of personal experience, or interior light. The result is 'a constant conflict that is worth stressing, for in it we can clearly see the contradictory conditions under which collective memory is sometimes obliged to operate' (Halbwachs: 100).

Sometimes the immediacy of the initial personal experience becomes translated into generalities and abstract meanings that reflect commonly perceived truths, but may not be faithful to the factual nature of the original experience. When that happens the dominant story, or dogma, grows into a system that often loses contact with its earlier reference point. According to Halbwachs, 'it is of the nature of remembrances, when they cannot be renewed by resuming contact with the realities from which they arose, to become impoverished and congealed' (Halbwachs: 106). It is often at this point that mystics step in and access neglected and little-known parts of the tradition, thus highlighting the dialectic between lived remembrance and tradition reduced to formulas.

When a religious community creates rites and rituals that reflect their beliefs about a lived experience that remains in their memories, their celebrations maintain direct remembrance of significant spiritual events. However, when the rites, rituals and beliefs become uniform and unchanging, but passing time allows the remembrance of religious history to fade away, the context for those rites, rituals and beliefs no longer adequately explains their value and purpose. They then need to be interpreted, and that leads to the birth of dogma, which is promulgated by those in authority. The result is often a system based primarily on perceived 'legitimate' group authority, rather than on a religious feeling emerging from direct contact with original spiritual experiences.

Related to Halbwach's work on collective memory are the achievements of another Frenchman, Pierre Nora, who gathered contributions from colleagues in a variety of academic disciplines in an attempt to identify 'memory places' from French history. Their purpose was to understand

and portray these places within a 'sacred context' as 'imaginary representations and historical realities that occupy the symbolic sites that form
French social and cultural identity'. In his introduction to the English-
language edition of Nora's *Realms of Memory*, editor Lawrence Kritzman
wrote that the authors had not wanted an historical, empirical approach,
but sought to

> construct a symbolic encyclopedia that attests to the values and belief sys-
> tems of the French nation. Conceived as a history of France through
> memory, Nora's work not only demonstrates how memory binds com-
> munities together and creates social identities but also dramatizes how
> one's consciousness of the past is symptomatic of the disappearance of
> certain living traditions. (Nora: ix)

This 'encyclopedia' includes stories related to geographical places like Lascaux; historical figures like Joan of Arc; monuments and buildings like
Versailles; literary and artistic works such as books; and emblems, com-
memorations and symbols like the French flag – all of which represent the
consciousness of France and 'signify the context and totemic meaning from
which French collective identity emerges' (Nora: x). Through these stories,
Nora showed how French memory has undergone a metamorphosis from
a 'unitary framework' of collective memory into 'smaller configurations or
identities' that caused the politicization of memory. In addition, the fact
that the term 'realms of memory' has significance today is a sign that some
memory has actually disappeared, and society needs to represent what effectively no longer exists.

This work is a form of 'genealogical revisionism' that gives people the
opportunity to recycle knowledge through new symbolic representations,
and to mediate cultural myths by infusing them with their own desires.
Though memory used to unify society, today it reflects nostalgia for what
has been forgotten or lost. As a result, Nora and his colleagues have shown
how rewriting the history of memory in this way can actually forge new
paradigms of cultural identity (Nora: xiv) by looking beyond historical
reality 'to discover the symbolic reality and recover the memory that it sustained' (Nora: xvii). In doing so, they seek to relate the symbolic whole
to its symbolic fragments. For example, Nora described the qualitative
difference in perspective between acknowledging the factual discovery of
the Lascaux caves and framing that discovery as something that provides
France with a memory that extends back in time to 'our ancestors the
Gauls' (Nora: xx). It reflects a history interested in memory as an overall
structure of the past within the present.

With that in mind, we turn to the emerging field of consciousness studies and its potential role in providing a better theoretical understanding of how our minds work and how we actually relate to ourselves, each other, and the world.

Consciousness

From a basic standpoint, consciousness refers to the state of being aware of self, another, or something beyond the self. According to Ervin Laszlo (a member of the Scientific Medical Network in the UK and known for his work on new paradigms, system theory, unified science, and unified philosophy), in order to cope with the accelerated rate of change occurring in the world today

> A new mentality is needed; a new way of envisioning ourselves and the world around us. This calls for a new consciousness, and evolving such a consciousness calls in turn for a significant leap in cultural creativity. With that leap we can not only see the world, and ourselves in it, in a new and more adequate light; we can also take more responsibility for our actions. Consciousness, creativity, and responsibility are three facets of one and the same – the *problematique* of sustained well-being and positive human and social evolution at the dawn of the next millennium. (Laszlo: 323)

In parallel with Laszlo's reflection of perspectives within the Science and Medical Network (formerly the Scientific Medical Network), an organization based in the USA and designed to identify, describe and facilitate paradigmatic shifts in consciousness towards the betterment of the planet is the Institute of Noetic Sciences (IONS). Founded in 1973 by Apollo 14 astronaut Edgar Mitchell, its mission is 'to explore the frontiers of consciousness to advance individual, social, and global transformation' (IONS: 80). In the spring of 2007 IONS published 'The 2007 Shift Report – Evidence of a World Transforming'. Not surprisingly, the focus of the report is on how the transformational changes occurring across the globe are shifting dominant views, or paradigms, about how the world is. Funded through a special research grant, the report describes aspects of an actual paradigm shift occurring now in contemporary society. Furthermore, it reflects many of the characteristics Thomas Kuhn said were part of any shift in paradigm. In other words, it describes how worldviews that have been dominant for centuries are now breaking down and colliding with others that are emerging in science and spirituality (IONS: 21–5). It also addresses the tension present in attempts to resolve this crisis.

Recognized expert in the field of consciousness studies, Ken Wilber, has stated that 'Consciousness, interiority, and awareness in the broadest sense – and science – empirical investigation based on reproducible evidence – are arguably the two most important branches of the human knowledge quest' (Wilber, 1999: 175). In a summary of diverse and sometimes contradictory schools of consciousness studies, Wilber notes that researchers often choose one school and ignore the others. However, he calls for an integral science of consciousness that measures its progress by its 'capacity to include, synthesize, and integrate' all of them (Wilber, 1999: 179–80).

Focusing on the approaches that require the researcher's personal involvement in consciousness studies, Ravi Ravindra says certain types of learning require the perception of subtler and higher levels of consciousness. Furthering his argument, he states that 'True knowledge is obtained by participation and fusion of the knower with the object of study, and the scientist is required to become higher in order to understand higher things' (Ravindra: 188).

Psychology scholar David Fontana has compared Eastern and Western ways of approaching consciousness, describing the Western worldview as one in which consciousness is seen as secondary to the external material world, and the Eastern worldview as one in which consciousness is perceived as being primary. Making a case for the latter, Fontana writes:

> In contrast to the Western view that consciousness is secondary and merely an epiphenomenon acted upon and arising out of the material world, the East sees it as primary, a spiritual reality which creates the illusory material world by the act of experiencing it. (Fontana: 195)

Though siding with the Eastern approach, he refers to the developments in Western scientific thinking based on the research into quantum physics by physicists such as David Bohm, who wrote about the implicate order of the universe; Dana Zohar, who has written about human nature and consciousness as defined by this new physics; and Ervin Laszlo, who was cited earlier (Fontana: 197).

Another related perspective comes from co-founder of the Consciousness and Transpersonal Psychology Research Unit at Liverpool John Moores University, Brian Lancaster. He claims that most authors distinguish between a passive phenomenal quality of consciousness, its 'is-ness', and its active informational quality, its 'about-ness' (Lancaster: 68–9). In a way similar to Wilber, Lancaster also describes four levels of inquiry into consciousness: neuro-physiological; cognitive and neuro-psychological; depth-psychological; and spiritual-mystical. According to Lancaster, human beings operate on all of these levels.

Not unlike Ravindra in his reference to consciousness being a focus in earlier centuries, he sees the roots of the current 'awakening to consciousness' as having already started in the self-consciousness of the Renaissance. In both eras, the known world expanded through exploration; people encountered different cultures and traditions; and communication capacity burgeoned. Relying on W.P.D. Wightman's analysis (Wightman, 1972), Lancaster contends that the roots of modern science grew from a Renaissance interest in magic and the possibility of aligning the human mind with 'supernatural' powers to bring about 'miraculous' changes. In effect, it fostered an experimental attitude that led to development of the scientific method; brought about a resurgence of Neo-Platonic concepts, such as the relationship between the macrocosmic and microcosmic realms; and restored interest in kabbalistic texts. He described these factors as having come together in the Renaissance magus, who integrated all of them in experiments designed to discover the secrets of nature, synthesize information gained from diverse sources, and reach knowledge of the divine through participation in the Neo-Platonic mysteries. Most importantly for Lancaster, who has drawn upon the work of D.R. Griffin (Griffin, 2000), the natural world for the magus 'was animate, imbued with a world soul' (Lancaster: 54–5).

This brief exposure to contemporary explorations of consciousness provides a partial background for another issue that is emerging in contemporary society – that of changing perceptions of faith and belief.

Faith and Belief

Often associated with religion and spirituality, how have the words 'faith' and 'belief' been understood over time, and what meaning and relevance might they have in contemporary society?

Cantwell Smith has traced the development of the word 'religion' from its initial Latin *religio* to its present usages – in great part to show how cultural context influences the meaning and use of words. He has also identified a contrast between St Augustine's interpretation of *religio* as a 'vivid and personal confrontation with the splendour and the love of God' and the more modern understanding of religion as a 'system of observances or beliefs' (Smith, 1991: 29). From this work Smith has drawn the following conclusion:

I have become strongly convinced that the vitality of personal faith, on the one hand, and on the other hand (quite separately), progress in understanding – even at the academic level – of the traditions of other people throughout history and throughout the world, are both seriously blocked by our attempt to conceptualize what is involved in each case in terms of [a] religion. (Smith, 1991: 50)

As implied in the above quote, Smith's research led him to determine that distinguishing between the terms 'faith' and 'belief' would be far more helpful than defining religion when trying to understand (contemporary) religious phenomena.

Perhaps surprisingly to modern ears, the earliest meaning of 'belief' was somewhat similar. Its etymology as the verb 'to believe' initially meant 'to hold dear' or 'to cherish' – other ways of saying 'to love'. Smith has traced its historical development through English and German, providing examples of how 'to believe' in someone meant 'to trust or hold in esteem and affection'. Even in Early Modern English, the noun 'belief' meant a holding of someone as a beloved or as one in whom confidence or commitment is placed (Smith, 1998: 106–7). Smith showed that the Oxford English Dictionary refers to 'belief' as the word originally used for what we now call 'faith', or 'fidelity'. He then described how belief came to be associated with a perceived objective truth – whether there was evidence or not of its veracity; in other words, in some cases it also connoted holding on to something that might be false. In any case, its meaning had moved away from the notion of commitment to an honoured relationship. At the same time, the meaning of 'faith' began to evolve to the point in which one of its meanings became something akin to 'belief' in 'objective truths'. According to Smith, the Enlightenment brought the first era of widespread discussion 'centred not on transcendent realities, and not on faith, man's relations to them, but on the conceptualizations of both, and on man's relation to those conceptualizations: on believing' (Smith, 1998: 123).

Similar to Smith in his approach to understanding the terms 'belief' and 'believing' and to reflecting on their implications for perceiving 'the Divine' is Marcus Borg, who has written extensively about the different ways in which the initial experiences of Jesus have been interpreted over the years. Borg notes that the 'most common modern understandings of God in the Church (as well as in our culture) are deist or supernaturalist'. According to Borg, these concepts of the 'divine' being 'out there' and separate were 'products of the Enlightenment, which removed God from this world' (Borg: 38). However, Borg claimed that another way Christians have traditionally interpreted initial Jesus events has been seeing Him as a spirit person, and therefore, someone with whom a relationship could be established. That view

> shifts the focus of the Christian life from believing in Jesus or believing in God to being in relationship to the same spirit that Jesus knew. (Borg: 39)

An example that supports this different way of interpreting initial spiritual events and of looking at authority comes from Dr William Shaw, minister, retired professor, and official observer from Scotland at the Vatican II Council in the 1960s. For years he has told audiences how he listened to Council participants discuss sources of revelation, with much discussion about whether scripture or tradition had more importance. However, when Council fathers finally reached a conclusion, it was to proclaim that Jesus was the source of revelation; scripture and tradition were there to support that reality (Shaw, 2003). At least in theory, their decision affirmed that the relationship with Jesus took precedence over the more 'objecti-fied' elements of scripture and tradition – important as they may be to the church.

Given the emergence of so many societal perspectives on the factors pre-sented in this chapter, an exploration of selected developmental theories may shed light on several aspects of this phenomenon.

Developmental Theories

Because humanity is currently immersed in such immense whole-system changes, this section reviews some of the research describing how women and men think, face life-stage crises, make moral decisions, progress through adulthood in order to integrate into the larger society, and grow in their 'faith'.

Lifespan Theories

Best known in the field of lifespan development is Erik Erikson, who intro-duced the concepts of developmental stages and tasks, along with their accompanying crises and opportunities for choice. In Erikson's mind, the results of those choices determine the nature of the path taken to the next phase of development. Unlike Freud, he recognized the importance of cul-tural factors in those processes, though he did tend to see white American males as the norm. This gender difference becomes particularly apparent at adolescence. From that time on, Erikson describes the challenge of form-ing a coherent sense of identity and moving into later life stages as centring on the process of becoming an autonomous and separate adult.

Carol Gilligan has argued that an equal voice should be given to women, whose developmental choices appear to be different. She pointed out that because men and women experience attachment and separation in different ways, 'each sex perceives a danger which the other does not see – men in connection, women in separation' (Gilligan: 42). In like manner, Nicola Slee, who has researched women's faith development, added that Erikson's model 'does not do justice to women's experience of connectedness and rela-tionality, nor to very different cultural models of development where indi-vidual identity is considered less important than kinship loyalty and commitment to the group (Slee: 18).

Cognitive Development

Piaget is known for having identified three primary levels of cognitive devel-opment – each containing stages within them. The first is *pre-operational* and includes ways of knowing that arise from sensory-motor functions and intu-itive thinking without logical thought. Following that is *concrete operational knowing*, which involves inductive and deductive logic that is applied only to specific situations or occurrences. The third level is *formal operational know-ing*, and it requires the ability to think abstractly and hypothetically (Fowler, 1995: 244–5).

Moral Development and Decision-Making

Building on Piaget, Kohlberg's research with males led him to conceptualize a progression of three levels – each with two stages. On level one, overlap-ping with Piaget's pre-operational and concrete operational levels, males were found to make moral judgements based on individual need – initially experienced as reward or punishment and then as reciprocal fairness. Level two, paralleling Piaget's early formal operational and his dichotomizing formal operational functions, revealed a conventional conception of fairness based on shared social conventions that began with interpersonal expecta-tions and then moved into rules, law and order. The post-conventional third level, compared with Piaget's distinctions between dialectic and synthetic functions at the formal operational level, started with forming moral judge-ments based on a 'principled understanding of fairness that rests on the free-standing logic of equality and reciprocity', perceived to have existed prior to the creation of laws. It then moved to a kind of 'loyalty to being' that involved identification with and love for the entire species – for all life (Gilligan: 27; Fowler, 1995: 244–5).

Responding to Kohlberg's initial application of his 'male' model to both men and women, in 1982 Gilligan published her research on the ways women tend to make moral decisions. In it she stated:

> Thus in all of the women's descriptions, identity is defined in a context of relationship and judged by a standard of responsibility and care. Similarly, morality is seen by these women as arising from the experience of connection and conceived as a problem of inclusion rather than one of balancing claims. (Gilligan: 160)

This discovery provided new information not accounted for in Kohlberg's theory of abstract moral principles, and showed how the relational and contextual ways in which women worked to resolve moral dilemmas were basically different from those of men. Both sets of research results reflected contrasting moral ideologies – one of separation, which is justified by an ethic of rights, and another of attachments, which is supported by an ethic of care.

However, what brings them together is the life stage described by Erikson as when 'the knowledge gained through intimacy changes the ideological morality of adolescence into the adult ethic of taking care' (Gilligan: 164). In other words, though men and women may approach intimacy in different ways and in different times of their lives, the processes of reaching that state and coming to understand each other's perspectives create a morality that includes integrity and care.

Building on this information, we now look at the process of faith development, which has some similarities with the section on faith and belief.

Faith Development

As Cantwell Smith was writing about faith, belief and religion, one of Smith's students, James Fowler, began conducting his own research on stages of faith development. He had read research published by Smith, Piaget, Erikson and Kohlberg. Also familiar with Paul Tillich's writing about 'ultimate concern', Fowler wrote:

> Faith is a person's way of seeing him- or herself in relation to others against a background of shared meaning and purpose. ... Faith as a state of being ultimately concerned may or may not find its expression in institutional or cultic religious forms. Faith so understood is very serious

business. It involves how we make our life wagers. It shapes the ways we invest our deepest loves and our most costly loyalties. (Fowler, 1995: 4–5)

Embracing a developmental theoretical approach, Fowler's research reveals faith as a general life orientation, but also one that can be sustained by religious traditions that bring a sense of alignment with chosen values.

Fowler provides parallels with Piaget, Kohlberg and Erikson by indicating the thought and decision-making processes operative at each stage of faith development. He also analyses the 'locus of authority' existing at each stage of development. As might be expected, the locus starts with attachment to visible symbols of authority and moves to incumbents of authority roles. From there, it moves to the 'consensus of valued groups and in personally worthy representatives of belief-value traditions'. Next comes 'one's own judgement as informed by a self-ratified ideological perspective' in which norms and authorities must be congruent. The final stage moves from 'various expressions of cumulative human wisdom' to 'a personal judgement informed by the experiences and truths of previous stages, purified of egoic striving, and linked by disciplined intuition to the principle of being' (Fowler, 1995: 244–5).

Fowler recently applied these faith development stages in research that correlates faith stages with overall consciousness, approach to religion, type of politics likely to be desired, and organizational approaches likely to be adopted within a given society (Fowler, 1996: 174). Not only does his model provide an opportunity for further analysis of faith stages within groups of people, but his developmental approach allows for similar analysis of how Piaget, Kohlberg, and Erikson's stages might provide insight into modern religious thought and behaviour on a collective level, not just an individual one.

Slee has praised the significance of Fowler's work in its presentation of faith as something 'dynamic and changing over time, involving cognitive, affective and behavioural aspects', though she has joined others who are concerned about some of its limitations regarding the faith lives of women. There is not space to present Slee's theories in detail. However, her research has revealed three overall patterns in women's faith development: *alienation, awakening* and *relationality*.

Spiral Dynamics

Finally, a rather complex conceptual model of transformational change is Spiral Dynamics. Based on the bio-psychosocial systems work of the late Dr Clare W. Graves, Spiral Dynamics was developed by Dr Don Beck as a tool to identify and describe worldviews, beliefs, and key drivers or personal descriptors actively functioning within eight stages that Beck says form a spiral of development for individuals, groups, communities and global cultures. In effect, each step along the spiral provides a paradigmatic framework for how people with that perspective see, interpret, and act in the world. Barrett uses this model in his work on whole-systems change (Barrett, 2006: 132–7), which Beck, in collaboration with Christopher Cowan, elaborates in the book *Spiral Dynamics* (Beck and Cowan, 1996).

The Dynamics of Stage Change

In these developmental theories, the movement from one stage to another is of significance in its overall uniformity and consequences. Initially, the existing stage is deconstructed by any number of internal or external changes, resulting in 'a time of maximum discomfort and confusion for the individual', because the normative way of operating has broken down. Whether this happens suddenly or gradually, it is a time of dislocation, intense dissonance, emptiness, and waiting for something new to emerge. The new stage does not appear overnight, but actually comes forth from what has just dissolved. Though it is a time of great bewilderment and anxiety, it is also when new possibilities can come into consciousness (Slee: 20). However, most people can cope with the cognitive and emotional dissonance of this situation only for a limited time before they either break through into a new way of functioning, or they revert back to the fragmented constructs of the stage that has been deconstructing and 'causing' the anxiety. One major influence in determining whether someone will grow into another stage, or fall back into the 'familiar' with great intensity, is the attitudes of those around that person. Supportive communities can inspire courage to move into the uncharted territory of growth, but fearful ones can generate insecurity, fear and withdrawal.

This chapter concludes by briefly examining what is meant by the patriarchal paradigm.

The Patriarchal Paradigm

Many have written about this, but one person who has brought together key elements in the paradigm and presented them in an understandable and articulate way is Joan Chittister, a Benedictine Sister who researched this topic during her fellowship in the UK in the 1990s. Chittister contends that though there is one humanity with two genders, and that the prevailing patriarchal paradigm has placed intrinsic value only on one of those genders – the male – and on what Western society has considered 'masculine' qualities. In this paradigm the male is the norm and, as such, superior to the female who, along with nature, is flawed. Patriarchy, according to Chittister, 'rests on four interlocking principles: dualism, hierarchy, domination, and essential inequality' (Chittister: 24–5).

Flowing out of these principles are polarities that do not lead to balance, but are perceived as being in competition, and therefore dominated by a 'winner'. Not surprisingly, the 'winning' polarity is usually a quality assigned by society as typically 'masculine'. Because both women and men share many qualities, Chittister says both are penalized when they exhibit qualities considered by society to be 'feminine'. A general listing of polarities highlights the parameters of this paradigm, showing how they emerge naturally from the worldview embodied in the above-mentioned principles. The polarities are competition over collaboration; authoritarianism over dialogue; spirit over matter; reason over feeling; 'power over' over empowerment; pyramids over circles and networks; violence over non-violence; exclusivity over inclusion; beliefs over experience; religion over spirituality; and humanity over nature (Chittister: 49, 59, 73, 109, 121, 133, 141, 159). The issue for Chittister is how to bring these polarities into a new paradigm of balance and choice, based on what serves all of humanity. From her standpoint, this paradigm confines each gender to half of its potential, provides severe consequences for stepping out of societal expectations to conform to the paradigm, and has provided a rationale for environmental destruction. Furthermore, it has been part of Western society for so long that women and men alike have unconsciously internalized the paradigm as normal.

Echoing Chittister's concerns is King, who has written that

Much spirituality in the past was developed by a social, cultural and intellectual elite that was exclusively male. A comparative study of the counsels of holiness and perfection in different religions reveals that the spiritual search of men was often related to their contempt of the body and the world. Frequently this included a specific contempt for women. (King, 1998b: 101)

As a result of this, King has noted that many women have been leaving traditional religious institutions in Western society and seeking spiritual experience and 'nourishment' elsewhere. King says the women's movement is one of many 'often situated on the margins of or completely outside traditional religious institutions, because these are seen as too patriarchal and oppressive to respond to women's deep spiritual needs' (King, 2001: 10).

Table 1: Critical Factors in the Transformation of Religion

Critical Factors	Aspects
1. Social and cultural change	*Sociological theories*: cultural and symbolic factors critical in understanding change; *Modernity*: fragmented belief systems, but emergence of religiousness; *Global interdependence, identity, and change*: emerging world system with levels of identity – self, national society, world system, humankind; *Post-modernity*: questioning and relativity; *Whole-systems change*.
2. Secularization	Decline of religion in the West; Relativism, diversity and pluralism; De-Christianization or post-Christian; Individualism and community.
3. Changing religious forms	Religion: from holder of universal cosmology to psychology of individual in private sphere; Spirituality seeks new forms and refocuses on initial experience or event during change; Globalization of religion and invisible, privatized religions; New religious movements.
4. Personal and collective memory	Importance of memory in passing on cultural and religious traditions/codes of meaning memory; Linking past and present; Power and control: determining orthodoxy and heresy; balancing dogmatics (tradition reduced to formulas) and mystics (lived remembrance); Memories that are mutating, metaphorical, and/or fragments often kept in folklore; 'Genealogical revisionism' and identity.
5. Consciousness	Growing awareness of bigger picture; Nine diverse schools of consciousness studies; Future steps: continue research; personal shifts in consciousness for researcher; move towards integral theory; Internal and external worlds: implicate and explicate orders; quantum physics; system theory; Shift towards universal participatory consciousness; Awakening to consciousness with roots in Renaissance.

Table 1: Continued

Critical Factors	Aspects
6. Faith and belief	Faith and belief – original and current meanings; Relationship between faith/belief; Belief and believing; Legitimate authority from relationship and/or tradition.
7. Developmental theories	Lifespan theories: cultural factors, emergence of identity; gender differences; Cognitive development: Piaget; Moral development and decision-making: research on males (Kohlberg) and females (Gilligan); Faith development for men (Fowler) and women (Slee); Spiral dynamics and dynamics of growth and changing stages.
8. The patriarchal paradigm	One humanity with two genders: 'socially assigned' male qualities are the norm and considered superior; rests on five interlocking principles that generate polarities that are competitive, rather than approached with balance and choice in service to humanity; Internalized by both women and men; Confines both genders to half their potential; Harmful effects for men, women, and the environment.

Though more has been written about the patriarchal paradigm, the purpose of this section has been to provide a brief overview of what comprises the paradigm, and how its presence in contemporary culture has been influencing and prompting many of the transformative changes taking place in society.

Conclusion

The factors explored in this chapter form part of a multi-faceted but loose 'system' of influences, research findings, concepts and experiences that are present in and at times contributing to the transformation of contemporary society. In-depth analyses of each factor have not been provided, but there is enough information to enable further understanding and to stimulate deeper insight into the issues and their potential relevance. Eight of these factors, listed in Table 1 (above), are incorporated into an analysis of the issues addressed in Chapter Eight.

Chapter Three

Seeking a New Definition of Religion

Why a New Definition?

As explained in Chapter One, most academic attempts to define religion have inadvertently resulted in excluding those who do not match the 'institutional' profile. A new definition of religion, with both theoretical grounding and flexible parameters, has the potential to address this problem and shed light on previously inaccessible information about marginalized religious phenomena. Hervieu-Léger's new definition stands as a useful model.

Hervieu-Léger as a Sociologist among Colleagues

Professor Danièle Hervieu-Léger is President and Director of Studies at the *Ecole des Hautes Etudes en Sciences Sociales* in Paris, and also chief editor of the *Archives des Sciences Sociales des Religions*. The respect she has gained from many of her academic colleagues is reflected in what they say about her, and about the importance of the research she has described in her book *Religion as a Chain of Memory*. According to Nicholas J. Demerath, Professor of Sociology at the University of Massachusetts,

> It is hard to imagine a student of religion who wouldn't gain from this book. Every generation of religious scholars tends to produce one eminent figure who has a way of digging beneath the surface to find and shape the most critical issues. This splendid book stakes Hervieu-Léger's claim to that mantle. (WCFIA, 2000)

From the Director of the Institute on Religion and World Affairs, Peter Berger, comes the following endorsement:

> This book establishes Hervieu-Léger as one of the most important contemporary sociologists of religion. In the best tradition of French

sociology, she places the problem of modern religion within a broad interpretation of modern consciousness. Her book will be a classic in the field.
(WCFIA, 2000)

One of the scholars who reviewed her book, Jerome Baggett from the Jesuit
School of Theology at Berkeley in California, called it a 'gold mine of
insights pertaining to the nexus of religion and modernity' (Baggett: 779).
He praised her originality, as seen in part by her refusal to dwell on the issue
of modernity destroying religion, and by her explanation of modern religiosity, which he said 'comprises the chief theoretical contribution
of her book', though the 'richness of her contribution' lies in the details
(Baggett: 779). Another reviewer, Hubert Knoblauch of the University of
Zurich, offered support for her efforts to define and refine religion, suggesting that she 'may be truly preparing the ground – if not for the discovery of new religious forms, then for the renewal of the sociology of religion
as a discipline that tries to account for the transformation of religion in
modernity' (Knoblauch: 528). Sophie Gilliat-Ray from the University of
Wales in Cardiff, also a reviewer of the book, referred to Hervieu-Léger
as being 'highly respected' within the sociology of religion community
and said that Hervieu-Léger's book 'poses some key theoretical challenges'
for the sociology of religion, and also provides broad insights into modernity and social relations. In these ways, 'it is a rich, original, thought-
provoking and rewarding read' that Gilliat-Ray contends will stimulate
'many future discussions in the field' (Gilliat-Ray: 125). With this kind
of support and encouragement from academic colleagues regarding the
quality of Hervieu-Léger's contributions, the next step is to present her analytical model and explore its key elements.

Overview of the Model

Published first in French in 1993, and then in English in 2000, Hervieu-
Léger's book *Religion as a Chain of Memory* is a sociological redefinition and
re-examination of religion. Convinced that no religion survives in the
modern world without 'deep roots in [the] traditions and times' in which it
is considered relevant, Hervieu-Léger developed the concept of religion as a
chain of memory. Her reasoning is that individual believers must become
part of a community that links past, present and future members; in that
way, 'religion may be perceived as a shared understanding of collective
memory that enables it to draw from the well of its past for nourishment in
the increasingly secular present' (WCFIA, 2000). Furthermore, this 'act of

believing together' is a process in which the authority of a tradition is invoked as support for the community and as evidence of its legitimacy. In that way, any communities which claim a 'heritage of belief' can be designated 'religious'.

To support her model, she explores concepts such as modernity and secularization, the sacred, believing and belief, legitimizing 'religious' authority, tradition, collective memory, and the future of religious institutions. Regarding secularization, Hervieu-Léger counters the assumption that people in modern secular societies have found secular substitutes for religion by claiming that they have, instead, become *amnesiacs* who are 'no longer able to maintain the chain of memory that binds them to their religious pasts' (WCFIA, 2000). However, like Berger and other researchers, she points out that the process of losing those historical religious connections is actually creating a new hunger for spirituality, and opening up a space that only some kind of religion seems able to fill. To the question of how a collective memory is transmitted, she suggests that the process in which a community invokes, celebrates, and otherwise elaborates its chain of memory is actually the very process in which it constitutes, transcends and transforms itself as a religion.

Making a distinction between the transformation of religion in modern societies and the disintegration of various traditional religions that had originally helped shape the very cultures and societies that now reject them, Hervieu-Léger describes how sociologists now are freed from the empirical study of religion's decline to explore instead the religious productions of modernity both within and outside historical religions (Hervieu-Léger, 1999: 74–5). In doing so, she shows that even though behaviours or practices are often out of alignment with identified beliefs, and former social supports for a religious culture have disappeared, 'religion' remains alive in various and surprising forms.

Hervieu-Léger states that her goal in designing the model she presents in her book is to 'enable religion in modernity to be considered the subject matter of sociology' (Hervieu-Léger, 2000: 4). Supporting that goal, she outlines in the first third of her book problems facing the sociology of religion when grappling with religion in modernity. In the second section she presents a definition of religion that centres around the concept of memory, with its particular form of belief – one that implicitly calls on the authority of a tradition as its reference. She concludes with an exploration of how this definition might be applied in modern societies that are characterized by no longer being custodians of memory. Throughout her book, Hervieu-Léger reminds us of the 'hypothetical nature of the propositions made', insisting that she is trying to find a way to impose 'some shape and meaning on the

profusion of empirically observable phenomena', not to make 'a definitive statement about the place of religion in the context of modernity'
(Hervieu-Léger, 2000: 4).

The purpose of this chapter is to present the Hervieu-Léger model in a
way that is understandable and coherently related to many of the diverse
issues she addresses. Doing so will support Hervieu-Léger's process of pursuing her objective:

> to untangle a number of highly intractable theoretical knots: the defini-
> tion of modernity, the problem of belief, an explanation of the concept of
> tradition, an elucidation of the question of collective memory, and so on.
> (Hervieu-Léger, 2000: 5)

At the end is a brief summary of five components drawn from this model and
used as a basis for the fieldwork interview questions and analysis presented
in Chapters Seven and Eight.

Modernity and Its Impact on the Study of Religion

Hervieu-Léger lays the groundwork for a sociological approach to religion
by describing its birth pangs as an academic discipline. For sociologists of
religion, recognition that their branch of sociology is capable of investigating religion and treating it as a social phenomenon able to be 'explained in
terms of other social phenomena' has over time been the source of considerable controversy (Hervieu-Léger, 2000: 9). Particularly in France, where
Hervieu-Léger lives and where a history of conflict and suspicion has
marked relationships between the Catholic Church and other educational
and research institutions regarding claims of authority on the nature and
role of religion, moving from what was formerly called religious sociology to what is now sociology of religion has been an uphill struggle.
As one might imagine, religious sociology implied in France that sociologists
were being used to promote church teachings, whereas sociology of religion
reflected a more independent role – one in which sociologists of religion
could, in the opinion of Gabriel Le Bras, 'identify a common aim, "the structure and nature of organized groups for whom the sacred provides both the
principle and the purpose"' (Hervieu-Léger, 2000: 11).

Momentum in the 1950s for French sociologists to move towards a more
empirical sociology of religious phenomena among diverse groups somewhat facilitated their emancipation from perceived church manipulation,
even though this movement skirted the issue of defining religion itself or

more clearly articulating what actually constitutes a religion. They did not want to incite further conflict with the church, nor did they want to become larger targets for those who already had decided that a sociologist of religion must be studying that field only to perpetuate personally held religious biases stemming from either membership of a traditional religion or rejection of that kind of membership. It appeared as if sociologists were in a no-win situation.

Acknowledging that all who work in the social sciences have some degree of personal investment when choosing their work, Hervieu-Léger cites Pierre Bourdieu's contention that

'The field of religion, like all fields, is a realm of belief, but one in which belief has the active role. The belief that is systematized by the institution (belief in God, in dogma and so on) tends to mask belief in the institution . . . .' (Hervieu-Léger, 2000: 13)

Hervieu-Léger's concern, however, is that belief in the institution is not necessarily indicative of belief in all articles included within the institutional structure's system of beliefs. To her, when belief in institutions of secularized society, such as schools, political institutions and universities, is perceived to be less of a threat to a scientific attitude than belief in a religious institution, religion itself is the stumbling block and must, therefore, be directly addressed as a subject in its own right. It is this insight that prompts Hervieu-Léger to face the challenge of defining religion by reviewing similar efforts by other scholars, reflecting on her own research in this area, and building on insights gained through both processes.

Contextually, the sociology of religion owes its origin to the birth of sociology itself, which was established as a social science whose purpose was to study society. Because religion has been perceived as a system of meanings that helps people make sense of the world and their experience in the world, sociological attempts to scientifically study religious systems initially met with fierce resistance from those within the systems who were incensed that 'outsiders' would dare to analyse and potentially question religion's traditional role of authoritatively mediating societal meaning. However, Hervieu-Léger points out that sociology and religion meet in a mutual understanding that human free will is typically bounded by religious dictates perceived to reflect divine purpose. This conflict between the church, fighting to retain its authority, and science, striving to remove scientific exploration from the control of religious institutions, has a long history that has ultimately brought Western science to define itself in terms of its historical break with religion.

In the process, religions have declined, but they have not been eliminated. Instead, changes in religion due to modernity, as expressed in science and politics, have actually stimulated the development of new religious movements and strong support for the legitimacy of a new way of understanding religion. As Hervieu-Léger says, religion, 'even in the act of disintegrating, shows astonishing resistance; it re-emerges, revives, shifts ground, becomes diffuse' (Hervieu-Léger, 2000: 24). Taking a broad social perspective, she also notes that religion has not declined just because science has claimed to be a superior form of knowledge, but because social change has eroded society's collective ability to set up ideals; and that has effectively loosened social bonds. Furthermore, science has no power to assume religious functions, such as providing moral guidance and attending to the need for ritual, which are found outside the realm of knowledge.

Drawing upon Durkheim and Weber in an attempt to understand this paradox, Hervieu-Léger builds a foundation for further exploration. Because Durkheim's ultimate goal was 'to uncover the universal character of religious life in order to disclose an essential, enduring aspect of social life' (Durkheim: xvi), he came to see religion as a system of symbols, including beliefs and practices, by which society expresses and represents its essentially sacred self, or soul, to itself. For him, society was not a substitute for God; however, he saw how the gap left by religion could be filled by making society the basis of morality and the herald of ethical ideals that could transcend individual instincts and self-absorption. Durkheim was charged with an 'evolutionary optimism' in his vision of a 'religion of mankind' that would require no church, rigid orthodoxy, or organization. This vision would stand with others as an example of how the question of religion was broader and far more important than analysing the loss of religion in modern societies (Hervieu-Léger, 2000: 26).

Weber's perspective on the future of religion followed a different line, though he addressed the question of what would replace historic religions in a world where supernatural references have declining credibility. According to Weber, 'polytheism of values' began to emerge on the religious landscape; however, shifts in belief that marginalize religion did not necessarily imply the disappearance of a need for meaning or transcendent moral imperatives. Weber did not clarify what new religious forms may be emerging, and unlike Durkheim, he did not define religion.

Wanting to create a new perspective that moves beyond Weber and Durkheim, Hervieu-Léger urges sociologists of religion to pay attention to the social reasons for religion no longer retaining a central place in modern societies. For her, the increasing divide between stated beliefs and actual practices for both individuals and communities is one reflection of the 'fragmented character of modern manifestations of belief' and the 'disappearance of the link between society and religion' (Hervieu-Léger, 2000: 29).

Nevertheless, Hervieu-Léger reminds us that religion still makes itself felt 'implicitly or invisibly throughout the gamut of human expression' and that the problem is to know what parameters to set in conducting an investigation (Hervieu-Léger, 2000: 29). Understanding that sociologists are not alone in trying to investigate complex phenomena, she draws upon Pierre Nora in identifying 'realms of memory' that make up the symbolic history of a people. What history and sociology share in this instance is the 'erosion of structured systems of representation (political in the one, religious in the other) linked to precise social practices and developed by clearly identifiable social groups' (Hervieu-Léger, 2000: 30). Hervieu-Léger suggests that the current move towards looking at a variety of social issues from a systems and interdisciplinary perspective reflects the need to re-establish coherence that has been disrupted by institutional differentiation and specialization.

In light of this background and the essentialist/non-essentialist orientations towards the need to define religion, she says that defining the scope of religion, identifying indicators that distinguish it from other phenomena, and wrestling with the fact that research methodology is guided by the definition one uses, remain blocks that must be cleared. Another challenge she sees is to differentiate between definitions of religion that are associated with the substance of belief, and those that provide a more functional, process-oriented approach. Using substantive criteria could restrict a researcher to the exclusive and narrow limits of established historical religions, whereas adopting a functional, or process, definition may be so inclusive that it could pose the problem of knowing where to set limits.

Moving beyond this kind of debate into action has been prompted by the development of new religious movements (NRMs), which Hervieu-Léger has described as

> an umbrella for a wide range of phenomena: cults and sects that have recently come into competition with traditional churches (dominant or the historic minorities), eastern-inspired syncretism, movements aiming to renew institutionalized religions; ... which show a marked ability to assimilate and recycle available knowledge, be it 'scientific' or marginal and fragmentary with roots in ancient learning, and which purpose and promise individual self-transformation. (Hervieu-Léger, 2000: 32–3)

Sometimes considered among the 'invisible religions', these are the groups that have prompted questions regarding the limits of religion and intense discussion over the relative merits of pursuing an intensive sociology of religious groups, an extensive sociology of belief systems, or both.

Prior to their emergence as a powerful presence, 'modern symbolic consumers' were already being explored by Luckmann to determine how they were incorporating a 'multitude of meanings' into a 'sacred cosmos of modern industrial societies' that could help them 'respond to ultimate questions' (Hervieu-Léger, 2000: 33). According to Luckmann, an expanded and modern view of the sacred emerged when modern societies stopped asking institutionalized historical religions to provide a framework for social organization and instead started to rely on individual or group ability to achieve direct access to available cultural symbols in constructing their own universes of meaning. Needing no institutional mediation for meaning, the personal freedom inherent in this shift has helped individuals transfer their attention from a transcendent other world to a more immediate experience of the sacred in this world. In many ways, it reflects Durkheim's philosophy of the sacredness of society and Max Weber's insistence on understanding religion as a 'galaxy of meanings' that can help humanity transcend the challenges of daily life. We find in Luckmann an inclusive, functionalist approach in which 'everything in humanity which lies outside biological survival taken in its most narrowly material sense has to do with religion' (Hervieu-Léger, 2000: 35).

In contrast, Bryan Wilson has constructed an exclusive, substantive type of ideal religion that draws upon the supernatural and directs its creativity to projects and activities designed to transform society. Hervieu-Léger says that this approach effectively excludes NRMs, because they 'strive to bring about individual regeneration and fulfilment, rarely to change the world' (Hervieu-Léger, 2000: 36). Even though she agrees with Luckmann's view, which she thinks represents a more expansive and needed approach to religion, Hervieu-Léger and Luckmann both doubt that the fragmented systems of beliefs present in the NRMs and perceived by them to focus only on individuals, not society, could coalesce enough to form new religious institutions or a coherent and modern sacred cosmos. I agree with Hervieu-Léger in her contention that both functional and substantive definitions of religion available thus far have contained radical limitations that continue to hinder a clear understanding of religion in modernity. However, I think more research is needed before declaring that most NRMs rarely strive to change the world. She and Luckmann are probably accurate in contending that the NRMs may not coalesce into new religious institutions, but that may be due to a paradigm shift among the NRMs – one in which individual growth within the context of community actually does foster a transformed and coherent understanding of sacred cosmos, but does not express that new-found understanding within familiar institutional forms. Follow-up studies on this are needed.

In an attempt to resolve this dilemma, Hervieu-Léger researched the work of Roland Campiche and Claude Bovay, who in their study of religion in Switzerland attempted to 'go beyond the substantivist and functional positions by bringing them together and finding in one a solution to the drawbacks of the other' (Hervieu-Léger, 2000: 39). Their writings incorporate an analysis of process on two levels: the disintegration and reintegration of belief due to modernity with its individualization, pluralization and uncertainty; and the demolition and reconstruction of social and cultural structures that provide denominational identification. Hervieu-Léger says that

> the relevance of the project to an analysis of the transformations undergone by religion applies best within a social and cultural milieu in which the structures of institutionalized religions, though no longer directly and exclusively arranging for individual and collective access to a state of transcendence, still offer major symbolic references and at the very least define the social functions of such a reference. (Hervieu-Léger, 2000: 40)

Because the split between traditional culture and religion is often more severe in some countries than in others, this type of analysis will not work everywhere. As such, Hervieu-Léger takes us to the next important component in striving for a definition of religion: the sacred.

The Sacred

Almost as difficult to define as religion, attempts to define 'sacred' and its relationship to religion in modernity have frequently brought more confusion than clarity. Likewise, in an age when the differentiation and individualization of modernity have wrested from institutional religions their monopoly on authoritatively responding to essential questions about existence, the space remaining is often filled in by individuals with an expanded notion of the sacred that encompasses any reference to mystery, the transcendent, or fundamental values. Even so, Hervieu-Léger suggests the possibility that

> the notion of the sacred may serve to cover a structure of meanings common both to traditional religions and to new forms of response to the ultimate questions about existence, extending beyond the beliefs developed on each side. (Hervieu-Léger, 2000: 43)

Perhaps, she says, the 'domain of the sacred' refers to an innate structure characterized by a commonality shared by all its diverse forms of expression. Though Hervieu-Léger does not specify this directly, I think that this innate structure is the inter-relatedness and interdependence of all existence. Following this, *the sacred itself would actually be a state of consciousness in which all aspects and expressions of existence are valued, and their interdependence is perceived and experienced on a personal level.* Naturally, awareness of this value and connection can grow slowly, or emerge suddenly in moments of spiritual or religious intensity.

One of the recurring challenges in modernity is the tendency for researchers to portray 'sacredness and religiousness' as 'mirror-images of each other' rather than as distinct, but potentially related, phenomena. Liliane Voye argues that 'the sacred must not be reduced to the religious', but her further description of religion as 'the means by which sacredness is given form, sacredness as the raw material of religion', brings the notion of sacred back into the lap of traditional religions as the ones holding 'the supreme imprint of the sacred within the social' (Hervieu-Léger, 2000: 45). Albert Piette also fell into this convergence. Trying to avoid tying religion and the sacred together, Piette referred to 'religiosity' as 'the presence of characteristic elements of religion in the different secular fields', and to 'sacrality' as 'the construction of a sacred dimension, based on contemporary values which are productive of meaning' (Hervieu-Léger, 2000: 46). However, when he attempted to use these separate meanings to study his own Christian religion, he found himself re-establishing the religion-sacred link. Because the notion of the sacred is so ambiguous, and it is difficult to distinguish its presence in symbolic productions of modernity, Hervieu-Léger thinks the problem of this continual linking of religion with the sacred lies in the genealogy of the notion of 'sacred'.

Francois-Andre Izambert's analysis of the sacred explains that there was no isolated concept of the sacred until Robertson Smith; then Durkheim and his followers began to address it. To the Durkheimians, defining a notion that appeared to be common to all peoples, and was generally found in all religions, was a way of giving voice to a mysterious power that stood in opposition and contrast to a profane world. Relying primarily on an Enlightenment rationality that cast soul against matter, Durkheim had already identified this profane world as being different from the sacred when he wrote that 'sacred things are cast into an ideal and transcendent setting, while the material [i.e. profane] world is left entirely to others' (Durkheim: 38).

I think Durkheim's desire to name and describe the sacred as something in opposition to the 'mere' physical led him and his followers beyond mere differentiation into the prevailing cultural paradigm of dualism and hierarchy. Not only did he limit matter, but also by ignoring the ability of the non-physical mind to reflect on and become aware of the value and interrelatedness of both physical and non-physical forms of existence, he limited the soul. His new definitions of sacred and profane moved these newly articulated concepts from descriptors of different types of experience into principles behind diverse religious expressions, through which all spiritual and religious paths converge (Hervieu-Léger, 2000: 49). Even though identifying the sacred came to be seen as a subject that binds all religions together and separates them from the rest of the world, in effect this perspective still operates out of a paradigm in which difference does not mean equal, and it naturally results in a hierarchical struggle for dominance and legitimacy.

To this day we see how the struggle for legitimacy continues to manifest itself in relationships among many existing organized religions, and between those religions and individuals as they differ with each other about whose voice more authoritatively reflects the sacred. One example of when the individual is perceived to be more highly valued than the authority of a religion or mediated revelation is the increasing use by individuals of the sacred as the new legitimizing authority for their subjective convictions about the nature of religious experience. Not only can more individuals now claim understanding of the sacred with greater confidence, but also their subjective religious experiences are often seen as validating the existence of the sacred as an objective reality. However, even with this development, the notion of the sacred as being attached to the image of institutionalized religions remains prevalent.

Though based on the Durkheimian contrast between sacred and profane, Izambert has noted that this concept of sacred does not actually correspond to the worldview of all religions. Referring to Eliade's work with indigenous and shamanic religions, in which the sacred can be experienced in any substance, she pointed out that this Durkheimian construct is not universal, but is valid only if one is studying institutionalized historical religions. In light of this, Izambert suggests that Durkheim's conceptual framework for the sacred appears to be a transposition of a Christian, specifically Catholic, perspective reflecting the opposition between church supporters and opponents. Though there may be truth in that, I think it also reflects a contrast between Enlightenment rationality and subjective experience, a difference between institutionalized historical religions and indigenous spiritualities, and as described earlier, an example of the prevailing cultural paradigm of dualism and hierarchy.

Izambert's analysis portrays a process in which the intentions of those who sought to separate the sacred from religion were hindered. Referring to the sacred was initially designed to further two primary goals. One was to help identify religious dimensions existing beyond the confines of institutionalized historical religions and thereby 'to wrest the definition of the religious from religion' (Hervieu-Léger, 2000: 50). The other was to prevent institutionalized historical religions from becoming the only authority for defining answers to fundamental questions about existence and meaning. For Hervieu-Léger, the conditions that created the need to define the sacred are the very ones that block its usefulness – 'namely, the preponderance of the Christian model in thinking about religion' and 'in analysing modern systems of meaning' (Hervieu-Léger, 2000: 51). I would add 'rationalist perspective' and its context of dualism and hierarchy to Hervieu-Léger's conditions blocking the usefulness of the term 'sacred'.

Though Hervieu-Léger moves away from Durkheim's sacred–profane dichotomy, she finds value in his analysis of the primary experience of the sacred as a 'wellspring of emotion'. In addition, she notes that this is aligned with a well-established sociological and psychological tradition, found in the writings of Joachim Wach, Henri Bergson and Roger Bastide, that

> religious expressions (beliefs, rites, types of community, etc.) are never other than transmitted (and limited) manifestations of a religious experience which merges with the emotional experience of the sacred. (Hervieu-Léger, 2000: 52)

Hervieu-Léger then describes the influence of William James. For him, validating the inner experience of human beings who communicate with that mysterious 'other' allowed him to distinguish between emotions, which are at the heart of religious feeling, and institutional manifestations of these emotions. Referring to Hubert's contention that religion can be understood as administering the sacred, Hervieu-Léger adds that individual and collective religious experience can never be fully reduced to doctrines or contained in liturgies. She makes a distinction between religious experience and administration of the sacred in order to enable identification of a 'pure religious core' that is separate from the forms in which those primary religious experiences are socialized (Hervieu-Léger, 2000: 53). In this she reflects Halbwachs in his reference to an initial spiritual experience that subsequently stimulates and is supported by memory; Cantwell Smith's focus on the original meanings of belief and faith as 'holding dear', or cherishing, the experience of a relationship; de Certeau's perspective that the experience of a significant spiritual event 'opens the heart' to new possibilities;

and Borg's contention that for many Christians over the centuries, the experience of a relationship with Jesus has taken precedence over dogmatic tradition.

In summary, religions were designed to mediate and pass on sacred experiences. However, in many cases the doctrines and dogmas defining those experiences have taken precedence over a conscious awareness of value and inter-relatedness; in doing so, they have effectively snuffed out the affective, experiential dimension that is the sacred. For Hervieu-Léger, 'the experience of the sacred may under certain conditions testify to the end of religion, not to its return' (Hervieu-Léger, 2000: 58).

Anticipating the question of how the modern emotional experience of 'sport' relates to the primary religious experiences referred to above, Hervieu-Léger acknowledges that sport does in some way fulfil a function that used to belong to religion. To describe their experiences, athletes often use language that sounds like religious mysticism when they describe 'the intoxication of transcending one's limits and becoming one with the elements'. Furthermore, there is a clear parallel between 'the mythological structure of sport and the mythological structure which characterizes traditional religions' (Hervieu-Léger, 2000: 54). Finally, the mobilization of crowds in a variety of symbolic rituals even shows how sport has incorporated yet another traditionally 'religious' activity.

However, Hervieu-Léger cautions us to refrain from assuming that the return of emotion or the presence of mass ritual equals the resurgence of the sacred. In addition, she warns that a return of the sacred does not necessarily equal religion or mark religion's return to the centre of modern society. In fact, for Hervieu-Léger, modern manifestations of ecstasy actually might be symptomatic of 'an impoverished religious imagination, manifesting itself in the quest for immediate contact with supernatural powers'; as such,

the emotional experience of the sacred in modernity may well mark not the final triumph of religion over the imperialism of reason but the completion of the process of ridding the modern world of its presence. (Hervieu-Léger, 2000: 57–8)

Citing examples of contemporary Christian communities that attempt to short-circuit doctrinal and ritual regulations in order to develop more suitable expressions of their subjective religious experiences, she acknowledges that 'sacred and religion relate to two types of distinct experience' (Hervieu-Léger, 2000: 58) that often conflict with each other. Again, a parallel exists in Weber's description of the prophet in relationship to the established norm and in Halbwachs' description of the differences between dogmatists and mystics.

Re-Thinking Belief

Influenced by Henri Desroche, who urges sociologists of religion to approach religion as something perceived and defined by society, and to examine other social manifestations, which *by analogy* seem to call for a similar approach, Hervieu-Léger introduces the work of Jean Seguy and his concept of metaphorical religion. Steeped in the work of Weber and his ideal-typical definition of religion, Seguy begins with Weber's contention that religion's distinguishing feature, the relationship between humans and supernatural power, lies at the convergence of a formal characterization of religious phenomena and a comprehensive approach to phenomena of belief. Building on this, Seguy sees religion as a meaningful form of collective action, something that determines the relations between humans and supernatural powers (Hervieu-Léger, 2000: 66).

Though his writing omits Weber's reference to social or political phenomena in which belief plays a part, Seguy seems confident that when Weber referred to those 'profane' phenomena in religious terms, he was 'making metaphorical use of religious concepts'. Rather than identifying 'authentic' religions in the theoretical sense, Seguy thinks that references to the conflicts of values in the modern world are actually analogical, or metaphorical, religion. In other words, though they do not refer to a supernatural power, they still produce meaning, are open to transcendency, and provide a foundation for moral obligations – factors typically ascribed to 'religion'.

The process of metaphorization for Seguy expresses a principle intrinsic to modernity, one in which modernity is 'at work on itself'. Because of modernity, societal components such as politics, art, science, sexuality and culture have broken free from the control of institutional religions and in the process, begun to manifest their inherent religious features differently – metaphorically. As this has happened, their new autonomy has made them available for a new kind of religious function that can now be compared 'with that performed by traditional religions in pre-modern society' (Hervieu-Léger, 2000: 67). For example, many business leadership books and quality training programmes call for leaders to develop organizational mission and vision statements, along with lists of company values and guiding principles, as part of preparing strategic business plans (Senge, 1992). Similarly, whole-systems change leader Richard Barrett refers to liberating the corporate soul (Barrett, 1998). International change management companies like the Pacific Institute provide programmes aimed at helping individuals, groups, organizations and businesses identify habits, attitudes, beliefs and expectations that help or hinder personal and/or collective goal-setting and achievement, including their ethical practices (Tice, 1976). Finally, modern spiritual figure Sri Sri Ravi Shankar, who primarily speaks of his work as spirituality, not religion, started the Art of Living Foundation, which is designed to help foster human values (Shankar, 1982).

An analogical approach to manifestations of believing that lie outside the bounds of institutional religions often leads to the conclusion that metaphorical religions have become substitutes, or replacements, for them. However, Seguy contends that institutional religions are themselves subject to this metaphorization process initiated by the 'ever-increasing intellectualization and spiritualization of the beliefs which form their basis'. As a result, metaphorical religions can be seen not as residues of past religion, but as 'the formative apparatus of modern religion' (Hervieu-Léger, 2000: 67–8).

Though Hervieu-Léger says there are few examples of this kind of self-transformative process, she does provide Izambert's description of the change in the Catholic liturgy of the sick, brought about by church reforms implemented in the early 1970s. These reflect the spiritualizing of dogma by reinterpreting meaning in order to retain relevance in modern circumstances. They also reflect the essence of the word 'metaphor', which points to a variety of symbolic meanings existing beyond literal understanding.

Motivated by Seguy's work, Hervieu-Léger incorporates the notion of loss by saying that the existence of a new metaphorical religion, or of an institutionalized religion that has been metaphorized, may mark

a transitional phase between a cultural world where to invoke supernatural forces is self-evident or plausible, and a world – the disenchanted world of modern rationalism – where such an appeal has become improbable, if not impossible. (Hervieu-Léger, 2000: 70)

This perspective is similar to Graham Ward's statement that modernity has tended to reflect the erasure of 'God' and 'God-talk' from the public arena. I would add that it has also ushered in a new opportunity to address the issue of spirituality – often called religiosity by Hervieu-Léger. What Hervieu-Léger finds most valuable is Seguy's profound insight that the loss prompted by modernity has been change in a *way of believing*. By showing how metaphorical religion also operates within institutional religions, Seguy has opened the door for seeing religion as 'a specific mode for articulating belief' and 'a way of believing' that can draw upon the pre-modern traditions of institutional religions, not just declare their erosion and imminent ending. Viewing religion as a way of believing, a concept Seguy has at least implicitly introduced, requires, in Hervieu-Léger's opinion, that metaphorical religion be valued equally with established historical religion, and as such, be recognized for being as fully religious as established historical religions.

Following this line of thought leads to a closer look at the concepts of belief and believing, and the logic behind contemporary religious transformations. By taking an approach that looks at these concepts from the standpoint of the change process itself, definitions become less about 'fixing' an object and more about identifying dynamic 'axes of transformation around which the object reconstructs itself'. Regarding belief and believing, Hervieu-Léger explains:

> it is important that all analysis be focused not upon the changing contents of belief, but upon *the mutating structures of believing* which these changes in content partially reveal. (Hervieu-Léger, 1999: 84)

In addition, these mutating structures are seen as part of a global dynamic that includes the encompassing, transforming, and reorganizing of the organized religions themselves. Thus, for Hervieu-Léger, the term 'to believe' has come to designate

> the totality of both individual and collective convictions which do not arise from verification, experimentation or, more generally, from isolation and control criteria which characterize scientific knowledge; convictions which have their basis in the fact that they give meaning and coherence to the subjective experience of those who hold them. (Hervieu-Léger, 1999: 84)

Rather than the substance of belief being separate, or distant, from the believer, that substance becomes an experiential enactment of itself through action, language and practice in the lives of its adherents. It reflects an alignment between convictions held and actions taken.

Hervieu-Léger explains that believing has several levels of structuring. One which is common to all humans was described by Bourdieu as a self-evident state generally experienced unconsciously as 'the way life is' (Hervieu-Léger, 2000: 72). At the opposite extreme is the 'range of formalized, rationalized beliefs' that are the subject of people's conscious attention and reflection about possible implications in their lives. Recognizing how central believing is in the lives of all people leads Hervieu-Léger to say that the act of believing is actually at the centre of human thinking, and therefore plays a major role in modernity.

She refers to those who were steeped in the rationality of science and technology of the last two centuries and assumed that by shifting the key question of meaning from *why* to *how*, they would remove 'most of the mystery of the world', and thereby eliminate the need for belief. Instead, the uncertainty brought on by modernity has raised society's need for assurance when facing the existential questions of meaning and survival. Whether one agrees or disagrees with Berger that the sacred is none other than a 'construct of meanings which humanity objectifies' and sees it as a separate power – a kind of sacred cosmos – to escape feeling overwhelmed by chaotic change, modernity still takes the form of

> many fragmented demands for meaning whose urgency reflects a world that is no long fixed and stable, representative of the natural order, but unpredictable and unprotected, where change and innovation have become the norm. (Hervieu-Léger, 2000: 73)

Because the dismantling of meaning systems has stimulated even more questions of meaning, Hervieu-Léger suggests that to identify modern believing, one must analyse how the different ways used to resolve uncertainty are 'refracted in a diversity of beliefs'.

Returning to Seguy and the implied expulsion of reference to a supernatural power contained in his description of metaphorical religion, Hervieu-Léger discusses how this in some ways exemplifies the classic understanding of the rationalist imperative of individual autonomy in determining belief. At the same time, she clearly points out that the process of believing has not died. The socio-symbolic systems of belief, their figures of transcendency, which ensured the stability and coherence of beliefs and practices, and their externally set norms for governing the belief of their members, may have been toppled. However, 'modernity has deconstructed the traditional systems of believing, but has not forsaken belief' (Hervieu-Léger, 2000: 74).

In light of her research, Hervieu-Léger proposes that we abandon the traditional markers of content and function when defining religious belief, and instead concentrate on the type of legitimation that is applied to the act of believing. She makes the assumption that 'there is no religion without the authority of a tradition being invoked' to support the act of believing. With that in mind, she refers to a study conducted in the 1970s to learn about intentional neo-rural communities, or utopias, that had been established in France, which reflected a variety of newly developing intentional communities springing up throughout the world. As their communities developed, members seemed to move collectively through several stages in what turned out to be a system of believing. In that process, they looked beyond the norm of primitive simplicity towards values that would ensure the group's survival (a settled way of life, controlled use of resources, action for a common purpose, etc.). (Hervieu-Léger, 2000: 78)

By doing that, they were creating a system to help them in this new life-style. This led to a deepening of their belief in the importance of the lifestyle they had chosen to adopt, setting them in symbolic opposition with those in society who had not chosen this kind of lifestyle. Durkheimian in approach, they had decided that their way of life was sacred, while that of others was profane. Furthermore, their vision of the world emerged from their day-to-day life in community, which included ritual observances. These characteristics appeared to researchers to be classic signs of construct-ing a sacred cosmos.

However, subsequent reflection led researchers to see that a more accur-ate indicator of a sacred worldview was the existence of a symbolic dialectic, which was reflected in each community's need to develop, shape, and clarify a way of believing that legitimized their decision to separate from mainline society and distinguish themselves by creating a new model of living.

To determine whether their way of believing had become religious, Hervieu-Léger identifies another factor whose importance the researchers eventually recognized: a community's choice to invoke 'a cloud of witnesses whose presumed existence gave validity to the experience'. Within these neo-apocalyptic communities

reference to witnesses enabled groups, which were isolated in their strug-gle to survive, to model themselves on any forerunners who had faced up to the dangers of destruction brought upon humanity by human self-sufficiency. (Hervieu-Léger, 2000: 80)

Researchers noticed the 'symbolic significance' that communities seemed to draw from seeing themselves as 'part of a prophetic tradition'. Rather than being of secondary importance, it became clear that of primary signific-ance to members of these communities was 'invoking a core lineage' that was 'seen to confirm the passage from a secular to a religious apocalyptic' (Hervieu-Léger, 2000: 80).

Apparently, what seems to matter here is not that the specific tradition invoked is religious in an objective or dogmatic way, but that it is a tradi-tion through which communities can appeal to past witnesses in a way that links them across time and binds them together in an all-absorbing chain of belief. Furthermore, this 'self-legitimizing of the act of believing by reference to the authority of a tradition' effectively moves a community from a *rational* perspective of doing something because it's the 'right thing to do' to a *relational* perspective in which they are 'begotten' from a lineage which confers membership in a larger spiritual community (Hervieu-Léger, 2000: 81). On this point we find echoes of Durkheim and Weber's 'collective sacred'; Weber's 'prophetic charisma' found not only in individuals, but within groups; Halbwachs's description of the mystics' desire for direct contact with the original spiritual experience, along with society's need for coherence when reconstructing the past to create a collective memory; Flood's claim that religions are narratives concerned about identity; and Cantwell Smith and Fowler's contentions that faith and belief originally referred to a beloved relationship.

Hervieu-Léger's comprehensive and multi-faceted study of phenomena such as religion, the sacred, belief and believing, and their interaction with modernity, and her observations about the significance of invoking a core lineage, or tradition, as a legitimizing authority for a community's way of believing, lead her finally to present her own working definition of religion:

> one might say that a religion is an ideological, practical and symbolic system through which consciousness, both individual and collective, of belonging to a particular chain of belief is constituted, maintained, developed and controlled. (Hervieu-Léger, 2000: 82)

Acknowledging that this raises objections and carries implications, she reiterates her understanding that this is a 'working concept' – one she hopes will enable researchers to grasp what justifies treating traditional and secular religions, along with their future within modernity, from a sociological viewpoint. Her objective is also to determine whether contemporary expressions of any traditions regarded by society as having to do with religion can be characterized as religious when viewed through her definition.

The Concept of Tradition

To consider the legitimizing authority of a tradition as an aspect of religion, we must understand the concept of 'tradition'. Hervieu-Léger refers to M. Gauchet, who described tradition as that which generated continuity in pre-modern societies. He explained how tradition has always symbolized a relationship with the past that imposed conformity with a code of meaning, and therefore values; in doing so, it has governed individual and collective life and has been transmitted from one generation to another. However, though tradition has continued to retain a core from the code's creation, it has consistently allowed for transformation in its expressions over time. In effect, the continuity that a tradition generates reflects a kind of evolutionary process in which old forms are plunged into disarray and chaos, only to be re-structured, re-employed and transformed into re-constructed expressions of the code within modernity.

Hervieu-Léger says that 'in the world of tradition, religion is the code of meaning that establishes and expresses social continuity' (Hervieu-Léger, 2000: 84). Countering objections that this understanding of religion relegates it to a passive and nostalgic function of 'remembering the old days', she responds in two ways. She first looks closely at the relationship between tradition and social change; then she considers whether an active and dynamic tradition can be a force for renewal in modernity.

Regarding the relationship between tradition and social change, her view is that the role of religion, as the code of a tradition, is to provide a norm for action in the present for societies that are changing and evolving over time. This religious code functions as a norm, because it is a set of constant values that are solid enough to withstand a variety of interpretations and expressions. It has 'the authority attributed to the past to settle the problems of the present' (Hervieu-Léger, 2000: 86). Furthermore, it confers 'transcendent authority on the past' in order to link past and present through the continuity of what is essential, and can incorporate the transformations demanded by the present.

People invested with the power and ability to regulate, shape and pass on a tradition are often challenged by those – sometimes considered prophets – whose personal revelations call for redefining aspects of that tradition. This kind of social conflict can be part of a dynamic in which 'a society creates itself and creates its own history', and is an example of what Louis-Marie Chauvet called a 're-reading', in which tradition actualizes the past in the present, rather than simply repeating that past. Familiar with Weber and Halbwachs's writings on the role of prophets and mystics, and steeped in her own research, which reveals the continuity of tradition as having a dynamic component, Hervieu-Léger thinks religion as a code of meaning within a tradition can play an active role in social change.

To help her consider how effective it can be as a force for renewal within society, she begins by asking how religion can play a significant role and not become marginalized as folklore – especially if modern society values change for the sake of change, questions continuity as foreign to change, and places tradition, perceived as rigid, in a minor role when producing and legitimizing societal norms and values. Building on the work of de Certeau, folklore in this sense refers to the sources of cultural heritage – stories, songs, customs and beliefs that reflect a way of life and are 'revered for their

historical significance and their emblematic function', but are not config-
ured to produce a coherent system of collective meaning. With the development of modernity, in which rationalization has gradually provoked and
dislocated systems of meaning that had provided coherence, and secularization has either eliminated or scattered the fragments of those systems
throughout society, folklore has become a logical repository for some of the
remains. As Hervieu-Léger reminds us, 'the marginalization of traditional
religions as folklore constitutes one of the outcomes facing religion in modernity' (Hervieu-Léger, 2000: 90). This mirrors researchers like Niklas Luh-
mann and de Certeau, who found religion in modernity destined for a
folkloric role.

In contrast, Hervieu-Léger points out that modernity itself has been
instrumental in 'mobilizing religious symbols for the cause of utopian politics'; in several cases, such as democracy in eastern Europe and identity for
North African immigrants in France, this mobilization has given religion an
active role in the production of meaning for actual social groups. This process also suggests that modernity's inability to address the overall need for
coherent systems of meaning without calling upon religion, with its authoritative tradition, may provide an opening for the renewal of 'belief linked to
the authority of tradition'. Hervieu-Léger asks us to consider that modernity may actually 'prompt' the need for individuals and society to call upon
the authority of tradition. She further argues that modernity and religion
can interact creatively.

Much like the dialectic between individual and family, the relationship
between individualism and collective meaning systems within society displays a continued and paradoxical dynamic. Modernity has not eliminated
the need to believe; in fact, the rate of change has deepened that need.
Research by philosopher Paul Ricoeur has shown that at some point in the
search for meaning, an individual needs to share that meaning with others
and in some way have it socially affirmed in order for the meaning 'to have
an effect' (Hervieu-Léger, 2000: 94). In modern society this social confirma-
tion has tended to be experienced by a person joining one or more affinity,
or support, groups, of his or her personal choosing, designed in many cases to
provide social recognition of individual meaning. Not only that, but support
groups typically appeal to their tradition of a shared past as the authority for
how they sustain each other. When that process of appeal or recall engenders development of a strong social bond with the tradition invoked, it
makes little difference whether or not that sense of continuity can be historically verified. Its importance has been established. To Hervieu-Léger, religious productions of modernity, like support groups and new religious
movements, are not residues of modernity; indeed, their source is the very

way in which modernity 'undermines the traditional foundations of institutionalized belief' (Hervieu-Léger, 2000: 97), and thus opens up new avenues for exploration of belief and meaning.

Hervieu-Léger contends that her concept of religion can identify religious believing in any social context. Referring again to sport, she acknowledges that there is a sacred quality in the immediacy and 'in the moment' emotion of many sporting events, but to her, 'sacrality' is one of many religious features in society, and its presence does not constitute religion. Likewise, traditional religions may be able to manifest the sacred, but they do not have a monopoly on contact with the divine. Sacredness for Hervieu-Léger constitutes one method of organizing collective meaning so that humans can make sense of their existence; it finds expression in emotional contact with an external force and in symbols and values found to evoke awareness of the 'absolute'. Religion, on the other hand, corresponds to 'another system of organizing meaning, based upon identification with a chain or line of belief' (Hervieu-Léger, 2000: 106–7).

In Hervieu-Léger's analysis of why the dimensions of religion and sacred do not necessarily link automatically, she describes how they did overlap in many pre-modern traditional societies, where their code of meaning encompassed the sacred in all life, and their prophetic heritage enabled change to be incorporated. She also reminds us that when modern societies dissociated the sacred from religion by pluralizing ways of producing meaning, the linkage broke. As a result, religion in modernity has not only lost its position as the only 'legitimate' access to the sacred, but at times it appears to have limited, if any, access at all. To support this claim, Hervieu-Léger refers to both external and internal ways in which religion has responded to the rationalism of modernity and to the freeing up of the sacred to be encountered in diverse ways.

Externally, institutional religions have distanced themselves from 'secular' modes of identifying a 'sacred cosmos' and instead, have become more ethically-oriented in their support of ascetic behaviours and practices that foster 'withdrawal' from a world seen as not being sacred. In addition, they have developed a perception that humans have the freedom to choose their involvement and its form. One result is inherent conflict between individuals and hierarchical structures of control over what constitutes ethics and morality.

Internally, many institutional religions have responded to rationalization by severely diminishing, and sometimes excluding, emotional experience that might help a community become aware of a divine presence. They have also initiated what Weber calls legal-rational forms of organization. Within those frameworks, church ministers and priests 'conduct their office according to abstract rules', and as church employees, 'exercise their command in the name of an impersonal norm, and not on behalf of a personal authority' (Hervieu-Léger, 2000: 107). In effect, by rationalizing religious power, many religions have tended to cut off emotional experience of the divine both within their own church communities and between those communities and the persons who have been designated to embody the chain of belief for them.

This split between religion and the sacred, which began with the gradual emergence of modernity many years ago, has found a focus in current attempts to define the sacred. Church, state and related movements are aware of society's search for symbolic systems of meaning. One response to that awareness has been to compete with each other in an intense struggle for the 'prize' of articulating not only what sacred means, but also what constitutes religion in the modern world.

Hervieu-Léger explains that the notion of 'religious field' developed at the same time that theories of secularization were developing. It was a way of giving religion 'its own strictly limited space' with a 'compact, organized, formalized appearance' during a time in which religion was losing its claim 'to govern society as a whole'. Not surprisingly, those boundaries have retained a fluid quality that motivates Hervieu-Léger 'to try to dissociate religion from its institutional, more specialized, aspects and to trace the way it has fragmented across the social spectrum' (Hervieu-Léger, 2000: 109). She wants to allow study of those fragmented religious expressions within social, cultural, and even scientific spheres, while avoiding the assumption that religion in modernity refers only to institutional religions.

Bourdieu developed the concept of religious field within the context of a general theory of social fields. From that perspective, a religious field has little relevance without being viewed as part of a system. Bourdieu found that belief in some form is a dimension of every social field. However, in the religious field, belief is not only the cause of its very existence as a field, but the dynamic operating principle that struggles for control of 'legitimate belief'. In other words, this field was born out of the sacred–profane dichotomy that emerged in the opposition between specialized religious professionals, recognized by society as exclusively possessing secret knowledge that allowed them to claim the monopoly for administering the sacred, and the non-professional laity, who were excluded from being recognized as possessing knowledge of the sacred. Though this approach seems to reduce religion to the single function of 'consecrating the social order', Hervieu-Léger says the questions raised by Bourdieu's work are helpful when considering struggles for control of legitimate tradition, especially within contemporary Christianity.

Knowing that a dimension of believing is present in all human activity, Hervieu-Léger asks how ordinary believing starts to assume a religious form and become 'an essential ingredient in phenomena we can term religions' (Hervieu-Léger, 2000: 111–12). She looks to Poland in 1989, where political and religious principles joined together in overthrowing a communist system that had undermined the system of government and code of meaning, which had formed the basis of Polish society. Hervieu-Léger reminds us that politics addresses how people live together and make sense of that togetherness by forming a system of government. It is a fundamental dimension of the symbolic in society, and its relationship to religion is organized around shared symbolic functions within society.

However, what follows is discovering how a society of individuals, created by and emerging from the process of rationalization, secularization, and fragmentation of coherent systems of meaning, can bind itself together in reciprocity, or common respect for the whole society, when that very process of individuation has destroyed the possibility of a collective determination of meaning. In response, Hervieu-Léger asks whether a compulsory transcendence of individual wills in favour of the collective will might point to a religious recoding of modern politics – indicating that when this kind of recoding cannot take place, social ties within society unravel.

This leads her to reinforce a sociological definition of religion that would prevent using as a religious component any reference to the transcendent value of a given social order. In her view, 'affording positive recognition of one's obligations to others as a means of realizing one's own humanity, is not in itself a religious reference' and does not become one, even if the basis, or source, of that transcendent reference is God (Hervieu-Léger, 2000: 116). It may become one if a society sees itself as a manifestation of a utopian community with transcendent values, but historically, when politics has been the initiator of an egalitarian utopian community and has subsequently formalized it institutionally, the result has been the establishment of utopia's antithesis – the very authoritarian type of structure initially rejected. This political distortion of utopia is particularly dangerous when its religious dimension confines social imagination by limiting its possible manifestations to one identified point of origin. Hervieu-Léger says this robs utopia of its ability to regenerate itself and grow with and through change. It also raises a question about the propensity of religion to become totalitarian (Hervieu-Léger, 2000: 117).

Rather than follow that line of thought, Hervieu-Léger suggests that the presence of the religious within the political may mean that politics and institutional religions are susceptible to the same methods of analysis, since autocratic tendencies in both search for ways to impose extensive external

control over religion, and to internally segregate those who actively participate in the chain of belief. Within religion itself, leadership generally places
initial emphasis on external control, while sects focus on internal control.
One challenge is discovering the degree of tension within a religious group
as it wrestles with integrating itself by balancing conformity with its tradition through expansion and discovery of ways to intensively apply that tradition internally. It is important information, because conflicts like these
embrace 'both the interpretation of the core tradition and the designation
of the authority properly empowered to supply this interpretation', significant aspects in Hervieu-Léger's definition (Hervieu-Léger, 2000: 118).

Collective Memory

Once tradition, which in this context is reference to a chain of belief, takes
the central role in a discussion of religion, the next step is exploring how a
tradition can be accessed, or remembered. That leads us to collective
memory, because an individual or a group must somehow draw upon memories from the past in order to consciously share them with others and extend
the linkage. As discussed earlier, a significant characteristic of modern
societies is change, not memory. Because of this, individuals and groups
caught up in this change are not socialized to nurture their innate ability to
remember, assimilate, or project a lineage of belief. Hervieu-Léger explores
how this phenomenon affects her attempts to define religion as a way of
believing that calls upon the legitimizing authority of a tradition.

Relating to Berger's statement that throughout history society's memory
has primarily been religious, she examines the structural connection between
memory and religion, noting that from the perspective she has adopted,
'all religion implies that collective memory is mobilized' (Hervieu-Léger,
2000: 124). Whereas traditional societies contained their memories of religious symbolism within their structures, language, organization and daily
observances, differentiated societies with established religions and distinct-
ive faith communities must constantly re-construct their religious memory
as a way of enabling the significant core events of their historical past to
be experienced as meaningful in the present. To do this, these core events
become 'symbolically constituted' outside time and history, capable then
of assuming new forms in different contexts. This normative character of
religious memory, which is common within any collective memory, allows
it to endure 'the processes of selective forgetting, sifting and retrospectively
inventing' (Hervieu-Léger, 2000: 124).

This is reinforced by the fact that a group holding a religious memory defines itself as a lineage of belief that embodies a continuity affirmed and manifested by recalling a past that gives meaning to the present and contains the future. Furthermore, the recalling of foundational events that enabled the chain to form in the first place generally takes the form of rites and rituals that contain regular repetitive patterns designed to facilitate the remembering. This perspective is also present in Berger's writings about how societies might live in right relationship with the sacred cosmos. Hervieu-Léger acknowledges that ritualized practice can give a religious dimension to secular ritual, and that some forms of religion, such as Quakerism and Baha'i, retain minimal, if any, ritual. However, she reiterates her contention that an authentic religion is a way of believing that calls upon a tradition, or chain of belief, as its legitimizing authority.

Religions manage their collective memories in different ways, but the core of religious power is the recognized ability to 'expound the true memory of the group'. Hervieu-Léger once more draws upon the work of Halbwachs and his description of how the main source of religious conflict often lies 'in the opposition between a rational, dogmatic type of memory (which he called theological memory) and memory of a mystical nature' (Hervieu-Léger, 2000: 126). Halbwachs described the dogma of a religious group as the end result of a process designed to maintain a unified religious memory and protect the chain of belief from disturbances caused by mystical memory with its claim to information gained through direct access to the divine. He also pointed out the dialectic between the internal process of emotive and symbolic evocation of the chain – the act of believing – and the external elaboration of the contents of belief – the beliefs themselves. To Hervieu-Léger this dialectic, which one can see as tradition in the act of becoming itself, constitutes the central dynamic of all religion (Hervieu-Léger, 2000: 127).

If memory is the crucial dynamic in accessing a tradition or chain of belief, and change has severely damaged individual and collective ability to retain an integrated and organized memory or coherence, the future of religion as defined by Hervieu-Léger may be dim. Continuing to explore this issue, Hervieu-Léger takes us back to the emergence and historical development of modernity as the crisis point for a comprehensive social memory. With its emphasis on the 'autonomous individual', the rational dismantling of 'sacred canopies', and the rise of 'institutional differentiation', modernity not only radically altered the role of institutional religion, but it effectively brought an end to societies based on memory. This crumbling of collective memory coincided with the growth of secularization, in which structures of religious meaning were dislocated and placed in a specialized religious field. As religious memory was marginalized, society also witnessed 'the differentiation of total social memory into a plurality of specialized circles of memory', which caused 'the piecemeal destruction of communities, societies and even ideologies based on memory' (Hervieu-Léger, 2000: 127). According to Nora, the various forms of globalization, along with democratization, the development of mass societies, and media encroachment then brought the final blow to these societies of collective memory.

Halbwachs identified two apparently contradictory trends that caused the disintegration of memory in modern societies. One was 'a tendency towards the expansion and homogenization of memory'. For Halbwachs, the emergence of the bourgeoisie brought a new fluidity of input from people in all areas of society, with one result being the destruction of a hierarchical social framework that had previously held the power to assure transmission of collective memories from generation to generation. In conjunction with that, he saw the advent of capitalism and technology as signifying all spheres of social life being aligned with production, and therefore stimulating only technical, neutral memories related to function.

The second tendency – one facilitated by conditions created through the homogenization just discussed – was for society to develop an unlimited fragmentation of individual and group memory. Without a unified social memory, individuals and groups have access only to fragments of memory contained within their areas of specialty. In that way, the collective social memory is primarily found in bits spread throughout society, not as a coherent whole. This raises the question of whether young people today have the capacity to organize the massive amounts of information they receive in a way that connects them to a lineage to which they see themselves belonging.

Halbwachs and Hervieu-Léger hold out some hope that in spite of the dissolution of its collective memory, a society might be able to reconstitute its sense of unity if enough individuals and groups within that society can develop sufficient unity of views. This clearly points towards the importance of social ties when considering the future of religion in modernity. It also raises the question of whether or not a group, whose context of memory has been 'reduced to fragments and made instantaneous', can actually 'recognize itself as a link in a chain of belief and [be] entrusted with the task of extending that chain into the future' (Hervieu-Léger, 2000: 130).

Tracking reactions against 'the official orthodoxy of modernity', Hervieu-Léger uses what Jean Baudrillard called 'psychological modernity' to describe the challenge to authority by those advocating the supremacy of individual, subjective experience (Hervieu-Leger, 2000: 132). Within the Christian churches this reflects a crisis in the authority of the priesthood and the institution, but even that is only one factor in a breakdown that in France extends beyond priesthood to the 'whole realm of religious practice and parochial culture' that 'gave substance to religious authority'. Hervieu-Léger proceeds to explain how the parish, which had functioned for centuries in the centre of village life as *the* society of memory and the main way people identified 'themselves as members of a lineage', eventually lost its dynamic function and became a 'register of observance'. That, along with breakdown in family structure, signified the loss of two significant ways the French had mobilized their collective memory in a religious sense: 'the ideal of continuous transmission and the ideal of rootedness in a locality' (Hervieu-Léger, 2000: 134). When collective social memory began to dissolve, that affected not only the dissolution of religious believing and its imaginative grasp of continuity, but also the disintegration of the religious dimension present in all forms of social behaviour. In all domains that meant loss of the conviction of believing, which was based on a tradition initially designed to be preserved and passed on.

Hervieu-Léger again draws upon the work of Nora to understand more clearly the social factors that in an advanced capitalist society effectively obliterate memory. One is the economic change that 'favoured pragmatic individualism at the expense of long-lasting forms of co-operation and social solidarity' and directed the economic system towards consumer satisfaction. Another factor is the chain of effects resulting from modernity's focus on individual 'rights' to happiness and self-fulfilment. When individuals began to face the insecurities that accompanied difficult economic changes, their general response was to seek the immediacy of getting by. In Hervieu-Léger's opinion, 'the individualistic pressure for immediacy ... has finally achieved the expulsion of memory from society' (Hervieu-Léger, 2000: 138).

These developments have had a significant impact on institutionalized religion and new forms of religious expression, especially as people make more conscious choices about what they believe and which forms of observance fit their individual needs. The question remains whether religion is totally disintegrating or being radically transformed into new patterns. If it is to be saved, Hervieu-Léger believes, modern societies must learn how to gather together those diffuse, fragmented and disassociated memories that are capable of forging new social bonds and promising some kind of collective identification, and form them into what she calls 'substitute memories' they can then invoke.

Referring again to Nora's research on realms of memory in French society, Hervieu-Léger says the challenge in this reconstruction process is that its lack of an organized and integrated social memory forces an equally fragmentary development. Nora's work has identified particular points when a 'reconstituted' memory crystallizes at the same time that other indicators reveal the 'loss of a unifying collective memory'. Despite this, research shows that the search for partial continuity has actually escalated and is evident in phenomena such as the passion for genealogy, historical novels, heritage days and pageants – not only in France, but also in other Western countries. Hervieu-Léger suggests that examining ways in which societies are reconstituting their fragmented memories should assist in understanding how this may also be happening in religious modernity.

This suggestion takes Hervieu-Léger directly to the notion of utopia, which she paraphrases from Seguy as being a reinterpretation and magnification of a golden age that projects an image of the future which is foretold to be different from the unsatisfactory present (Hervieu-Léger, 2000: 143). From there she moves to Desroche's major study of 'contraband religions', which he characterized as typically accessing religious imagination by drawing upon a past for help and inspiration while projecting a new vision of the future. Linking religion and utopia in a genealogical way, Desroche described seven 'constellations' of traditional utopian populations that stood as 'milestones and witnesses of the alternative route taken by religion in modernity' (Hervieu-Léger, 2000: 144). Considered hopeful by Desroche, these utopias reached as far back as the eleventh century, and they covered locations such as Russia, Britain and America. They also exhibited a motivating force from within religion that extended beyond institutional religion and were parallel to revolutionary movements, utopian forms of socialism, and experiments in communal living. For Desroche, this supports his argument that a religious dynamic of society functions steadily through and beyond all forms of secularization.

A utopia fosters renewed ways of creating an alternative imagined continuity that feeds the consciousness of the chain, and provides a vision of hope that inspires action in the present. Of course, this invoked memory turns into a reinvention that involves some loosening of the original tradition, or authorized memory, in order for its transformation into a new memory to occur. The new order of memory then allows for the redefinition of ways in which society operates and functions. However, drawing upon the work of Seguy, Hervieu-Léger says that the utopian dynamic must materialize as a social movement if it is to move beyond the limitations of a voluntary group and develop broader social consequences.

Interestingly, Desroche's analysis of the internal dynamics of utopia reveals a complex process in which memory is both secularized and religiously recharged. Another paradoxical utopian dynamic is its search for its own realization and the inherent dilemmas discovered therein. Desroche points out how any utopia faces a series of options: it either creates the new vision, or it fails; if it succeeds, it may lose its momentum by achieving cultural integration, rather than maintaining its unique quality; or if it succeeds, it may become institutionalized and rigid – representing and preserving the new authorized memory in the face of alternatives.

However, utopias generally maintain a fidelity to their initial inspiration, often identifying with a founder whose message can be invoked or explored, and whose life can be an example to be followed. Furthermore, some kind of religious stabilization may help a utopia become incorporated into a culture without losing it identity – as evidenced in the history of religious orders. Alternatively, sometimes when traditional religions have allowed alternative readings of their foundational stories, that allowance has triggered its own internal protest – as witnessed in radical movements of the Reformation.

To Hervieu-Léger, the collapse of memory in traditional societies became the condition that freed the imagination of modern societies to construct history. Likewise, the intensifying social and cultural contradictions that have prompted social change can also be catalysts for renewal of utopian potential and its association with the possible emergence of religious innovation. Pointing to base communities in Latin America and denominational feminist movements in the United States, Hervieu-Léger contends that

> the innovative resources of religion now find expression through a different articulation of this reference, which is itself inseparable from the formation of individual and collective identities. (Hervieu-Léger, 2000: 149)

One articulation is that of elective fraternities, which develop through 'shared interests, experience and hardships' among people not necessarily related by blood, but whose relationships embody a sense of 'real solidarity, transparency of thought and communication, and common values and memories' (Hervieu-Léger, 2000: 50). Hervieu-Léger says that members of an elective fraternity often attach themselves to the charismatic founder, who is frequently designated as 'father' or 'elder brother' in this extended family of choice. They provide freedom of commitment and a stability that is different from that of the natural family. When a group starts seeking ways to represent itself beyond the context of the inter-relationship of its current members and calling upon a common spirit that transcends its individual members, that group is beginning to present religious features. Furthermore, its transformation reflects a powerful change that depends on the strength of emotional ties uniting the individuals who have made this choice.

Hervieu-Léger tells us that according to Hegel (1988: 114), the love that permeates an elective community does not make it a religion, and in some cases prompts it to clash with religion, especially when commitment to the relationships takes precedence over fidelity to the chain of belief (Hervieu-Léger, 2000: 152). When an elective fraternity does not initially develop as an intensely emotional community that centres on a charismatic leader, it often faces an intense struggle when some of its members do intensify their emotional commitment, thereby raising larger group suspicions that the minority members, in some cases, should be expelled. Of course, this can work in the opposite way. Sometimes the increased emotional intensity and 'union of hearts' is experienced as transcending individual experience, and seen as evidence of a spirit that pre-dated and will survive the group's break-up. With all this in mind, the decisive factor in a decision to institutionalize an elective fraternity is a rejection of the volatile nature of these emotional states. This rejection opens the way for a community of people to imaginally reconstitute their cloud of witnesses, and possibly re-formalize what they consider an authentic chain of belief in which the authorized memory is preserved.

Elective fraternities, with their characteristic re-socializing of religion, find themselves both outside and within traditional religions. As forums where men and women can take authentic personal initiative that finds expression and recognition, sometimes reference to a chain of belief turns out to be of secondary importance or of no value. One example Hervieu-Léger provides of an elective fraternity outside traditional religion is what grew out of an affinity network that followed singer Jim Morrison of The Doors. After Morrison's early and sudden death, this network effectively turned itself into a religion that twenty years later still buys his recordings and song texts, makes pilgrimages to his grave, gathers to read his poetry and sing his songs, and affirms his dream of another life.

Sometimes groups operating within the parameters of traditional religion decide to maintain a high visibility in endorsing a given lineage as a way of avoiding the pitfalls of communal excess. This means that as the emotional ties strengthen for those experiencing a deeper spiritual commitment through membership in the group, the push for a more public symbolic display of 'membership in a religious family' becomes prominent. Examples in the Catholic Church include Pax Christi, an international Catholic peace movement, which draws upon church traditions of non-violence and social justice; the Women's Ordination Conference, which points to elements of church tradition that they consider supportive of women's ordination; and Call To Action, a lay and clergy group that advocates dialogue, collaboration and shared leadership within the church. All of these 'elective fraternities' have existed for at least three decades, consistently invoke 'original' elements in the Catholic tradition, and hold fast to their right to speak with a 'different' voice from within the institution. Hervieu-Léger suggests that references to past witnesses, or saints, also may be an example not of wanting to return to a pre-Vatican Council state, but of emotionally stabilizing the group by imagining its genealogy, and also of validating it as something permanent.

When the issue of symbolic representation of religious affiliation arises, Hervieu-Léger leads us into a discussion of what is ethnic and what is religious in the reconstruction of ethnic memory. She describes how an ethnic revival calls upon a naturalized genealogy relating to soil and blood, while a religious revival invokes a symbolized genealogy constructed with belief in, and reference to, a myth and a source. Examples of ethnic and religious memory joining together include Northern Ireland, Poland, Israel, Kosovo, and immigrant communities in the USA and Eastern European countries. Referring to Dominique Schnapper's research into ethnic and religious renewal, Hervieu-Léger outlines how a modern convergence between these two processes started with the modernization of conventional religion in a way that converted a personal God into a moral and ethical ideal. That process, along with the increasing tendency to view objects of religious belief as symbols, resulted 'in the transformation of religion into a system of ethics which, taken to its extreme, can allow one to confuse it with a morality of human rights' (Hervieu-Léger, 2000: 158).

One might conclude that this 'ethical standardization' would cause institutional religious traditions to assume a universalist design which would prevent individuals and groups from appropriating religious symbols for their own use, but Schnapper asserts that the opposite has occurred. Religion has instead become a fragmented mass of symbols and values that can be moulded, changed and re-appropriated by those wanting to restore a sense of identity, including ethnic identity. This is complicated further by ethnic groups who take on a religious function by assimilating the symbols and values of religion and by marking their place in history as transcendent, thus claiming meaning for their existence.

This interplay between disintegration and re-integration in the process of referring to the continuity of a line of belief implies access to new ways of inventing a common memory – whether using symbols derived from historical religions, or resources available from 'profane' history and culture. For Hervieu-Léger, this perspective marks a shift in the nature of religion and makes it now possible to believe only in the continuity of the group, while still preserving symbols from traditional religion that provide meaning.

The Future of Religious Institutions

From a sociological perspective, the late twentieth century brought the first of the post-traditional generations – groups that find themselves living in the midst of structural uncertainty within society, including the final collapse of the world of tradition. Alain Touraine describes this situation as post-modernity, but Hervieu-Léger recommends we concentrate on Anthony Giddens's notion of high modernity. Acknowledging the prevalence of risk and uncertainty, which he says are the result of globalization in modern societies, Giddens refers to individuals who 'are adrift in a universe without fixed bearing', living in a world 'no longer one they can construct together', and holding self-fulfilment as their 'chief aim' (Hervieu-Léger, 2000: 165). Given this context, Hervieu-Léger suggests that deliberately choosing to invoke the authority of a tradition, thus becoming incorporated into a continuing lineage, may be a viable 'post-traditional way of constructing self-identity among others, all of which call upon an individual's affectivity and are fed on his or her search for community, and his or her memories and longings' (Hervieu-Léger, 2000: 165).

With that in mind, Hervieu-Léger invites a discussion of differentiating between the rise of the religious and the existence of post-traditional religion. Evidence for the rise of the religious is seen in individuals' attempts to reconstruct meaning for themselves through reflection on their experiences, and their imaginatively reconstituting a chain of belief in order to acquire religious coherence and provide an organizing principle for their lives. This reference to a chain of belief affords a symbolic resolution to the loss of meaning, but it does not necessarily lead to the establishment of a religion.

For that to happen, the tradition called upon would have to be capable of generating minimum conditions for a 'collective validation of meaning necessary for a community of believers to be able to establish itself' (Hervieu-Léger, 2000: 166). Those conditions would include taking the form of 'a tangible social group – whose organization may range from very informal to very formal – and an imaginary lineage, both past and future' (Hervieu-Léger, 2000: 166). In addition, this pattern of relating and believing would have to arise from individual commitment to membership in a 'genuine spiritual community'. For Hervieu-Léger, a post-modern religion would focus on the 'effectiveness of individual commitment' in recognizing the power of a tradition to generate continuity, rather than on the assumption that a tradition must impose obligations upon its individual adherents. In this way, an authoritative system of belief would be less able to 'impose itself in society' in an effort 'to exercise exclusive control' over what is believed and how those beliefs are proclaimed.

For sociologists, the resulting issue is not whether secularization is reversible, but what this 'radical de-institutionalization of the religious' means for traditional institutions of religion. Hervieu-Léger contends that the challenge faced by these institutions is their ability to give serious attention 'to the flexible nature of believing as it affects them' and to a new role they would need to play in 'the propagating and reprocessing of religious signs' – understanding clearly that grappling with these issues would be 'an essential part of their function and a mark of their credibility in the world of high modernity' (Hervieu-Léger, 2000: 168). It would also require that they reform their own system of authority and stop seeing themselves as 'dispensing the true memory'. In that way, the 'repository of the truth of belief' would shift from the institution to the believer, which brings its own set of challenges. Moving to the question of how this crisis of authority affects those institutional religions that formalize their tradition under a recognized magisterium that regulates religious observance, Hervieu-Léger describes how the Catholic Church has reacted strongly by reaffirming the 'doctrinal authority of Rome' not only for their own believers, but for all people. Though attempting to provide some stability in a changing world, their ability to offer meaning at this time in history is countered by the overall societal attitude of primacy for the subjectivity of the individual. Even in the Reformed Church there is the problem of legitimate interpretation of the Bible, reflecting conflicts about recognizing the legitimate authority for conveying the true memory. A further issue is the Protestant 'inclination to institutionalize ideological power' as a way of constructing and reconstructing religious memory.

In Hervieu-Léger's opinion, the problem facing major religions today is how to manage their relationship with the truth as they perceive it, particularly when the 'capital of memory' held by each one may 'continue to create tradition'. The challenge for all religious denominations, according to Hervieu-Léger, is to attend equally to those members searching for authority in a message, rather than an institution, and to those choosing allegiance to the community, not to a set of beliefs and values. She thinks institutional religions can transcend some of these conflicts by 'recreating an individual and collective consciousness of emotional belonging' and by 'playing down conflict by giving it the appearance of a worthwhile expression of diversity in culture and feeling' (Hervieu-Léger, 2000: 173).

In her conclusion, Hervieu-Léger reiterates her purpose to 'prepare the ground' for ways in which the sociology of religion can move beyond lamenting the damage caused to traditional religions by secularization,

Table 2: Components in Hervieu-Léger's Model of Religion

Key Component	General Characteristics
1. Forming community	Types, sizes, purposes; Creating, maintaining, supporting.
2. Understanding tradition	Religious or spiritual backgrounds; Plurality of ways, multicultural sources; Kinship with all life forms.
3. Invoking tradition	Calling upon 'cloud of witnesses'; Begotten into core lineage; Affirming commitment to set of beliefs.
4. Determining legitimate authority	Link with cloud of witnesses; Commitment to set of beliefs; Chain of belief legitimized by community.
5. Believing	Process of joining with others; Shared content of beliefs; Shared determination of beliefs and meaning.

and instead shed light on how the transformations inherent in religious modernity may actually contain the seeds of renewal and the insights necessary for understanding the new religious phenomena emerging throughout the world.

Summary

In summary, Hervieu-Léger's model of religion as a chain of memory has emerged from extensive research into underlying issues at work in the transformation of religion in contemporary societies. The solid academic grounding she has established provides a comprehensive context and rationale for the following key components that represent the essence of her model: forming community, understanding tradition, invoking tradition, determining legitimate authority, and believing. These components are addressed specifically in the fieldwork described in Chapter Seven, and in the 'model of religion' portion of the analysis in Chapter Eight. A brief summary can be found in Table 2 (above). The next chapter introduces contemporary shamanic practice in Scotland as a doorway to further understanding the issues of religion and spirituality raised thus far.

Chapter Four

What is Shamanism?

Introduction

This chapter focuses primarily on shamanism in indigenous cultures, though it also contains an introduction to contemporary forms of neo-shamanism. The context is set with a historical overview of shamanism and the various ways it has been understood over the years by many scholars who have studied it. Out of that context comes a series of working definitions that support a fairly comprehensive description of several basic terms commonly associated with shamanism. Following that is a model of cross-cultural shamanism composed of seven elements found in many different indigenous shamanic cultures, yet understood and expressed in ways that reflect those different cultures. The chapter concludes with a brief discussion of current challenges present in this kind of study. Table 3 at the end summarizes the seven elements in the cross-cultural model, which are also integrated into the presentation of fieldwork in Chapter Six and its analysis in Chapter Eight.

Historical Perspective

For over 500 years, people from various backgrounds have observed and/or studied shamans. Intrigued by accounts from 'travellers and traders who had visited among indigenous people' (Harvey: 5), academics from disciplines such as ethnology, 'anthropology, archaeology, gender studies, history, performance studies, psychology, and religious studies' (Harvey: 1) have sought to learn more about shamans and their communities. Naturally, their interpretations of those observations have often been filtered through the cultural lenses of their time. A short review of how this has occurred may illustrate the point.

Scholar Margaret Stutley's research has revealed 'large numbers of shamanesses in China during the second century', and that shamanism 'deeply influenced Taoism (and to a lesser extent Confucianism) with its concept of an ideal society' (Stutley: 22). Stutley also found evidence of shamanism in Korea dating back to the first century CE, though as new religions arrived in the country, practitioners of shamanism began to lose various privileges (Stutley: 23). In addition, during the last century, many Korean shamans suffered persecution from the occupying Japanese government and hostility from numerous Korean Christians, often resulting in these practitioners going underground. In his study of Korean shamanism another scholar, Chongho Kim, describes how this history of alternating between both high and low status during various centuries and/or eras has caused the presence of contemporary shamanism in Korea to represent 'a cultural paradox'. He discovered that 'Koreans still use shamans as indigenous healers' in a way that places those shamans in the category of 'traditional medicine', but that many of the users feel shame for having accessed what is officially looked down upon (Kim: 6). Prior to Kim's research, scholar Laurel Kendall had written about a shamanic, female-centred 'folk religion' that existed in Korea during the latter half of the twentieth century (Kendall, 1987). Though focused on the seer as healer in Japan, rather than on shamanism *per se*, scholar Carmen Blacker has described an ancient Japanese cultural premise that 'most of the ills of the world have their cause in invisible spiritual beings which impinge forcefully on the human community' in the form of ancestral ghosts, intrusions of animal spirits, and *kami* spirits, or divinities who are understood to feel neglected (Blacker: 116).

Two other scholars who have studied and trained with indigenous female shamans in the twentieth century are Barbara Tedlock and Bonnie Glass-Coffin. Tedlock writes about how prevalent women have been in shamanic traditions throughout the world – particularly in relationship to religion and medicine (Tedlock, 2006). In a similar vein, Glass-Coffin describes her discoveries about female spirituality and healing in northern Peru (Glass-Coffin, 1998). In both cases, they conducted fieldwork that led them to academic scholarship and to personal experience. Furthermore, both wrote about those two aspects of their research.

Scholar Geo Trevarthen's research into Celtic shamanism from approximately 500 BCE to around 500 CE has revealed evidence of shamanism and/ or a shamanic worldview playing a part in Celtic religion, even into the early days of Christianity (Trevarthen: 10–11). Another scholar, Brian Bates, has been looking at shamanism during the time of the Anglo-Saxons in England. He has presented much of his academic research in the form of novels about the meeting of a Christian scribe and a 'pagan' shaman, who worked together based on an agreement in which the shaman was to teach the scribe about his work (Bates, 1983). Though the story is fictional, most of its historical information about shamanic ways emerged from scholarly sources describing Anglo-Saxon sorcery. Bates later wrote another, related, novel (Bates, 1996).

Regarding shamanism in North Asia, Ronald Hutton tells us 'there are no accounts of Siberian shamans which date from before the sixteenth century,' but travellers like Marco Polo and Franciscan friar William of Rubruck, who went to the courts of the Mongol Great Khans during the thirteenth century, 'reported figures who were culturally similar' (Hutton, 2001: 30). In the mid sixteenth century, an Englishman named Richard Johnson visited Siberia and wrote an eye-witness account of what he called 'devilish rites' in North Asian shamanism as practised prior to Russian rule (Hutton, 2001: 30). This was followed by an equally pejorative late-seventeenth-century description of shamanic practitioners among the Tungusic and Samoyedic-speaking peoples of Siberia, written by Nicholas Witsen, who portrayed the shaman as a 'Priest of the Devil' and whose writings actually popularized the term 'shaman' in Europe (Hutton, 2001: 32).

During the sixteenth and seventeenth centuries, when witch-hunts and persecution were prevalent in Europe, and when many believed that any spirits other than those sanctioned by the official Christian churches were evil, most Christian clergy saw shamans as 'ministers of the devil' (Thevet: 13), because they communicated and worked with spirits not always understood within a Christian context. In the 1700s, Enlightenment rationalists tended to view shamans as impostors and jugglers who deceived 'their fellows with song and dance, tricks, and sleight of hand' (Narby and Huxley: 22). For example John Bell, a Scottish surgeon who travelled throughout the Russian empire in the early eighteenth century, concluded from his observations that most shamans were a 'parcel of jugglers' (Hutton, 2001: 33). This eighteenth-century pattern of hostility and prejudice was reinforced by another European traveller to Siberia, Eva Felinska, who called shamans 'corruptors and parasites' and contributed to a social milieu in which it was 'dangerous for natives to discuss such matters with Europeans' (Hutton, 2001: 34).

When the study of social anthropology began in the late 1800s, observers began to write more objective accounts of who became shamans, and what they did. This was also the time when one of the founders of anthropology, Englishman Edward B. Tylor, 'proposed the term *animism* to refer to the belief of spiritual beings in nature and in humans' (Tylor: 41). Towards the end of the nineteenth century V.M. Mikhailovskii, Vice-President of the Ethnographical Section of the Imperial Society for Natural History, Anthropology and Ethnography, compiled a general survey of information known about Siberian shamanism, incorporating the work of three well-respected and effective anthropologists: Waclaw Sieroszewski, Waldemar

Jochelson, and Waldemar Bogoras. Sieroszewski and Jochelson, in particular, 'showed a sympathy for the natives, and an imaginative ability to understand the appeal of shamanism to them' (Hutton, 2001: 35).

By the twentieth century, when some anthropologists and ethnologists began to record first-hand accounts by shamans about their work, scholars Sergei M. Shirokogoroff and Vilmos Dioszegi provided extensive data about shamans in Siberia. In addition, other scholars like Claude Lévi-Strauss, Mircea Eliade, Knud Rasmussen, John Neihardt, Anna-Leena Siikala, Mihály Hoppál, M.A. Czaplicka, Alfred Metraux, Verrier Elwin, Lorna Marshall and Ronald Rose deepened available understanding by contributing valuable information about shamans from various cultures throughout the world. In Lévi-Strauss's case, he went so far as to call shamans 'psychoanalysts' (Lévi-Strauss, 1949: 108).

Building on this research during the last half of the twentieth century, scholars such as Francis Huxley, Holger Kalweit, R. Gordon Wasson, Barbara Myerhoff, and Harner went on to embrace Malinowski's method of 'participant observation' by taking part in actual shamanic sessions (Narby and Huxley: viii). Their experiences and subsequent writings led many other observers to pay closer attention and gain deeper respect for what they were seeing. More anthropologists and ethnologists began learning native languages and tape recording interviews with shamans in a variety of settings – sometimes publishing their transcripts (Narby and Huxley: 185–6). Piers Vitebsky has conducted research in a number of shamanistic cultures, while I.M. Lewis, a former Professor of Anthropology, has specialized in studying and writing about shamanism and spirit possession.

Finally, a topic addressed extensively in popular literature, but minimally included in academic research, is that of contemporary forms of shamanism. Fortunately, this situation is beginning to change – due in great part to the efforts of scholars such as Wallis, Hoppál, Graham Harvey, Vitebsky, Marjorie Mandelstam Balzer and Ward Churchill. Wallis tells us his aim in writing about what he calls neo-shamanisms 'is to encourage people who may currently think neo-Shamanisms have nothing to do with them to think again' (Wallis: xiv). Furthermore, he contends that his study 'explores the complex and controversial issues neo-Shamanisms raise for archaeologists, anthropologists, indigenous communities, neo-Shamans themselves and related interest groups' (Wallis: 3).

A number of scholars have come to see shamans and the shamanic systems within which they operate as having much in common with global issues facing the world today. Lévi-Strauss has placed 'magic, which includes shamanism, on the same intellectual footing as science' (Lévi-Strauss,

1962: 245). In an article based on his own book about shamanism, anthropologist and medical doctor Roger Walsh contends that shamans are pioneers in exploring the human mind (Walsh, 1990: 257). An ethno-botanist with training in anthropology and biology, Wade Davis 'considers shamans to be researchers and intellectual peers' who can work with scientists to promote folk medicine and save the rain forests (Davis: 286). Focusing on the 'animistic' quality of Siberian shamanism, Mihály Hoppál, a shamanic scholar from Hungary, writes about 'ecologically conscious animism (eco-animism) – for the protection of the environment', because 'balance has to be maintained in all respects – and this is typically a shaman's task' (Hoppál, 1997: 9).

Working Definitions

As the term implies, working definitions are not exhaustive. Their dual purpose is to establish a solid grounding and to provide a common language. To facilitate a basic understanding of shamanism, I will provide working definitions for the terms *shaman, shamanism, core shamanism, neo-shamanisms, shamanic culture, shamanic spiritual allies, spirit possession, mastery of spirits, soul,* and *shamanic healing*. In several cases, my definitions will be preceded or followed by those from known scholars of shamanism.

Shaman

According to Eliade, the word shaman 'comes to us, through Russian, from the Tungusic *saman*' and refers to a person who 'specializes in a trance during which his soul is believed to leave his body and ascend to the sky or descend to the underworld' (Eliade: 4–5). He further acknowledges the possibility of *saman* actually coming from the Pali *samana* (Sanskrit *sramana*, meaning 'an ascetic person') through the Chinese *sha-men* (Eliade: 495).

Though scholars Siikala, Jakobsen and Åke Hultkrantz also note the possible Sanskrit origin, they have stated their consideration of Diószegi's theory that the root of *saman* is the Tungus-Manchu verb *sa* meaning 'to know' (Siikala: 14; Jakobsen: 3; Hultkrantz, 1973: 26–7). However, Hutton effectively shows how 'the Tungusic term "shaman" is itself a crude and convenient piece of European labelling' – primarily because 'it was not the word which would have been used of such figures by the great majority of native Siberians', who instead used comparable terms from their own distinct languages (Hutton, 2001: 47).

Narrative definitions help to provide a sense of diversity, yet commonality, when describing shamans. Shirokogoroff, a Russian authority on the Tungus, wrote that shamans were 'persons of both sexes who have mastered spirits, who at will can introduce these spirits into themselves and use their power over the spirits in their interests, particularly helping other people, who suffer from the spirits' (Shirokogoroff: 269). He also said that the main objectives of a shaman were 'to discover the causes of present troubles and to divine the future', which is similar to Siikala's characterization of shamans as 'troubleshooters' when dealing with human crises (Hutton, 2001: 51). According to Harvey, 'In the language of Tungus-speaking peoples of Siberia, shaman (pronounced *sharmarn*) refers to a communal leader chosen and trained to work for the community by engaging with significant other-than-human persons' (Harvey: 1). Jakobsen states, 'The shaman is, as I have argued, first and foremost a master of spirits in the traditional society. His role is to contact and to possess spirits so that a communication on behalf of an individual or society as a whole can be established' (Jakobsen: 9). For Vitebsky, 'a shaman is a man or woman whose soul is said to be able to leave their body during trance and travel to other realms of the cosmos' (Vitebsky, 2000: 55). Finally, Hoppál says the shaman is a mediator – a religious specialist whose functions include maintaining 'communication between the world of daily routine and the transcendental world, i.e. between the microcosm and the macrocosm' (Hoppál, 2001).

Because a shaman is considered a master at entering a state of consciousness that facilitates direct communication with spirits in the non-physical realms, I would define the term as one who undertakes each ecstatic soul journey, also called a soul flight, in order to work with spiritual allies and ultimately bring information, inner power, and/or soul healing back to individuals and the larger community within which the shaman lives. This view is advanced by scholar Hultkrantz, who says we 'may define the shaman as a social functionary who, with the help of guardian spirits, attains ecstasy in order to create a rapport with the supernatural world on behalf of his group members' (Hultkrantz: 34). This is similar to psychologist of religion Peter Connolly's view that a shaman could be a 'person who, on behalf of a community, enters a trance state and, by means of spirit helpers, obtains a range of benefits for that community (Connolly: 12). It also finds commonality with anthropologist Metraux's 1944 definition of a shaman as 'any individual who maintains by profession and in the interest of the community an intermittent commerce with spirits, or who is possessed by them' (Narby and Huxley: 4).

Like Metraux, American anthropologist Michael F. Brown has acknowledged that shamans can use their power to harm others (Brown, 1989: 251).

In her thesis on Celtic shamanism, Trevarthen has also addressed this issue and described how in Celtic Scotland, one understanding of this ability of a shaman to harm has been described as using the 'evil eye'. Drawing upon Kalweit's research into the ways in which a shaman can use power, Travarthen noted that shamans are known to gather a kind of neutral spiritual power through their partnership with spiritual allies, but that power can be directed to heal or harm depending upon their intentions and upon what they think any harm would accomplish (Trevarthen: 157; Kalweit: 177–91). Though I agree that this can and does occur with some shamans, I also think the proper use of power is an ethical challenge for any person with the ability and leadership position to influence and, in critical ways, control others. This research has relied primarily on evidence gathered by scholars who have focused on the healing, helpful dimensions of shamanism. However, this in no way diminishes the power and control issues that are present within shamanism.

Shamanism

I define shamanism as a system of inter-relatedness that exists among shamans, their cultures, and the spirits, as each interacts with the other(s) to provide and maintain spiritual healing, support and guidance for both individuals and the community. As a system, these inter-related components express themselves differently according to the cultures in which they function. Because a shaman is designated as the one to intercede with the spirits for others through a soul journey, or flight, that involves a type of ecstasy, Eliade has said that 'a first definition of the complex phenomenon, and perhaps the least hazardous, will be shamanism = *technique of ecstasy*' (Eliade: 4). Supporting that, but expanding upon it, Louize Backman and Hultkrantz state:

> The central idea of shamanism is to establish means of contact with the supernatural world by the ecstatic experience of a professional and inspired intermediary, the shaman. There are thus four important constituents of shamanism: the ideological premise, or the supernatural world and the contacts with it; the shaman as an actor on behalf of a human group; the inspiration granted him by his helping spirits; and the extra-ordinary, ecstatic experiences of the shaman. (Backman and Hultkrantz: 11)

According to Nevill Drury, whose Masters degree thesis compared traditional shamanism and Western magic:

A distinguishing feature of shamanism, then, is the journey of the soul. It is because the shaman can project consciousness to other realms that he or she is called a 'technician of the sacred' or a 'master of ecstasy'. It is this capacity to venture consciously among the spirits and return with sacred information for the benefit of society, that is all-important. (Drury: 13)

Another related, but different, perspective is that of Siikala, who says that 'the technique of communication used by the shaman as a creator of a state of interaction between this world and the other world is fundamentally ecstatic role-taking technique' (Siikala: 28). This is consistent with Lauri Honko's view that

> the shaman actualizes a large number of frames of reference and takes the roles of different beings. We may here speak of the momentary 'picking' of different roles, as a result of which there is actualization of that role-set which makes the most important integrating factor, that is to say the shaman's own role. (Honko: 41)

Stutley contends that all forms of shamanism share three things: a 'belief in the existence of a world of spirits'; the 'inducing of trance by ecstatic singing, dancing and drumming'; and the treatment of 'some diseases, usually of a psychosomatic nature', but also including 'various difficulties and problems' experienced by clan members (Stutley: 2). Though there are more definitions by worthy scholars, this section ends with Vitebsky's view that 'Shamanism is not a single, unified religion but a cross-cultural form of religious sensibility and practice' (Vitebsky, 2001: 11).

Core Shamanism

In the words of Harner, core shamanism consists of 'the basic principles that are common to most shamanic practitioners in most societies' (Wallis: 51). Building on his definition of a shaman as 'a man or woman who enters an altered state of consciousness – at will – to contact and utilize an ordinarily hidden reality in order to acquire knowledge, power, and to help other persons', Harner starts to identify what he calls the fundamentals of shamanism (Harner: 20). Generally through initiation experiences, a shaman achieves a state of consciousness that allows him or her to travel back and forth between a non-ordinary reality, where 'spirit helpers' are met and acquired as protectors and teachers of shamanic divination and healing, and the ordinary reality of daily life (Harner: 44–5). This state of consciousness is usually facilitated by steady, monotonous drumming or rattling (Harner:

50–1), and the non-ordinary realms reflect a cosmology of at least three areas: a lower world, an upper world, and a middle world (Vitebsky, 2001: 5–17). Harvey says that

> The label 'Core Shamanism' is used by many practitioners, indicating that it is based on the identification of central themes and practices within the different localized shamanisms known from ethnographic and historical texts as well as from significant encounters with indigenous shamans themselves. (Harvey: 304)

Harner has been criticized for 'decontextualizing and universalizing' traditional shamanism through his teaching of core shamanism. Indeed, in Wallis's fine study of neo-shamanisms, he supports that criticism and places core shamanism in the same category as other neo-shamanisms. One of his points is that any shamanism is reflective of its cultural context and, as such, cannot be politically neutral. Because Wallis interprets Harner's intention to teach common basic principles of shamanism as a belief that cultural context is not important, I think he misses a valuable insight. Denying the importance of cultural context and expression is not the same as identifying underlying patterns that appear to exist in shamanic societies regardless of their cross-cultural expressions. I also think Wallis's response to Harner's statement that core shamanism, especially in its healing dimension, is not inherently political, may also reflect different understandings of the term 'political'. Taking political action as an extension of one's shamanic worldview and call to participate in healing the planet is not the same as changing the focus of one's shamanic vocation from a soul healer to an activist consistently engaged in governmental politics. However, Wallis raises important issues that must be addressed by those engaged in neo-shamanisms.

Neo-Shamanisms

As mentioned in Chapter Three, 'neo-shamanisms' is a term used by Wallis to sensitively encompass the variety of contemporary shamanic expressions that otherwise tend to be lumped together as one type of shamanism. By using this term, Wallis is not suggesting that all forms of contemporary shamanism must be accepted without study and critical analysis. However, he thinks the term 'neo-shamanisms' 'does require that we address the diversity of neo-shamanisms and shamanisms, and the subtleties of their engagement and interaction' (Wallis: 32).

Hoppál addresses what he calls 'the phenomena of today's (post-) modern shamanism', which he says include two main classes. One has survived within its culture up to the present time – whether continuously keeping tradition alive or having barely survived near-extinction through persecution. The other is represented by 'neo-shamanism (or urban shamanism), which has arisen mainly in an urban context' (Hoppál, 1996: 2–3). According to Hoppál, 'The representatives of neo-shamanism have appeared in Siberia, as in other parts of the world, and their role is just as deserving of attention as that of their predecessors' (Hoppál, 1996: 5–6).

Finally, we find (neo-) shamanic teacher and practitioner Sandra Ingerman, who learned about shamanism from Michael Harner and has continued with her own shamanic research into soul retrieval and healing the environment. Not only has she revived the contemporary practice of soul healing, but she also currently includes as a primary shamanic teaching and practice what she has written about in her book *Medicine for the Earth – How to Transform Personal and Environmental Toxins* (Ingerman, 2000). It appears that many neo-shamanisms are focused on addressing contemporary needs within individuals and society.

Shamanic Culture

I define a shamanic culture as a society whose worldview encompasses an experience of the spirit realms as a legitimate reality; an appreciation for the ability of the shaman to travel between realms and work with spiritual allies as a valid source of maintaining equilibrium for the community; and an understanding that the shaman's sharing of information, power and healing is actually necessary for their well-being. The society, or culture, calls forth a shaman to work on its behalf. As Eliade wrote about shamans and their relationship to their communities:

> This small mystical elite not only directs the community's religious life, but, as it were, guards its 'soul'. The shaman is the great specialist in the human soul; he alone 'sees' it, for he knows its 'form' and its destiny. (Eliade: 8)

Shamanic Spiritual Allies

In this context, I refer to shamanic spiritual allies as those beings in the non-physical spiritual realms who protect, guide, inform, strengthen and partner with a shaman in the process of soul flight on behalf of others. Though some shamanic cultures distinguish between powerful guardian or tutelary spirits and the less powerful familiars, or helping spirits, the concept is similar. Whatever their apparent status, these spiritual allies can reveal themselves in human forms, such as gods or goddesses, heroes, or ancestors; or they can show themselves as animals, plants, or other nature spirits (Eliade: 88–9).

Harvey disagrees with using the word 'spirits'; he says it 'unhelpfully mystifies matters', especially when according to Warren's *Dictionary of Psychology*, 'the concept of "person" is not, in fact, synonymous with human being but transcends it' (Harvey: 10). Instead, he uses the term 'other-than-human persons' in order to encompass the variety of forms that spiritual allies take. His point is well taken; in fact, I have experienced very clear conversations with Native Americans who refer to the stones in a sweat lodge as 'the rock people'. I also think that this kind of personification for all creation promotes a sense of oneness with what the Lakota call 'all our relations' – a concept that is not only shamanic, but also is common in many spiritual traditions. However, I think using the word 'person' for animals, plants and rocks is generally more confusing than clear. As a result, I will occasionally refer to spirits when I mean spiritual allies.

Spirit Possession

Related to working with spiritual allies is the concept of spirit possession. There is little question that a distinguishing feature of shamanism is the reality of shamans working closely with spirits. However, understanding that working relationship, how it develops, and what effect it has on shamans and their communities is a challenge that includes sensitivity to differing cultural worldviews within shamanic societies and among those studying this subject. Because an extensive discussion of spirit possession is not my primary focus here, providing my own working definition, along with an overview of key scholarly perspectives, seems appropriate.

Cited by Lewis in his research on spirit possession, British anthropologist Raymond Firth has defined spirit possession as involving 'phenomena of abnormal behaviour which are interpreted by other members of society as evidence that a spirit is controlling the person's actions and probably inhabiting his body' (Lewis, 1996: 107). The main question is whether or not this possession is voluntary or involuntary, pointing towards the shaman's ability to consciously 'allow' this experience to occur, and to stop it at will. While possession for some people means their personality is completely displaced, leaving them amnesic of the experience, that condition is not what characterizes shamanic possession. For shamans, it is better understood in T.K. Oesterreich's description of lucid possession, in which the one possessed

... does not lose consciousness of his usual personality but retains it ... he remains fully conscious of what is happening; he is the passive spectator of what takes place within him .... (Connolly: 6)

Connolly does not distinguish between trance and possession (Connolly: 3); instead, he identifies a trance as the way in which a shaman contacts spirit helpers and works with them on behalf of the community (Connolly: 12). Disagreeing with those like Connolly 'who regard trance primarily as a form of supernatural possession', Lewis argues that 'possession thus has a much wider range of means than our denatured term trance' (Lewis, 2003: 25).

Drawing upon these perspectives, I define spirit possession for a shaman as a conscious and voluntary choice to enter a trance-like state in order to unite with a spirit in a type of role-taking experience of intimate partnership that facilitates communication with the spirit and enables the shaman to receive direct access to information, gifts and/or powers available from the spirit. In this the shaman is not completely overtaken or controlled, but retains choice and consciousness (Eliade: 6). In fact, this union reflects a 'contractual relationship' that 'binds the shaman and the spirits which he incarnates' in a mystical 'fusing of man and divinity ... part of controlled spirit possession everywhere' (Lewis, 2003: 50).

Mastery of Spirits

Tied closely to spirit possession is the concept of mastery of spirits. According to scholar Daniel Merkur, some cultures, like the Inuit, generally perceive certain types of spirits as malevolent and dangerous, thereby resulting in the need for their shamans to overcome those spirits, much as one 'tames' wild animals (Merkur: 226). Others may not hold that initial malevolent image of the spirits, but still believe that to be effective and respected the shaman must be in charge, or control, of the spirits and not be overtaken by them. Referring to shamanism in Greenland, Jakobsen says:

Mastery should therefore be understood in its broadest sense: an *angakkoq* masters his spirits insofar as he is able to use their power. (Jakobsen: xiii)

I define mastery of spirits for shamans as the ability to develop and maintain the kind of close relationship of mutual respect and understanding with spirits that allows the shaman to 'count on' and 'know' that the spirits will always provide assistance, help and guidance whenever asked, because that is the nature of these relationships. Also worth considering when trying to understand this concept is Merkur's comment about the role of thought and intention in mastery of the spirits: 'It is significant that Inuit shamans are well aware that shamanic power consists of a mastery of their own thought, i.e., of auto-suggestions' (Merkur: 237). In other words, control over one's thoughts and intentions can be a very powerful aspect of knowing that the spirits will respond helpfully to a request.

Soul

Inherent in these concepts and fundamental in the process of shamanic healing is the term 'soul'. For our purposes, soul refers to the intangible essence of life, which precedes and survives material existence. One of its counterparts is the Latin *anima* (Pearsall: 52), which suggests a life force, power or energy present in humans, animals, nature and the entire world. In one of his *Collected Works* – on alchemy – Swiss psychiatrist Carl Jung, who spent many years developing a theory of soul, stated that the soul's 'essential characteristic is to animate and be animated; it therefore represents the life principle' (Jung: 213).

Some scholars of shamanism refer to *soul dualism*. That term reflects a view that there are actually two types of soul: a body-soul needed to maintain human life, and a free-soul that is able to leave the body and return at will (Hultkrantz: 30). According to this theory, it is the free-soul that enables the shaman to take soul journeys. From another perspective, Paul Johnson refers to Harner's first-hand description of three kinds of soul among the Shuar and their shamans. One is an *arutam wakani*, which must be acquired by seeking a vision or by stealing it from another. Its function is to protect a person from being assassinated or dying in warfare. A second one is a *muizak*, an avenging soul whose mission is to avenge the death of its owner. The third soul, *nekas wakani*, is called the true or original soul. It is born with each person, is present in the individual's blood, and it hovers around the community until its transformation into an impersonal, formless mist (Johnson: 340–1).

Building on Jung's work with soul and his understanding of shamanism, C. Michael Smith states the following about Jung and shamanism in dialogue:

> The shaman views the soul as a plurality of psychical energies which must exist in some loose harmonious balance within the individual; Jung similarly viewed the soul as a multiplicity-in-unity. When stressing its mystery, variety, and impenetrability, he tends to use the word *soul* (*Seele*). When stressing its integrity, ordering, archetypal patterning, and striving

towards wholeness, he tends to use the term *psyche*. Whatever the termino-
logical usage, psyche and soul are largely synonymous for Jung. (Smith,
1997: 101)

Shamanic Healing

Specializing in soul work in a culture that sees the dimension of soul to be as
important as, if not more important than, the physical, emotional and
mental dimensions of human life, it naturally follows that when illness or
disease occurs, the shaman helps with healing on a soul level. Shamanic
healing as I use it here refers to soul healing provided by a shaman primarily, though not exclusively, by retrieving lost power animals or soul parts,
removing harmful soul intrusions, and conducting souls of the dead to the
spirit realms (Eliade: 181–2, 215–16). Hultkrantz says the three main reasons for shamanic soul flights, those ecstatic soul journeys into the non-
physical spirit realms, are to gather information from the spirits, escort a
deceased person to the realm beyond, and restore a lost soul part (Hultkrantz, 1973: 29). Though lost soul parts will be addressed in more detail
when I discuss shamanic healing in my model of cross-cultural shamanism,
from a shamanic perspective, when a person experiences a severe emotional,
physical or spiritual trauma, sometimes a part of that person's soul spontaneously separates from the whole soul, travels into the spirit realms, and
stays there until someone like a shaman finds it and brings it back to be
reunited (Eliade: 300–1; Ingerman, 1991: 27–8). In-depth descriptions of
the soul retrieval concept and process presented from a contemporary perspective are found in Sandra Ingerman's books *Soul Retrieval* (Ingerman,
1991) and *Welcome Home* (Ingerman, 1993).

   With these working definitions in mind, we now turn to a model of cross-
cultural shamanism.

A Model of Cross-Cultural Shamanism

As shamanism has become better known, scholars like Eliade, Harner,
Lewis, Vitebsky and Harvey have identified components that appear to be
significant in distinguishing shamanism from some other forms of mystical
or magical practice, and to be present across many shamanic cultures.
For example, Vitebsky provides three key characteristics he sees as 'distinctively shamanic': a 'layered cosmology, with the flight of the shaman's
soul to other levels of this cosmos, and the power to use this journey to
fight, command, and control spirits' (Vitebsky, 2003: 278). Though there

are cultural variations in how key components are described and experienced, what follows are descriptions of those fundamental elements that form what I think is a basic model of cross-cultural shamanism. They include *shamanic vocation and initiation*; *shamanic cosmology*; *shamanic soul flight/journeying*; *shamanic consciousness*; *shamanic spiritual allies*; *shamanic soul healing*; and *community support*.

Shamanic Vocation and Initiation

Shamans usually receive the call to a shamanic vocation through illness or suffering, dreams, or spontaneous ecstatic experiences with spirits. According to Vitebsky,

> Though there is much variation across societies, shamanic power and practice are often inherited within a lineage or kin-group. But at the same time it is generally said that a future shaman does not choose his or her profession, but is chosen by the spirits themselves to serve them. The young candidate may be made aware of this through dreams or by other signs. (Vitebsky, 2000: 60)

Even when the vocation is expected because of heredity, Eliade says that one or more 'death and resurrection' processes still occur – often during soul journeys, but sometimes through physical illness. According to him, these experiences usually have three components: dismemberment and renewal of the shaman's body, ascent to the sky, and descent to the lower world (Eliade: 34–5). Hutton argues that the visionary experience of 'death and resurrection' Eliade described was not clearly cross-cultural. He states that 'The truly universal pattern was that the prospective shaman underwent a period of withdrawal in order to develop her or his skills and knowledge' (Hutton, 2001: 74). In any event, the shaman must in some way(s) die to the life that existed before the call came in order to ultimately accept that the new abilities of experiencing ecstatic soul flight and providing spiritual healing are actually gifts. That often includes some kind of apprenticeship that involves initiation experiences. According to Harvey,

> Initiation establishes relationships, knowledges and abilities that define who shamans are and what they do. Relationships with powerful helpers are not only formed but also cemented in dramatic encounters which demonstrate or negotiate power, control, authority, and boundaries. Shamans are taught what their helpers require and offer, what etiquette will maintain and enhance their ongoing relationship. (Harvey: 27)

For many, the experience of travelling to the spirit realms or communicating with the spirits is frightening; for others, seeing themselves as healers is equally frightening. Facing these fears, allowing the new gifts, and participating in traditional instruction regarding shamanic roles and functions can provide intense and powerful initiation experiences for one who becomes a shaman (Drury: 11; Smith, 1997: 26). With the Inuit shamans, part of their initiation process often involves obtaining from 'the spirits' a song that fills them with power (Merkur: 199). For East Greenlanders, rock grinding to call forth spirits that become helpers (Jakobsen: 52), and successfully initiating a soul journey and song while tightly bound with ropes in order to ask spirits for release from the ropes (Jakobsen: 63–4), are two initiation rites described as ways of mastering the spirits during a potential shaman's apprenticeship.

An initiation crisis occurs for a small percentage of shamans, raising a concern about whether the newly emerging shaman is having a psychotic emergency or a spiritual emergence. It is helpful to remember that a community's recognition of the experience as 'initiatory', and its support for the new shaman throughout that process, are important in the shaman's healing or recovery (Walsh: 41; Cameron: 3). According to Lewis, a shaman's career follows three main phases: first is an involuntary, uncontrolled possession by spirits; next is a time of accommodating to, or domesticating, those spirits; finally, it culminates with the shaman either dying or successfully learning to initiate controlled, voluntary and solicited trance and possession as a healer (Lewis, 1996: 118).

Shamanic Cosmology

A shamanic cosmology is possible when one distinguishes between an ordinary reality that is material and visible to our physical eyes, and a non-ordinary reality that is not material, but is seen through the eyes of imagination or experienced through intuitive ways of knowing – a reality often called a vision (Eliade: 226). It is in the spirit realms that the shaman finds a geography usually made up of three primary cosmic regions: a lower world, sometimes called an underworld; a middle world, often described as the spiritual dimension of the physical earth; and an upper world, referred to at times as the sky. Generally these upper and lower regions are accessed through a kind of hole, or opening, in the sky or the earth, depending upon the direction of the journey (Vitebsky, 2001: 17). A journey to the upper world may begin with a soul ascent from the top of a hill, mountain, tree, or other high place exiting from the earth in ordinary reality (Drury: 17); a journey to the lower world may begin with the soul descending into a cave, body of water, root system of a tree, or other natural passage that can take one downward into the earth (Harner: 24–31).

Common in descriptions of sacred space, a centre axis, often called the tree of life or the world pillar, is identified by many shamanic cultures as a symbol connecting the three cosmic regions (Drury: 38–9). A further aspect of this cosmology is that both the upper and the lower regions contain numerous levels through which the shaman may travel (Eliade: 259–60).

In her book about Yup'ik Eskimo oral tradition, scholar Ann Fienup-Riordan describes a slightly different cosmology – one of circles within a circle, reflecting the Yup'ik 'structure of daily life and movement in the world at large' (Fienup-Riordan: 259). This daily movement of people within a circular village space is mirrored in the seasonal movement of villagers as they circle around their land at different times of the year. All of this movement takes place within a circular framework of universal space, which is experienced as inhabited by the *ellam yua*, 'the person of the universe' who watches the world. Though shamans may still journey up or down, within this cosmology, one journeying quite far in one direction might 'eventually arrive at a point where the earth folded back up into the skyland home of the spirits of land animals' (Fienup-Riordan: 259).

An important point when identifying a shamanic cosmology is that one journeying from ordinary reality to the non-ordinary reality of the spirit realms usually discovers a non-ordinary reality geography that can be explored and revisited – a geography that provides special meeting places with spiritual allies. Furthermore, that territory often has characteristics not unlike those of the land in which the one journeying lives.

Shamanic Soul Flight/Journeying

Central to shamanism is the soul journey, or flight of ecstasy, taken into the spirit realms by the shaman, in partnership with spiritual allies, for the purpose of helping self and others. With this in mind, Vitebsky tells us

> So while it is reminiscent in some ways of mystical experience in the mainstream historical religions, shamanic journeying is at the same time extremely pragmatic and goal-oriented. (Vitebsky, 2000: 61)

He elaborates by describing how this pragmatic process functions in ways that include re-enacting central experiences in the shaman's initiation, performing seasonal rites that maintain order, and responding to a problem experienced by an individual or the community (Vitebsky, 2000: 61). Examples of this are ritually and dramatically portraying an initial meeting of the shaman's guardian spirit, enacting the seasonal battle between seasons as one gives way to another, and providing something like a soul retrieval for an individual or a divination to access information regarding a community problem, for example how to deal with young people who no longer want to maintain cultural traditions. Harvey reminds us that Korean shamans are good examples of people who do not 'journey' beyond their bodies (Harvey: 19). However, I think the commonality is in the experience of something shifting when a shaman meets with spiritual allies who partner with him or her in doing shamanic work.

Consistent with the cosmology described earlier, the shamanic journey has a basic structure in which the shaman: begins at a starting point in ordinary reality; ascends or descends into the non-ordinary realm of 'the spirits' to partner with them for information or healing; and ends by returning to the ordinary-reality starting point. Though the unique aspect of this journey is the ecstasy experienced by the shaman, it is worth noting that soul flight is accomplished by using a fairly straightforward methodology. This ecstasy is often compared to 'magical heat' – a kind of burning with joy that occurs when the lost connection is restored, and spirit and matter are reunited. For this reason, from both a metaphorical and a physical standpoint, a shaman is sometimes said to have 'mastery over fire' (Eliade: 272–6). The experience of journeying has its parallels with meditative processes like guided imagery and 'active imagination' – a term coined by Jung. Guided imagery is generally directed by another person who instructs the one meditating in what to do, but active imagination is more interactive and less dependent on another's guidance. It is closer to a shamanic journey in that the one meditating takes control of focusing and of wilfully interacting with images that appear in the realm of imagination (Noel: 170–1).

This soul journey can take place alone or in the presence of one or more people, often the family and friends of one asking for healing, but sometimes members of the community who have asked for shamanic assistance regarding a common problem. Researchers who have observed these more public journeys have often called them séances. During a 'séance', the shaman will often enact what is occurring in the journey. In that sense, this kind of 'shamanistic séance is high theatre' – a 'performance' in which the shaman embodies his or her spiritual allies and 'tells the story' of the healing or the information gathered from the spirits (Lewis, 1996: 120).

Shamanic Consciousness

What shamans do is inseparable from the music they (or their helpers) play, the costumes they wear, the art they create, the movements they make, the performances they enact. A shaman banging a drum, wearing mirrors, moving like an animal, chanting, is someone shamanizing. (Harvey: 155)

In order to take flight, or journey on a soul level, the shaman must access a state of consciousness that facilitates that process. Most shamans utilize the rhythmic music of consistent drumming, rattling, singing, and/or dancing to enter into a trance. To further deepen the trance state, some wear costumes or masks that reflect their spiritual allies, or which have bells or shells sewn into them. Many possess objects of special spiritual significance to them – objects they believe actually strengthen and align them with their spiritual power. Hoppál describes this well in his article describing the shaman's garments, head-dress, crown, belt, and footwear (Hoppál, 2001: 76–84). Furthermore, during ritual 'performances', the participation of everyone present not only facilitates a shaman's own spiritual work, but involves those present in accessing and enhancing their own spiritual power.

One example of the importance of ritual dress is given by James Cox during his shamanic research in Kivalina, Alaska. Though applied in a Christian setting, not a traditional shamanic ritual, the officiating priest at an Episcopalian service asked Cox to assist with distributing elements of the Eucharist, but would not allow him to do so without wearing a clerical shirt. Cox tells us 'The costume of the religious practitioner thus mediated the spirit world to the people, and without the costume, such mediation could not occur' (Cox, 1999: 275, 278).

There are shamans who use drugs to enhance their soul journeys, but that is not a universal practice. Drury describes some of the ways shamans from Pakistan, Singapore, Indonesia and the Arctic Regions move into a shamanic state of consciousness 'following periods of fasting, sensory deprivation, meditative focusing, chanting, through the beating of drums, or through a particular response to a dream' (Drury: 15). Connolly emphasizes the fact that 'trance is rarely an end in itself. Usually it is a means to the attainment of some other end' (Connolly: 5). For shamans, that end is passage into the spirit realms, or non-ordinary reality, to work with spirits for healing and/or information. To an observer, this passage may appear to be quite intense and frenzied, or it may seem rather quiet and inward. This depends in great part upon the shaman's personality, his or her susceptibility to trance states, and the nature of his or her relationship with spiritual allies.

Shamanic Spiritual Allies

As discussed in the working definitions, a shaman works with spiritual allies of various types in a kind of partnership. Drury expands upon this:

In the shaman's world, spirit allies have many functions: they can detect the origins of illness, be dispatched to recover lost souls, be summoned in acts of aggression, and show a clear path past obstacles which might arise on the shaman's quest. As we have already seen, spirit guides may appear to shamans in dreams, in visions, and spontaneously after initiations. In some societies, shamans also exchange or inherit spirit guides. In all cases, however, spirit guides are perceived as crucial to the shaman's resolve and power: a literal embodiment of psychic and magical strength. (Drury: 42)

Because of this close relationship, shamans often sing, dance and perform certain rituals as if they were these allies; they are uniting with the power and energy that the allies are sharing with them in order to more effectively fulfil their functions in society (Eliade: 93). According to Harner,

To perform his work, the shaman depends on special, personal power, which is usually supplied by his guardian and helping spirits. Each shaman generally has at least one guardian spirit in his service, whether or not he also possesses helping spirits. (Harner: 42)

This guardian spirit corresponds to the 'tutelary spirit' of Siberian shamanism, the 'nagual' in Guatemala and Mexico, the 'assistant totem' in Australia, or the 'familiar' in European literature; without it one cannot be a shaman, though possessing a guardian spirit does not automatically make one a shaman (Harner: 42–3). Often a (power) animal, a teacher in human form, or a plant (possibly tree) spirit, the guardian spirit protects, serves and guides the shaman when he or she is journeying on behalf of others. In conjunction, helping spirits support the shaman in diverse and specialized ways – much like a crew of assistants available when needed for specific tasks (Harner: 43).

Sometimes a shaman's alliance with a spiritual ally who appears in human form takes on aspects of a spiritual marriage with a beloved. Lewis states that

the relationship between the devotee and the spirit, which he or she regularly incarnates, is often represented directly in terms either of marriage or of kinship. (Lewis, 2003: 52)

This kind of union is another way the shaman can be helped through initiation into spiritual power and fulfilment of his or her healing vocation (Eliade: 79–81; Cameron: 3).

Regardless of the diverse descriptions of spiritual allies, their categories, or their names, research points to the fact that they are essential to the successful functioning of a shaman. It is in partnership with these allies that a shaman is initiated, learns to discern the shamanic path, and serves the needs of the soul for those in the communities in which he or she lives. Their presence does not necessarily eliminate the need for apprenticeship with human teachers, but without these spirits, shamans would be unable to do their work.

Shamanic Soul Healing

Shamans gather divinatory information for themselves and others, but that function serves primarily to help them in their main work of soul healing. Referring to Siberian shamanism, Hutton tells us

> A function of shamanism which was as widespread as healing and almost as prominent in the records, was divination, either in the form of clairvoyance, to trace lost or stolen goods or animals, or of prophecy, to advise people on how best to prepare for hunting, fishing, journeying or seasonal migration. (Hutton, 2001: 54)

We also learn from Chungmoo Choi that contemporary Korean shamans regularly use divination to obtain information helpful in working with those who come to them for shamanic assistance (Choi: 171–4). Examples from Siberia and Korea underscore the importance of good relationships with spirits as part of maintaining the health of individuals and their communities.

As mentioned in the definitions, the shaman is a specialist in soul issues. For that reason, when a person or a group experiences some kind of disease, illness or malady, the shaman operates on the soul level to cure, or heal, the problem. Fienup-Riordan tells us that the Yup'ik peoples in Alaska 'primarily regarded healing as a spiritual enterprise aimed at either exorcism of unclean essences or restoring wholeness by recalling something lost' (Fienup-Riordan: 196). Therefore, when the shaman, with the help of spiritual allies, determines that the underlying cause of that problem is loss of power, then retrieving a power animal, a spiritual ally in animal form, for the one(s) with the malady is usually the healing practice used (Harner: 69–70). Similarly, when an individual or group has experienced a severe trauma, as is likely to happen in war, disasters, accidents, various type of abuse or other terrifying occurrences, the shaman and his or her allies will often diagnose the underlying issue as soul loss (Ingerman, 1991: 12–13).

In other words, from a shamanic perspective, a part of the soul reacts to a trauma by separating itself and travelling into the spirit realms for protection. While Hultkrantz suggests that the free soul is what departs, Sandra Ingerman, pioneer in modern-day shamanic soul retrieval, contends that any lost part is a fragment of the vital soul, what Hultkrantz calls the body-soul. It is essential to life, and the reason healing is needed (Smith, 1997: 189; Ingerman, 1991: 11–12). The shaman's role is to journey into the spirit realms, find any lost parts, bring them back in a ritual of reunion, and support the process of integrating the parts (Ingerman, 1993; Jakobsen: 251–2).

Sometimes individuals or groups feel as if an 'evil spirit', or a harmful illness, attitude or belief has intruded into their physical or emotional space. If a shamanic diagnosis (via consultation with a spiritual ally while journeying) confirms the presence of a spiritual intrusion, the shaman may remove that intrusion by performing an extraction on a soul level (Harner: 115–23). Some Yup'ik shamans accomplish this by putting a frog on top of a sick person's head – holding the belief that 'the frog could draw sickness out of the body and carry it away when it left' (Fienup-Riordan: 201). Other methods of extraction include the shaman physically removing the intrusion with his or her hands, or by a sucking technique; with each method, the shaman uses divination to determine the problem, and then works with spiritual allies to conduct the extraction (Harner: 115–22).

A shaman may be called upon to help one who is about to die, or one who has just died. From a shamanic perspective, teaching a person close to death about how to journey and how to meet spiritual allies can increase that dying person's sense of familiarity with the spirit realms, and bring comfort in the dying process. Likewise, when necessary, a shaman may function as a 'psychopomp', one who helps those who have already died to cross over into the spirit realms (Eliade: 215–17). Disagreeing with Eliade's claim that shamans in general always functioned as psychopomps, Hutton identifies the work of the Nanais *kasanti* as only one Siberian example of those who

> conduct the souls of recently deceased tribespeople to the land of the dead, in a long and elaborate ritual which allowed the bereaved an opportunity to work through their grief and conclude their relationship with the dead. (Hutton, 2001: 55)

Regardless of whether or not every shaman specializes in psychopomp healing, it seems clear that work with those who are dying and those who have died is part of an overall soul healing function provided by many shamans throughout the world.

Community Support

Shamans function within the context of the societies in which they live. Though they may feel alone in their shamanic call, it is for the community that they do their work. It is also the community that acknowledges their vocation, supports them in their work, or chastises them if they refuse or ignore what is theirs to do. According to Vitebsky, after a shaman passes through a severe initiation experience, he or she

> must always be re-socialized and psychologically reintegrated to serve a social function within the community. The mystic is also a social worker. (Vitebsky, 2000: 63)

In Alaska, Yup'ik communities want their shamans to help them prevent illness, rather than cure disease, and their ceremonies reflect that focus (Fienup-Riordan: 203–4). Likewise, with the Sora, an aboriginal tribe in eastern India, 'instead of being called in for a crisis, the shaman is involved in a constant regulation of social relations' (Vitebsky, 2000: 64). In essence, shamanism as a system is fairly practical in that it encompasses and attends to a network of relationships that a community and its shaman(s) deem important for their health and well-being, and vital for their overall survival.

Conclusion

These are basic elements that appear to exist cross-culturally, though it is unlikely that every shamanic practitioner or shamanic culture always exhibits each component at all times. Highly influenced by Harner's concept of core shamanism, the elements in this model reflect an underlying pattern of shamanic characteristics that exists globally, but is expressed locally. Not alone in exploring this concept, Vitebsky also presents a list of distinctively shamanic aspects: a layered cosmology, the flight of the shaman's soul, and 'the power to use this journey to fight, command and control spirits which inhabit these realms and affect human destiny' (Vitebsky, 2003: 279). He, too, sees shamanism as a system, but one 'of contemplative thought with an implicit set of propositions, and a blueprint for action' (Vitebsky, 2003: 279). I agree with his insights, and his contention that shamanic thinking has important implications for our world.

At the same time, several challenges present themselves when looking at shamanic practice. One is whether the elements I have identified actually do exist cross-culturally. I believe there is evidence that they do, but I also realize their expression may differ according to culture. Another is how contemporary shamanic practitioners see themselves and relate to indigenous shamans – especially in light of legitimate concerns about appropriation. Finally, as Linda Tuhiwai Smith points out, any researcher must use

Table 3: Model of Cross-Cultural Shamanism

Key Element	Examples
1. Shamanic vocation and initiation	Hereditary or spontaneous call; Illness and/or dreams; Death and resurrection experiences; Bestowal of spiritual allies; Possible power song.
2. Shamanic cosmology	Ordinary/non-ordinary reality; Upper, lower and middle worlds; Earthly starting points for journeys; Tree of Life/Axis Mundi.
3. Shamanic soul flight/journeying	Ecstatic experience; Either ascent or descent; Partnership with spiritual allies; Magical heat/Mastery of fire; Focused and interactive.
4. Shamanic consciousness	Rhythmic music: drumming, rattling, chanting, dancing; Costumes; Fasting.
5. Shamanic spiritual allies	Protective and supportive partnership; Source of power; Guides to information and healing; Human, animal and plant form; Spiritual marriage.
6. Shamanic soul healing	Divination; Power animal retrieval; Soul retrieval; Extractions; Death and dying/Psychopomp; Environmental healing.
7. Community support	Call acknowledged; Work supported; Effectiveness monitored.

research methodologies that respect those who have agreed to tell their stories – especially when those stories come from indigenous peoples who may have endured colonial imperialism (Smith, 1999).

Table 3 (above) portrays the elements just described in the model of cross-cultural shamanism. Chapter Five introduces the fieldwork participants, the contexts in which they work, and the process and methodology used in this project.

Chapter Five

A Case Study of Three Shamanic Practice Groups in Scotland

Overview

In Chapter One I described how I realized that the shamanic people with whom I was working actually saw the world differently. Furthermore, their paradigm of religion and spirituality was new. In this chapter I introduce them and provide a brief context for their lives and work. Following that I explain my methodology, and then conclude with several descriptions of my participant observation sessions.

General Context

Those who agreed to participate in this study are in some way related to the Foundation for Planetary Healing (originally named the Edinburgh Shamanic Centre in 2003), the Findhorn Foundation and Lendrick Lodge. These three organizations have at least one not-for-profit charitable dimension to their organizational structure, though private ownership allowed each of them to begin functioning initially. They are intentional spiritual communities with three different ways of coming together as a community. In addition, all of them have websites that describe their philosophy and shamanic programmes (Edinburgh, 2004b; Santoro, 2004; Findhorn, 2004; Lendrick, 2004c).

I interviewed six shamanic practitioners who lived in Scotland – a key criterion for choosing them. One was female, and five were male; an additional female functioned occasionally as a shamanic assistant for one of the practitioners. Four practitioners were in their thirties, and one was in his fifties. Two were born and raised in Scotland; one grew up in Brazil; another came from Denmark; one is a native of Italy; and another was raised in Ireland. Those who migrated from elsewhere arrived as adults who had chosen to come to Scotland for a variety of reasons. However, once here, they found enough receptivity to their work that they decided to stay.

Of the twenty-three people who were not practitioners, but participated in shamanic communities with the practitioners, I interviewed five women and one man. I also spoke informally with seventeen other community members – thirteen females and four males. Two of those people functioned as members of staff, and the remaining community people were participants in an 'astroshamanism' workshop at the Findhorn Foundation. All twenty-three came from countries that included Scotland, England, Holland, Italy, New Zealand, the USA, Germany and Sweden. The age cohorts included four in their twenties, seven in their thirties, five each in their forties and fifties, and two in their sixties.

Each of the communities focuses on shamanic work that includes both individual healing, and/or divination and group work that usually occurs through shamanic drumming sessions, trance dance, or training workshops. Furthermore, most of this shamanic work takes place within the centres that form the locus for their communities, though practitioner Franco Santoro, who lives at the Findhorn Foundation, also offers a number of workshops in other countries. All must in some way determine how to earn an income that can sustain their work.

The Edinburgh Shamanic Centre

Meeting Cláudia Gonçalves

I first met Cláudia Goñalves at a shamanic journey drumming group we both attended in Edinburgh in the winter of 2002. A year later we met again, rather unexpectedly through her shamanic work at a metaphysical book-store in Edinburgh. Cláudia said that during the previous year she had begun practising as a shamanic healer and was regularly attending various health fairs throughout Scotland. At those fairs she had met other shamanic practitioners who were living in Scotland; together they formed a loose network of shamanic colleagues. She also told me she was expanding from primarily working one-to-one with clients, to starting trance dance groups.

About a month later Cláudia rang to ask if I would be one of her helpers at a trance dance she was leading at the Salisbury Centre. Though I had pre-viously experienced a trance state while drumming, dancing and singing with various shamanic groups, I had never been to a trance dance and was curious to know what it was like. She told me she would be asking particip-ants to close their eyes during the dance, which meant that the helpers would act as a 'wall' or shield to protect people from bumping into each other when that seemed likely to happen. Pleased that she trusted me, I agreed to help. A partial description of that event can be found in the Participant Observation section.

Founding the Edinburgh Shamanic Centre

Cláudia and I continued to communicate over the next several months. Due to the time involved in finding, organizing and renting various venues needed in order to conduct shamanic group events, and based on the desire for a regular place to hold individual shamanic healing sessions, Cláudia began looking for premises to start a shamanic centre in the Edinburgh area. The following summer she and Mark Halliday, another shamanic practitioner, found a suitable building at a price they could afford, bought it, and began refurbishing it the better to accommodate the type of work they would be doing. In September of 2003, they opened the Edinburgh Shamanic Centre in Portobello; by late that month they had created a website and prepared a publication describing the Centre:

> Here you will find a spiritual library, a meditation room and a Shamanic shop. Daily groups and classes, healing circles, personal shamanic guidance, readings, workshops, Shamanic Healing with Cláudia Gonçalves, Solar Shamanism with Mark Halliday, and much more. (Edinburgh, 2003)

Though Cláudia and Mark own the Centre, they created it as a registered charity. As such, they have committed themselves to holding annual general meetings, building a membership of shamanic and financial supporters, receiving feedback and guidance about Centre business, and relying extensively on volunteer help.

By January of 2004, Cláudia and Mark had invited shamanic practitioners Preben Eagle Heart Olsen and Alistair Bate to provide shamanic work at the Centre; they also asked other guest practitioners, including Franco from Findhorn, to teach occasional shamanic workshops. At the same time, another woman named Collette helped the Centre move forward by volunteering several hours a week; she also participated in some of the Centre offerings. As I met both paid and unpaid core staff and asked if I could interview them as part of my research, each one said yes.

On 17 January 2004 they held an open day, which I attended, in addition to many other visitors. Groups of about fifteen gathered every hour for an introductory talk and meditation facilitated by one or more of the Centre staff. Though most of the time I remained upstairs talking with people, during the introductory session I attended, Cláudia talked about the purpose and offerings of the Centre, Mark provided a guided meditation and

Preben played the Native American flute. Visitors came in waves throughout the rest of the day. It appeared that the ages of those who visited ranged
from early twenties to early seventies. There was a substantial mix of male
and female, though with more females. Most visitors said they were curious;
some had shamanic backgrounds themselves; and others had heard the
term, but wanted to know what shamanism really was.

During one of my visits to the Centre, I participated in a shamanic journey drumming session with Preben. That, too, is described in the Participant Observation section.

Follow-Up

Since then, I have remained on the mailing list as a member of the Centre,
and I have occasionally visited there. On 11 December 2004, I participated
with about thirty people in the Centre's first annual general meeting. That
group was a fairly equal mix of women and men – most of whom had not
been present a year earlier at the open day. Cláudia and Mark had asked a
trained facilitator to organize and conduct the meeting. That helped exped-
ite a number of organizational decisions that freed them to do more of their
shamanic work, and allowed others to help more extensively in different
aspects of the business, such as membership and marketing.

In the last half of 2004 Preben, Alistair and Collette stopped working
out of the Centre as practitioners and volunteer. However, the Centre
still offered regular shamanic groups, in addition to weekend workshops
conducted by local and international shamanic facilitators (Edinburgh,
2004a). One of the international facilitators was from the Czech Republic;
another was from the Andes in South America. The Centre has also entered
into global partnerships with two charities that help people with HIV/
AIDS, based in Brazil and South Africa.

In early 2005 through the Sacred Mountains Foundation, located in Colorado, USA, Mark spent six months living in Colorado, doing voluntary
work for the Navaho Nations, all the while under the supervision of a
Navajo medicine man. During that time, he published his experiences in
the Centre's newsletter. With Mark away, Cláudia relied even more on
volunteer help, and she opened the Centre to practitioners who wanted to
rent space for events or workshops.

After Mark returned, he and Cláudia continued to develop their work
and expand their programmes. Their commitment to help people in poorer
parts of the world, and to hold a global vision, was reflected in their 2006
decision to change the name of the Edinburgh Shamanic Centre to the
Centre for Planetary Healing. They participated in the first gathering of

the UK Society for Shamanic Practitioners in August 2006, held in Glaston-bury, England. In addition, they facilitated workshops and were leaders of some of the spiritual practice sessions held at the Shamanic Spiritualities Conference in Edinburgh, in May 2007.

The Findhorn Foundation

Meeting Franco Santoro

Cláudia suggested I meet Franco. A resident staff member of the Findhorn Foundation since 1999, Franco works with people individually, but also conducts training workshops in astroshamanism throughout the year in sev-eral countries. When I learned that he would be facilitating a two-day astro-shamanic workshop at the Salisbury Centre in April 2003, I decided to participate as a way of meeting him, observing his style, and determining with him the feasibility of our working together on my research project.

Called 'Astroshamanism, The East Gate – A Voyage through the Inner Universe', the Salisbury Centre's winter/spring programme described his workshop as designed to explore shamanic states of consciousness as they relate to planetary energies and seasonal cycles. Using traditional shamanic methods such as drumming, singing, trance dancing and shamanic jour-neys, Franco would help participants focus on the energies of spring as a way of releasing grievances or blocks and embracing new possibilities (Salis-bury, 2003). One workshop brochure described Franco as:

> a shamanic facilitator, experiential astrologer, member of the Findhorn
> Foundation, the developer of astroshamanism and supply director of the
> Sacred Cone Circle. In 1964 he started regular connections with non-
> ordinary dimensions that led him to live a parallel life which was often
> a cause of conflict in his relationship with conventional reality. In 1976
> he had a transformational experience which, after years of practice with
> shamans and medicine people, allowed him to find clarity about his con-
> nections and acknowledge his function as a bridge between dimensions.
> His path of apprenticeship encompassed both the archaic traditions
> of his Italian natal descent and those of other adopted lineages. From
> 1996 he has run the Operative Training in Astroshamanism, an intensive
> programme for shamanic practitioners and healers. (Santoro, 2003b)

The workshop ran for several hours on Friday night, and continued on Saturday morning and afternoon. By the end we both knew we would like to collaborate, and we agreed to discuss the process in the following months.

Learning About the Findhorn Foundation

In May 2003 I checked the Findhorn Foundation website and re-read the brochure Franco had given me describing the week-long astroshamanism workshop he planned to conduct at Findhorn near the end of June. Both sources stated that it would be facilitated by 'Franco Santoro and Faculty', and called it

> A workshop and retreat which offers practical tools and experiential understanding for journeying into shamanic dimensions beyond conventional time and space. The purpose is that of exploring archaic roots and original lineages, connecting with significant past lives or planetary memories, releasing grievances, discovering potential and bringing healing in our current life and environment. Cluny Hill College and its natural territory will be used as a geomantic Sacred Circle to inspire and ground our experiences. The programme includes soul retrieval, past life regressions, shamanic time voyages and trance dances, and a basic vision quest and rite of passage (Quiure Saike). An astrological map will be drawn and journeyed for each participant. This workshop is also a shamanic celebration of the Summer Solstice and the South Gate. (Santoro, 2003b; Findhorn, 2004)

That seemed a rather ambitious agenda, but one that contained the opportunity for new experiences and for participation in numerous shamanic elements with which I already had some familiarity. It occurred to me that attending the workshop would give me not only a more extensive chance to observe and understand Franco and his work prior to our interview, but it would also allow me to observe and interview other people who would be there as participants.

When I emailed Franco to ask about my potential involvement, he responded favourably and even supported my receiving a bursary from the Findhorn Foundation to assist with some of my fees. It was then settled that I would be a participant observer at the June workshop. During that time I would interview as many participants as I could, and once the workshop had ended I would conclude by interviewing Franco. As part of my preparation, I was to send Franco some birth information needed for my astrological chart. An abbreviated account of that workshop is provided in the Participant Observation section.

The Findhorn Foundation, which sponsored and hosted Franco's June workshop on Astroshamanism, started in 1962, and by its own description grew into the centre of one of the best-known intentional communities in the world. Its main focus continues to be on education, community and environment, demonstrating the links between the spiritual, social and environmental aspects of life. (Findhorn, 2003)

Though it began in a caravan park, Findhorn has developed into the Findhorn Foundation, a registered charity in Scotland and an NGO associated with the Department of Public Information of the United Nations. Based on research about the Findhorn Foundation conducted in the 1990s, Sutcliffe wrote that Findhorn

is a substantial settlement of spiritual 'seekers' (Sutcliffe, 1997) on the north-east coast of Scotland, which since 1962 has hosted three generations of religious individualists engaged in the exploration of alternative spiritualities, psycho-physical therapies, craftwork and gardening. (Sutcliffe, 2000a)

An in-depth analysis of the Findhorn Foundation, 'New Age' spiritualities, and the concept of 'spiritual seeker' is not the overt purpose of this thesis, but Sutcliffe's work provides a valuable contribution to understanding these issues, which relate closely to my own work.

Follow-Up

Franco keeps me on his email list and has expanded his workshop offerings beyond what they were in 2003. Not only does he continue his individual shamanic work, but also he conducts some workshops at the Findhorn Foundation, and in other countries including Germany, Italy, South Africa, Spain, Ireland and the Netherlands. In May 2007 Franco travelled to Edinburgh to participate as a workshop facilitator and leader in some of the spiritual practice sessions at the Shamanic Spiritualities Conference.

Lendrick Lodge

Meeting Stephen Mulhearn

During my time talking with people at the Edinburgh Shamanic Centre, Lendrick Lodge surfaced periodically as a good place for shamanic study and experience. Told that the Lodge had a website, I checked it initially and found material about fire-walking opportunities, but very little describing shamanic training. As a result, I delayed further exploration. However, after hearing about the Lodge again in early spring of 2004, I revisited its website and discovered the posting of a comprehensive programme of shamanic training. Based on that, I decided to contact Stephen Mulhearn, co-owner of Lendrick Lodge, and ask if I could visit him and perhaps include what I would learn from him in my research. During our telephone conversation I also explained who I was, some of my own shamanic background, and what I was studying at the university. He readily agreed to meet with me, and we set a date for early June of 2004.

I took a morning bus from Edinburgh to Callander and a taxi from Callander to Lendrick Lodge, which is situated near Brig O'Turk in the Trossachs, Scotland, and described in their materials as one of many scenic locations in the country. The Lendrick Lodge website says it is a 'residential spiritual centre, nestled in remote wilderness amidst the hills, lochs, forests and natural beauty of the Scottish Trossachs' near what is often called the 'doorway to the Highlands' (Lendrick, 2004c). Its vision is to 'create a safe space for healing, empowerment and the guidance to awaken your inner spirit' (Lendrick, 2004a). Experiences available at Lendrick Lodge include attending courses, accessing holistic treatments and therapies, undertaking a private retreat, and using the space for a private group. It is the UK centre for the Sundoor International Fire-walking School, and the home of a school of shamanic training called the Spirit of Shamanism (Lendrick, 2004b).

The Lodge itself has a large living room with big windows, a spacious kitchen next to a large dining room, and several group rooms ranging in size from small to large. Designed to accommodate various numbers of people, it contains sleeping arrangements that range from single to double and triple rooms. Outside there is a labyrinth, a sweat lodge, an area for fire-walking, paths winding through the land and near a stream, and many beautiful flowers and trees. Upon my arrival, a staff member welcomed me warmly and took me to the living room, where I waited until Stephen joined me.

Stephen was born near Glasgow. He told me about his many life experiences in Scotland and other parts of the world that prompted him to buy Lendrick Lodge in January of 2001. It had previously been a hunting lodge, a youth hostel, a yoga centre, and a holistic centre. When Stephen and his wife Victoria purchased the Lodge, they expanded its scope by establishing it as a residential holistic centre offering personal growth, healing, empowerment, retreat opportunities and the programme of shamanic training. They are the owners, but associated with the Lodge is the Lendrick Trust, a charitable trust set up to support individuals who would like to participate in centre activities, but are restricted by finances or in other ways; the Trust is also designed to promote public education about holistic principles and practices.

Stephen said he designed his shamanic programme with the input of several shamans from North and South America – focusing especially on training those who see their shamanic work as a lifelong path. As part of a long-term case study, he does follow-up work with the people he trains by asking for reports about what they do in their shamanic practice. He said he tries to help these people develop the gifts they already have, but occasionally he finds people whose gifts he thinks are better utilized in areas other than shamanic practice.

Talking with the Staff

After interviewing Stephen, I explored the grounds and was then invited to stay for lunch. No groups were using the Lodge that day, which meant I was able to talk casually with the staff during and after our lunch of homemade soup and fresh bread in the kitchen. Staff members seemed quite willing to tell me about their own involvement and experience with Lendrick Lodge.

The gardener was from Fife, and came to the Lodge fortnightly to tend the grounds. In reference to the labyrinth built on the property, he said he was aware of it and of other spiritual work going on in Fife. One with the most longevity and first-hand knowledge of Lendrick Lodge was a woman who helped clean the Lodge. She had worked there as a volunteer and as paid staff for fourteen or fifteen years. For all that time she had lived in nearby Callander and watched the facility evolve through its various forms until Stephen and Victoria purchased it. She talked about how she had become friends with many who frequent the Lodge, enjoyed the good environment it supports, and participated in yoga and fire-walking activities, but not the shamanic training.

The chef, in his mid-to-late twenties, had lived in Glasgow, where he had attended 'cooking school' before taking time out to travel around Scotland. After returning to Glasgow and starting work as a cook about three years ago, he had met Stephen, who with Victoria had been facilitating meditation classes in Glasgow at the time. Eventually he started working at a wholefood shop, where he met Stephen again. The result of that was his being hired to work as a chef at the Lodge. He explained that they buy wholefoods from Tesco and other produce from the Farmers' Market. Thorn, the office administrator, had been at the Lodge for almost a year and had only recently begun to learn about shamanism. From that exposure, he said, he thought most spiritual paths contained some shamanic elements.

I left in late afternoon to return to Edinburgh – wishing that I had found a way to participate in one of Stephen's shamanic workshops or experiences. A Peruvian shaman was coming to Lendrick Lodge for one week in late June, but the workshop was already full. In August a two-week fire-walking course that centred on Initiation, Certification and Spiritual Leadership was scheduled. Though it had shamanic elements, the course would not be focused directly on shamanism or shamanic training. As a result, I chose not to participate.

Follow-Up

On the day I initially visited Lendrick Lodge, I joined as a member who supports the work of the Lodge. Based on that, I have received regular newsletters and mailings that have kept me informed about activities and offerings. Since that time Stephen has continued to train with shamanic teachers in other parts of the world and to offer his own shamanic training at Lendrick Lodge. In 2006 he terminated the members' newsletter saying that he would be devoting more time to the Lendrick Trust. At the Shamanic Spiritualities Conference in Edinburgh in May of 2007, he facilitated one of the workshops and also announced that Sandra Ingerman would be offering Medicine for the Earth training at Lendrick Lodge in the spring of 2008.

Conclusion

Of the three intentional shamanic communities included in this research, the Findhorn Foundation is the one that has been established for the longest time. Its support for Franco and his work enables him to have more flexibility in travelling beyond Findhorn to do his shamanic work. He is also older and more experienced in shamanic ways than are the other practitioners. However, because he travels more and draws people from various parts of the world, developing a sense of community over time with participants at his workshops is probably quite challenging.

Those at the Centre for Planetary Healing continue to grow, and to attract people willing to volunteer as a way of supporting their work. In 2003 they were younger and less experienced not only at doing shamanic work with individuals, but also with groups. However, Cláudia and Mark, in particular, have successfully survived a steep learning curve that has included developing business ownership skills and working with other practitioners. Unlike an established intentional spiritual community such as

Findhorn, the Foundation for Planetary Healing is located in an urban setting and is non-residential, though various ceremonies and retreats are conducted outside in natural surroundings. Cláudia and Mark's understanding of community, its role and importance in shamanic practice, and their perceptions about how communities form and grow, appear to be developing rapidly.

Lendrick Lodge is another kind of community that is actually the home of a married couple with a small baby. The staff members who live there have more flexibility to move as their lives change, and they are not the ones responsible for paying the bills. Being in a rural setting, Lendrick is the most secluded. All of this makes the challenge of building a community a bit different. The community at Lendrick Lodge is more like an extension of family and friends who come to visit on a regular basis – sometimes staying for days and weeks at a time.

People who are part of all three intentional shamanic communities form a very multicultural network. Furthermore, most of them know each other. Among the practitioners, Stephen at Lendrick Lodge is the one who invited Franco to do a shamanic workshop, and it was at that workshop that Cláudia and Mark discovered how many of their own spiritual experiences had actually been of a shamanic nature. Their time with Franco at Lendrick turned out to provide some of the profound initiatory experiences that opened them up to the path they now follow with deep commitment.

Methodology

Selection of Research Methods

This study is fundamentally a qualitative research project that incorporates quantitative tools when they serve a functional role (Corbetta: 37). It was designed to serve the multi-layered approach to shamanism I described briefly in the Introduction and more fully in Chapter Three. My study is supported, guided and semi-structured by *quantitative* aspects, such as the theoretical underpinnings of shamanism, Hervieu-Léger's model of religion, and basic elements in the transformation of religion; however, *qualitative* methods, such as participant observation and interviewing, are needed to gather and understand the stories and experiences shared by shamanic practitioners and participants. This mixture of methodologies provides perspectives that are both *etic* and *emic*. Not only have I used *etic* cross-cultural models with identified criteria and/or characteristics, but I have also correlated those external models with *emic* information gathered from groups of people who are living in culturally specific areas and willing to provide internal viewpoints about what they are doing, their motivations, and the meanings they experience from their shamanic work (Pike: 29).

Research is generally formed and guided by an overarching paradigm with its own characteristics that frame the research questions. This project has operated primarily from an interpretive paradigm concerned with 'what's going on within and between individuals' who share some common social context; focused on discovering meaning for what is said and done by those people; and oriented towards comparing results to other related processes or phenomena, in addition to developing workable and shared understandings about what has happened (LeCompte: 60). The study has a phenomenological dimension in that it utilizes methods of empathic interaction between the researcher and the one being studied in order to help the researcher understand meanings that the individual perceives (Corbetta: 24).

Relevant at this point is a brief discussion of the insider/outsider issue in the study of any religion. Phenomenologists attempt to move beyond explaining facts that are observed from an outsider perspective to a closer understanding of the meaning which people on the inside attach to their beliefs and actions. Another approach described by Russell McCutcheon is that of methodological agnosticism, or neutrality, in which the researcher 'selects a number of tools, or methods of research, that purposely avoid asking questions of truth where there exist no means of acquiring empirical evidence to determine that truth' (McCutcheon, 1999: 8).

Though each of these approaches contributes to scholarship, McCutcheon concludes that a fourth one, best understood as a reflexive stance, may help researchers see how their own experiences and positions are intertwined with what they observe. He points out that the questions chosen shape the answers received; in that way they reveal as much about the presuppositions and biases of the researcher as they do about those interviewed. 'Reflexive scholars, therefore, are more interested in questions of point of view and the stance of the observer than they are with issues of neutrality, objectivity, and fact' (McCutcheon, 1999: 10). McCutcheon also cautions scholars to conduct a theoretical analysis of the research results, rather than simply presenting participant self-reports of meaning and affirming them through self-reflexive accounts. If this analysis does not occur, the researcher may 'miss an ideal opportunity to make a significant contribution' to scholarship (McCutcheon, 2005: 15).

Determining whether my field research could be described as case studies or ethnographies has been another methodological issue. For case studies, questions of 'how' or 'why' are asked about contemporary events 'over which the investigator has little or no control' (Yin: 9). Though case studies can include 'direct observation and systematic interviewing' (Yin: 8), Yin warns about incorrectly confusing 'the case study strategy with a specific method of data collection, such as ethnography or participant-observation', because case studies do 'not depend solely on ethnographic or participant-observer data'; indeed, some can be conducted without ever leaving the library or telephone (Yin: 10–11).

Ethnography is a scientific approach used to investigate and discover within a given community, or culture, what community members do and the reasons they give for those actions. According to LeCompte and Schensul in their book *Designing and Conducting Ethnographic Research*, 'The basic tools of ethnography use the researcher's eyes and ears as the primary modes for data collection,' and they do this 'by interviewing and carefully recording what they see and hear, as well as how things are done, while learning the meanings that people attribute to what they make and do' (LeCompte: 2). As with case studies, ethnographers do not control what happens in field settings, and they use both qualitative and quantitative data sources. However, ethnographers work in the field through face-to-face interaction with participants in order to accurately reflect participant behaviours and perspectives, and ultimately to construct local cultural theories based on those interactive data collection and analytic strategies (LeCompte: 9). They conduct their research locally, but they seek to understand how local experiences relate to national, regional and global issues (Schensul: 7).

This research project has characteristics of both the case study and the ethnography, though as a whole, it falls primarily into the category of ethnography. Beyond what both approaches have in common, the design and application of pre-determined research questions used to interview participants who are part of three distinct 'communities' makes the 'case study' category seem appropriate. However, the interview questions include the element of community, which makes the culture of each community an important aspect. Combining the study of community culture with the role of participant observer tipped the balance towards ethnography as a better descriptor of this project. Regardless of category, the goal was to reflect accurately what participants do, how they feel and what their experiences mean to them.

Interview Process

Due to prior experience with interviewing, when I discovered that a free-flowing conversation guided by selected questions had yielded good results for me, I decided to do the same for these field research interviews. I wanted those I interviewed to know I was listening, trying to understand, and doing my best to reflect their stories accurately in the way I wrote their responses. To ensure that, once I had written my account of their interviews, I sent each one a copy, along with the questions I had used to guide our discussions. I asked them to read what I had written and let me know if I had understood what they had meant or intended to say; I also encouraged them to make any changes they thought were appropriate. All of them responded to my request by providing either minor changes or telling me the account was fine.

In those fieldwork chapters and in the analyses provided in Chapter Eight, when I refer to responses related to all who were interviewed, I use the term 'participants'. If specifically referring to the shamanic practitioners, they are called 'practitioners' or 'shamanic practitioners'. For reference to those who have formed the respective shamanic communities, the term 'community members' is used. All of those interviewed gave me permission to use their first names. Because the shamanic practitioners also advertise their work publicly, I have included their surnames as each is introduced initially.

For ease of reference, the interview questions used to explore the model of shamanism are listed towards the beginning of Chapter Six – prior to presenting the participants' responses. Likewise, those questions used to explore religion and spirituality, specifically through Hervieu-Léger's model, can be found near the beginning of Chapter Seven. Each set of questions reflects the key elements or components found in the respective model.

Participant Observation as Method

My role as a participant observer actually began when I decided to attend the trance dance with Cláudia Gonçalves. This was followed by participating in Franco's weekend shamanic workshop at the Salisbury Centre. In both cases, my participation in these preliminary events helped us decide we could proceed together with the larger research project.

The theoretical underpinning for each set of interview questions I wrote also guided my process of participant observation. However, the interpretive paradigm from which this research was designed required that I be open to 'discovering theory' and to observing actions that might not match my expectations, but may provide insight. Participant observation calls for looking at areas such as physical and social settings, formal and informal interactions, and participant interpretations of social interactions

(Corbetta: 246–9). I have provided that kind of data, along with observations that may not be obvious to participants.

Participant Observation

What follows are abbreviated descriptions of three participant observation sessions: trance dancing with Cláudia; a week-long workshop with Franco and other participants; and a shamanic journey session with Preben. These accounts describe what I observed and heard, and how I responded. I have included them as a way of providing the reader with a perspective on the work of these practitioners, which can be understood only partially through interviews.

Trance Dancing

I had heard about and visited the Salisbury Centre prior to this trance dance with Cláudia. 'Founded in 1973 with the aim of serving the community of Edinburgh and promoting personal development' by offering 'educational courses, workshops and therapies for spiritual, emotional and physical well-being', the Salisbury Centre describes its philosophy in the following statement:

> The interconnectedness of body, mind and spirit, as symbolized in the Celtic Trine, is the foundation of our work and we believe that healing arises naturally from this recognition. (Salisbury, 2003: 1; 2004: 1)

However, this would be the first time I had attended a function there. I arrived about thirty minutes early on 28 February 2003, to visit Cláudia and help prepare the meeting room. Because that room was not yet available and four of us were early, we were all shown to the kitchen, where we informally introduced ourselves while we waited. One woman came from Galicia in Spain and said she was very interested in Celtic culture; a young man from Fife told us that until recently he had focused more on Native American spiritual influences than on his own Scots heritage; and Cláudia herself said she had moved several years ago from Brazil to Scotland. This first encounter had brought together four people from four different countries. When the room was finally ready, we went to prepare our meeting space.

It was a large square room with a polished wooden floor, large windows on two sides, green plants and soft lighting, all contributing to a welcoming atmosphere. As more people arrived, Cláudia asked a couple of them to help her place about six small lanterns around the room; they provided an even warmer atmosphere when the other room lights were eventually turned off. After informal introductions by people as they came into the room, participants were encouraged to pick up large cushions from the back of the room and use them for sitting on the floor in a large circle for the opening session.

There was silence for about five minutes as participants watched Cláudia light some sage and use a feather to wave the smoke from the burning sage around her own body and over some of the objects she was going to use for the evening, including several necklaces she then put around her neck and wore during the session. I recognized this as a purification or smudging ceremony, variations of which I have seen many times in the last eighteen years. The process of smudging herself and the necklace before wearing them appeared to be part of her personal preparation for the trance dance. It is something I have watched other ceremonial leaders do, though I could not determine how many other participants understood her actions, because Cláudia did not speak or explain herself during the ceremony. In fact, she sat outside the circle at one end of the room with her side and back to the participants in a preparation that was essentially separate from the group.

Though I had seen this kind of preparation before, most of the previous purification ceremonies I had witnessed had actively involved group members in the ceremony itself; several had also included explanations about the meaning of what was happening. When she had finished, Cláudia joined the circle and officially welcomed everyone. She told them how pleased she was that they had come to this group trance dance, the first she had ever facilitated in Edinburgh. She explained that most of her experience with trance dance has been on her own or working with individuals during healing sessions.

Cláudia told participants she had started trance dancing when she was thirteen years old and that it was one of her passions. According to her, its purpose is to connect with the spirits for healing. She said this happens by letting the energy of the music and the movement of the body help each individual tune into an issue or issues, such as depression, sadness or hurtful memories, and then release what needs releasing in order to bring about the desired healing.

Participants were told to start by keeping their eyes closed, paying attention to their breathing, and then 'going within' to experience the music and allow their bodies to respond; they were not to speak or sing, but to let internal prompting be expressed only through movement. Cláudia explained that since participants would have their eyes closed, she had asked another woman and myself to keep our eyes open and help prevent people from bumping into each other – telling the group that she had chosen special people to fulfil this role of helper. She said they would dance for ninety minutes and that as the music slowed down towards the end of that time, those who wished could lie down as a way of finishing the experience.

Before beginning the dance, Cláudia asked participants to take turns saying their names and where they lived. Among the twenty participants, most of them women there were people from Scotland, England, South Africa, Germany, Spain and the United States. When we were ready to begin, Cláudia instructed everyone to put their cushions near the side of the room to make way for the dancing. Soon the music began. It consisted of CDs carefully selected by Cláudia, and supplemented with sounds from rhythmic instruments that she also played occasionally throughout the evening. Those instruments included a rattle, a shaker egg and a rain stick. Some songs were slow; some were faster; and most had a distinct beat that was hard to miss.

A few participants were more active than others, though as the evening progressed, more people appeared less inhibited. Most seemed in a trance-like state, moving to the beat of the music and clearly experiencing something that their bodies were expressing. As the music played, Cláudia lined up other songs that would follow throughout the evening. Periodically, she played a percussive type of instrument like a rattle, shaker egg or rain stick, and walked through the group making rhythmic sounds that enhanced the mood of the recorded music.

When the CD music ended, leaving Cláudia's rhythmic shaking of a shaker egg as the only remaining sound, most people were lying on the floor. Once back together, she told us we had gone past our closing time deadline, and those who needed to leave could do so. Most stayed. She then invited us to say 'thank you' and 'goodbye' to the spirits – not with words, but by taking turns shaking a small wooden percussive instrument, which she passed around the circle in a counter-clockwise direction.

My own experience at the trance dance had been a mixture of familiar elements that were packaged in somewhat different ways. I had relaxed and enjoyed the music – allowing myself to move with it. However, my attention had been focused primarily on participants and not on my own emotional or physical responses to the music.

Astroshamanism Week-long Workshop at the Findhorn Foundation

Arrival and Settling In

Grateful for Findhorn generosity, I arrived by train in Forres shortly before noon and was met by a middle-aged woman who was standing near a

Findhorn Foundation van and would take me to Cluny Hill College in Forres, where the workshop was being held. During the ride to Cluny, she explained that the Findhorn Foundation was 'like a living organism' in the way it was organized. The original site was called the Park and was located about five miles outside Forres, near the sea. In November of 1975 the Findhorn Foundation had also purchased the Cluny Hill Hotel, which they then converted into Cluny Hill College. Some of the Findhorn Foundation staff live at the College, but most of that space is for workshop guests, Foundation students participating in the Living Education Staff Programme (LESP), and short-term visitors. Also affiliated with the Findhorn Foundation are those people who live in the surrounding areas, not at the Park or Cluny, but who still participate in community activities and initiatives. Once at Cluny Hill College I was directed upstairs, where I met Katharina, another Findhorn Foundation resident staff member who had moved there from Germany. She welcomed me and said she would be Franco's shamanic assistant during the week, especially regarding administrative matters. Then she took me and a couple of other participants to our rooms, pointing out along the way an area for coffee or tea, a lounge or parlour, a computer room for internet access and email (five pounds for the week), and the meeting rooms.

I shared a room on the first floor with three other women who were there for the workshop. One was a forty-eight-year-old woman whose family had moved from Scotland to New Zealand when she was nine. Another woman, in her late twenties or early thirties, was from Italy. She had been staying at the Findhorn Foundation for several months and was trying to decide whether she would continue at the Foundation or return home to Italy. For most of the week, another middle-aged woman who lived at the Park, the Findhorn Foundation's second campus, joined us at Cluny. This saved her from having to travel back and forth between the two campuses on the Findhorn Foundation bus each day.

Before the workshop actually began, I met two other participants, Susan and another woman, who were in their forties, and we began to learn about each other. Both of them had Christian backgrounds as children and younger adults, and they had also been quite actively involved in their churches. Susan had taught Sunday School for years in New Zealand, and the other woman had been part of an evangelical community in Colorado, USA. Each said that at some point she had begun to experience religion as a block to her unfolding, growing spiritual development. Both displayed strong feelings about how stifling they thought religious rules and dogmas could be, especially when those rules and dogmas become ends in themselves, rather than tools to aid and support spiritual growth.

The Workshop

The workshop began on Saturday afternoon in the ballroom, which is a large open square room with many big windows that provide a view of the beautiful trees and surrounding landscape. As we entered, we were invited to take one of many large floor pillows that we could use for sitting in a circle on the polished wooden floor. Franco began by welcoming all of us and asking for a minute of silence. When the minute ended, we saw that he was holding a small sphere, which he explained would be used as a kind of 'talking stick'. This appeared to be the same sphere he had used during the Edinburgh shamanic workshop I had attended in April, and he used it in a similar manner. Including the two facilitators, Franco and Katharina, there were twenty-one people, and they came from countries including Holland, Italy, Scotland, England, the USA, New Zealand, Germany and Sweden. They ranged in age from one woman in her early twenties to two in their early sixties. Most were about evenly divided among those in their thirties, forties and fifties. In addition to Franco, there were only two other men.

When the sphere came to me, I explained to the group not only that I was there as a participant who had some background and experience in shamanic practice, but also that contemporary shamanism in Scotland was the subject of my PhD research. I told them I would be taking notes about the workshop process, interviewing Franco after the workshop, and asking for interviews with any of them who might be willing to talk with me at mutually chosen times available outside the workshop sessions. Most people seemed open and accepting of that. In fact, as the week progressed, I spent most of my 'free' time talking with people, and there still would not be enough time to interview all who had volunteered.

Franco then described how our meeting room, the Cluny Hill 'territory' (land surrounding Cluny Hill College), and the astrological charts he would be giving us were all containers for the experiences we would be having during the week. We were encouraged to use the entire environment as part of the workshop. He then explained that later on we would be taking a walking tour of the grounds not only to familiarize ourselves with the area, but to 'physically activate' the energy of the place in order for that space to work in partnership with us by containing and supporting our shamanic experiences. Furthermore, throughout the week we would be spending time outside and holding various rituals there. He also acknowledged that today was the summer solstice and that we would honour that occurrence in the evening.

Franco utilized a fairly standard and effective group facilitation opening. He welcomed everyone; encouraged them to gather their thoughts; facilitated introductions by using an object that helped make clear whose turn it was to speak and when that speaking role changed; and explained the purpose of the workshop and the types of activities to expect. After that, he described the physical layout of the areas we would be accessing during the week, and addressed internal group guidelines and external expectations for living co-operatively with staff and guests staying at Cluny Hill College. He also set the tone by presenting his overall paradigm of shamanism and his understanding of its role in the world.

We were then invited to do a brief shamanic journey – one in which we acknowledged where we had been and what our energy had been like, not only during the previous twenty-four hours, but from the time we had chosen to come to the workshop. Franco asked us to find a comfortable position; then he did a five-minute meditation about the season of summer, followed by drumming designed to help us take a shamanic journey. Afterwards, as we sat in the circle, he passed around the 'talking stick' sphere for sharing experiences from the journey and the intentions we had brought for both the journey and the entire week.

Highlighting the Rest of the Workshop

The rest of the week was filled with rituals, shamanic journeys, teachings about shamanism and astrology, experiential exercises, music, dance and other expressive arts processes too numerous to include without detracting from the main purpose of this field research. The overall framework for the week included identifying individual life intentions; accessing and enlisting the help of spiritual allies and energies associated with various aspects of the zodiac; experiencing and utilizing the grounds around Cluny Hill College as reflective of astrological energies available to help participants grow in wholeness; reflecting on and healing from life memories that may be current barriers to personal and spiritual growth; and celebrating moments of healing, friendship and unity. Throughout the week each particular journey, ritual or experiential exercise was generally structured by setting our specific intentions; connecting with spiritual allies; releasing whatever needed to be released; asking for and accepting gifts that we were ready to receive; sharing with the group what we were willing to share of our experiences; and utilizing various tools to help us integrate all that had just happened.

As the week progressed, I participated fully in workshop events. Because my own familiarity with shamanic methods allowed me to experience a great deal – much of which I shared with the group at appropriate times – many participants seemed to recognize my sincerity and my respect for what was happening. That recognition, along with Franco's clear support for my presence, helped create an atmosphere of trust that apparently made it safe for a number of people to talk with me as part of my field research interviews with individuals and small ad hoc groups during breaks. Most interviews took place during afternoon or evening breaks on the last three or four days of the workshop. By intention, Franco's interview, held on the morning after the workshop ended, was the last one scheduled.

Follow-Up

After the workshop I contacted those I had interviewed to ask how they were doing, and to request feedback that would ensure my account of their interview accurately reflected what they had intended to say. They all seemed pleased to hear from me, and were generally satisfied with what I had written. In a few cases, they supplied me with minor modifications, which I gratefully accepted. Nanna, Heleen and Tessa, three of the women I had interviewed, told me they had continued to train with Franco; Jonathan said he had embarked on more in-depth study of astrology, rather than continue with shamanic training; and Susan explained that she had allowed the astroshamanism experiences to help her make major positive changes in her life when she returned home – even though she currently was not actively pursuing shamanic training as such.

Participating in a Shamanic Journey Session at the Centre

After I interviewed Cláudia on 21 January 2004, I remained to participate in the weekly shamanic drumming group that Preben facilitated. We joined together in the lower room, sitting in a circle on the floor. Preben is from Denmark, but he had trained with Native American shamans and drew upon some of the Lakota customs. Just as Cláudia had done in the ceremony I had attended with her, Preben acknowledged the unseen spirits and called upon them for purification and protection. His way of 'honouring the spirits of the directions' and of using sage for purification were familiar to me, because I had grown up in the USA near Lakota territory, and I too had learned some of those same practices from First Nations spiritual teachers.

Preben told us that he uses different drum beats for going to the upper and lower worlds, and that today he felt guided to send us on a lower world shamanic journey. Though I had previously learned about using different drumbeats for various healing ceremonies, using them to distinguish between upper and lower world journeys was new to me. However, I was open to what he said and went to the lower world. Perhaps because I was still processing the cross-cultural elements in the opening ceremony, I did not remember much of my own journey. At the end, Preben led us in ceremonially 'releasing' the spirits – a practice Cláudia had also followed in the trance dance I described earlier. After the ceremony was over, those present spoke quietly for a few minutes and then went home.

Summary

This has been a general introduction to most of the shamanic practitioners who worked with me on this project. It has included descriptions of how I met them, the primary contexts in which they work, the methodology I used to gather information, and some of the participant observation experiences I had with them. By using this approach, I have tried to set the stage for a more in-depth presentation of the personal stories they shared with me during our interviews. Their responses to my questions about shamanism, which are found in Chapter Six, provide insights into the paradigm shift occurring in their lives and in the larger society. Likewise, their views on religion and spirituality, which are presented in Chapter Seven, reveal concrete examples of how that paradigm shift is being expressed in religion, spirituality and their relationship to each other.

Chapter Six

Exploring Connections Between Cross-Cultural Shamanic Elements and Neo-Shamanic Expressions in Scotland

Introduction

Having provided in Chapter Five a context for the fieldwork, we now turn to actual participant interviews and the insights they contain about the paradigm shift occurring in the areas of religion and spirituality. These insights emerged from my discussion with participants about their understanding of shamanism and how it relates to their lives. However, that discussion began as an attempt to determine a possible correlation between their neo-shamanic experiences of shamanism, and the elements of cross-cultural shamanism I had identified in the model described in Chapter Four.

Below is a brief review of those shamanic elements, followed by a list of the questions I asked. Next are the participants' own verbal descriptions of what they call shamanism and how they first heard about it. This information sets the tone for their other responses organized under the headings corresponding to each of the seven elements in the model of cross-cultural shamanism. The chapter ends with a few observations and themes that are incorporated in an analysis of this data in Chapter Eight.

Overview of Cross-Cultural Shamanic Model

The model of cross-cultural shamanism used in this book contains seven key elements existing cross-culturally in most shamanic communities. Those elements include: vocation and initiation; cosmology; soul flight/journeying; consciousness; spiritual allies; soul healing; and community support. My interview questions were designed to solicit information from participants about their understanding of and relationship to these elements.

Interview Questions

Below are the questions that guided the shamanic portion of the interviews:

1. What is your understanding of shamanism?
2. When did you first hear about shamanism?
3. What made you decide to learn about or practise shamanically?
4. Have you had what you would call an initiation experience or experiences? If so, please describe what you are willing to share.
5. How do you experience your spiritual helpers, or allies? What are they like? How do you work with them?
6. Have you had experience with shamanic healing? If so, please describe.
7. What helps you enter a state of consciousness that facilitates shamanic journeying or work?
8. How does community fit into your experience of shamanism? Or does it?
9. What does non-ordinary reality look like to you? Do you experience travelling to upper and lower realms?

Shamanism Defined and First Discovered

I began the interviews by asking the first three questions listed above. The responses I received are found below, starting with the six shamanic practitioners and then moving to six of the community members who were just beginning to learn about shamanism through workshops, reading, and/or volunteering at a shamanic centre.

Franco Santoro, Age 45 in 2003 – Shamanic Practitioner

Franco considers shamanism to be an ancient and widespread spiritual method or system of healing – one in which shamans, who are familiar with states of consciousness that enable communication and collaboration with spirit guides in the exploration of the spiritual dimension of reality, help themselves, their communities and their planet achieve a direct and experiential sense of the unity and interconnectedness of all life. He defines astroshamanism as 'a spiritual system of healing aimed at enlarging human perception through the integration of the basic principles of shamanism with experiential astrology, the ancient Mystery Religions, pagan and early Christian traditions in the context of contemporary society'. Shamanism for Franco, especially astroshamanism, offers an alternative to the prevalent world belief system of separation by revealing a sacred way of receiving information about the original and continued unity of the world – one which helps people come to know their multidimensional selves in a very practical way.

Stephen Mulhearn, Age 38 in 2003 – Shamanic Practitioner

Stephen created *The Spirit of Shamanism* training programme, in which he identified key elements that 'have assisted the shaman throughout history'. Those elements include: journeying and facilitating healing; connecting with the Spirit of Nature; transmitting the information; working with the Spirit of Fire; and doing the work on yourself (Lendrick, 2004b: 1). However, when I asked about his understanding of shamanism, he laughed and said shamans are 'glorified donkeys with (spiritual) allies' – people whose intention is to serve others by allowing Spirit to work within. He further explained that his use of the word 'donkey' harked back to the story of an Apache shaman who described his healing work as 'travelling over the mountain to bring back healing for the people'. His humorous response actually reflects a deep commitment to the personal development he perceives is necessary for anyone following a shamanic path of partnership with Spirit in healing service to others.

Cláudia Gonçalves, Age 33 in 2003 – Shamanic Practitioner

Cláudia said shamanism was home, her culture, living in communion with spirits, and sharing her gifts and medicine with others. For her, these gifts include healing, accessing spiritual insight and teaching others about the shamanic way.

Though the word shamanism may not have been used, Cláudia grew up in a Brazilian culture that was shamanic. She told me her neighbour was a medicine woman, or healer – also called a *cuarandera* – and there were many spiritual centres in the city where she lived. According to Cláudia, Brazil then and now reflects the spirituality of the native indigenous people, African spiritual traditions that came with African slaves, European Catholics, and Allan Kardec from France, a nineteenth-century systematizer of spiritism and author of *The Spirits' Book*. She said that the African and indigenous traditions clearly incorporate the understanding and practice of partnering with spiritual guides when doing spiritual work. Furthermore, that process of incorporating a spirit guide is understood as long and arduous, usually taking years of study and practice for the practitioner to become familiar and at ease with it.

Mark Halliday, Age 34 in 2003 – Shamanic Practitioner

Mark said shamanism is communion with all life. It involves a journey to the spirit realms, working with spiritual allies to return a lost soul part or to do some other healing for someone.

Though Mark did not actually start reading about shamanism until his late teen years, he began having 'other-worldly' kinds of experience as a young boy growing up in Methil, a coal-mining community in Fife. At an early age he said he could see auras and heal animals by hugging them. When he was four, his maternal grandmother, who had recognized his inner gifts, gave him a tepee, some Native American-style clothes, and an African drum – sharing with him stories about the culture of the Native North American peoples. He says he had a happy, joyful childhood and was brought up a Church of Scotland Christian. His grandmother, to whom he was very close, and with whom he lived for a while, was killed by a drunk driver when he was ten. He said he felt her presence when she died, but after he went on to secondary school that stopped, and he had few spiritual experiences. During these years he was drawn to the writing of William Blake, the music of The Doors with Jim Morrison, and to the music of Nick Cave, an Australian musician and novelist. He also learned that Jim Morrison believed himself to be a shaman. As a result of these experiences, Mark decided to read and study what he could about shamanism, especially Native American shamanism. After much self-learning, at twenty-three he entered the University of Dundee to study English. Once while drawing in an art class at college, he said he felt ecstatic as he completed a picture of Christ. All of these experiences prompted him to include soul, God and more shamanism in his studies.

Alistair Bate, in his thirties – Shamanic Practitioner

Alistair's understanding of shamanism is found in the context of his Druidic practice, which is discussed in Chapter Seven. When he works with spiritual allies in his own spiritual practice, but especially on behalf of others – using ritual, sound and journeying for divination and healing – he considers that shamanic. To him, shamanism is one of the four pagan denominations that also include Druidry, Wicca, and the Northern Traditions of Norse and Anglo-Saxon. Alistair said all of these denominations contain shamanic elements: guided visualization, similar to journeying, within the Druid Ovates; pathworking within Wicca; and working with runes to connect with trees as spiritual entities in the Anglo-Saxon tradition. For further reference, he suggested books such as Ronald Hutton's *Witches, Druids and King Arthur*

(Hutton, 2003) and *The Triumph of the Moon* (Hutton, 1999), and Brian Bates's *The Way of Wyrd* (Bates, 1983).

Alistair said he started opening up to a shamanic connection in 1999, when he became aware of the Edinburgh High Street shops Golden and Wildwood, which have supported alternative spiritualities for a number of years. At that time he also learned about an Edinburgh esoteric Christian group that was open to druidic and shamanic worldviews. It was then that he began a correspondence course to gain a more in-depth understanding of the Order of Bards, Ovates and Druids, with its shamanic dimension. When he joined the Ovate grade of Druids, Alistair's tutor was a man who incorporated shamanic healing in his work with the dying. Being exposed to a shamanic aspect, which included learning to journey, helped Alistair change from what he described as a fairly rigid, magical, liturgical Druidic style to a more flexible approach that aimed to balance the individual with the collective order. To Alistair, the shamanic approach has helped him 'loosen up' in his work and has encouraged him to celebrate diversity in ways he had not previously done. Alistair attended a shamanic class taught by John Matthews from Oxford; in 2003 he began more formal and ongoing shamanic training with John and Caitlin Matthews.

Preben Eagle Heart Olsen, Age 33 in 2003 – Shamanic Practitioner

Preben says he does not like the word 'shamanism', in great part because it does not adequately convey what shaman practitioners do. To Preben, shamanism is 'medicine' work, or work that provides healing (medicine) for the soul. Though multi-dimensional and holistic, it remains essentially simple and calls for shamans, or 'medicine people', to work with spirits of nature and others in the spirit realms to move without judgement beyond ego and the polarities of good and bad, yin and yang, holy woman and holy man, and the reality of different ways, to a global 'bigger picture' of life – one that encompasses many paths towards healing and oneness.

Born and raised in Denmark, Preben described numerous experiences of spiritual awakening, training and growth from the time he was small. However, he first heard of shamanism in his twenties, when twenty Lakota Native Americans visited Denmark for a week of sharing their teachings, culture and spiritual practices, including a pow-wow and sweat lodge. Preben realized that much of the spiritual work he had been doing all his life was essentially shamanic. At age nine he had started working with spirits who have continued providing him with much guidance and 'spiritual schooling'.

Contact with these Native Americans and the return of his childhood memories helped Preben to re-frame much of his work, and understand it in more of a shamanic context. He then began learning drumming and rattling techniques, shamanic journeys, the spiritual significance of the four cardinal directions, and how to conduct spiritual ceremonies. He also travelled to Wales, where he met Lakota Medicine Man Wallace Black Elk who was visiting there. Though Preben knew that the term Star Nations referred to beings from other parts of the universe, especially the Pleiadian star system, he learned from Wallace that the Lakota believed the Stone People came from the Star Nations early in the formation of the earth. As Wallace continued sharing stories of his people's spiritual tradition, Preben's response was to feel 'I'm home.'

Collette from Scotland, Age 28 in 2003 – Volunteer at Edinburgh Shamanic Centre

Only in the last few years has Collette come to use the term 'shamanism' to describe the spiritual system of healing, and the work with spirits that was part of her childhood. She grew up in the Highlands north-east of Inverness with parents who ran a healing centre. Her father was a healer and a medium who also used medicine cards and wheels. Clairvoyant herself, Collette felt close connections with nature and investigated angels, Reiki and colour therapy after she and her family moved to Edinburgh during her teen years.

While at the University of Edinburgh, she heard about shamanism through an indigenous religions course at New College and another course through Open Studies. That gave her a good theoretical framework for shamanism as a possible religion that involved work with spirits and rituals of various kinds. In addition to reading about shamanism, Collette also began to explore more directly the connection between spirituality and health, especially mental health. This was relevant to her, because her own family had a history of struggling with mental illness. However, all of this reading still did not provide the experiential and cross-cultural components that she wanted to explore in order to better assimilate what she was learning. She said she knew from her own experience that 'spirit' was the unconscious part of everything.

Heleen from Holland, Age 60 in 2003 – Astroshamanism Workshop Participant

When I asked Heleen what she understood shamanism to be, she said it was the connection between fire, water, earth and the heavens – something that brightens your brain and allows you to look at life in a different way.

To Heleen, that 'different way' involves moving from an objective view to *feeling* — to something more, behind what the physical eyes see.

Heleen said she first heard about shamanism about two or three years earlier, when her daughter had a friend who worked as a shaman with stones, purification, and intuitive choices. When she checked the Findhorn website and saw Franco's astroshamanic workshop, she knew she needed to come and 'let it happen'. That workshop was her first experiential exposure to shamanism. She said she came with an openness to learn, and within the workshop began asking for guidance from spiritual allies.

Jonathan from England, Age 47 in 2003 – Astroshamanism Workshop Participant

When asked about his understanding of shamanism, Jonathan said it was attuning to a level of consciousness that is always present, but separate from everyday chatter and survival. For him, shamanism stills senseless and trivial chatter, and takes someone to a different world dimension where 'one can see the pattern of life differently — with great meaning and joy'.

Jonathan's first exposure to shamanism was by reading about it in books, such as those describing the philosophy of Gurdjieff. Then in April of 2003 he went to a lecture by Jose Stevens, an American shaman and psychologist, who spoke about shamanism and business. In an individual conversation with Stevens, Jonathan experienced him as a level-headed man, who was calm and had considerable academic training. Stevens had spoken at St James Piccadilly in London. Jonathan said that St James is a very open Christian church that provides alternative means for spiritual growth. At St James he found the information about the astroshamanism workshop at Findhorn, and later decided to participate in it.

Susan from New Zealand, Age 47 in 2003 – Astroshamanism Workshop Participant

Susan did not define shamanism for me, but she indicated that much of what was being taught in the astroshamanism workshop seemed familiar to her. She said she had been journeying (shamanically) since she was a child, though she did not call it a shamanic journey at the time.

Susan was born in Scotland, but her family moved to New Zealand when she was a young girl. Because she was planning to visit Scotland on holiday and wanted to participate in something related to personal and spiritual growth while there, Susan checked the Findhorn website via the internet. When she saw the astroshamanism workshop and its dates, she decided to sign up and see what happened. She said she has always been interested in ancient traditions, and has had a curiosity about what she could learn or what tools she could add to her body of knowledge. Because she and others with similar perspectives about spirituality have often felt like round pegs in square holes – on the periphery – she decided that participating in a group experience of this kind of spiritual learning would be helpful.

Nanna from Italy and Holland, Age 51 in 2003 – Astroshamanism Workshop Participant

Though Nanna did not define shamanism directly, when I asked her what she understood shamanism to be, she started talking about the existence of so much more than we can see – about another dimension in which there are 'presences' that can guide us to where we want to go, help us in a very wide context, and provide answers needed to reach our life goals.

She first heard about shamanism in a field museum in Holland, where there were exhibits showing older traditions of people in faraway countries like Egypt, Africa and Japan. Connected to the art and masks was information about shamanism. This experience immediately reminded her of a picture from Africa, which she had seen when she was three years old. It also brought back other memories that had started when she was three – memories of 'the most important experience' to her, which was talking with her grandmother about 'other world stuff'. While working and crocheting, her grandmother had taught Nanna about her own experiences of seeing more than the physical eye can see.

When Nanna was forty-four years old, she awoke suddenly at 6 a.m. at her home in the Netherlands, feeling a draught from a closed window and hearing a voice saying 'good-bye'. Later that day she learned her ninety-one-year-old grandmother had died in Italy at 6 a.m. As the family gathered to read her grandmother's will, they discovered she had left Nanna her crocodile bag and had included a note saying, 'Nanna is my spiritual heir.' Nanna knew that crocodile meant 'Old Wisdom' to her grandmother. She said it was as if her grandmother's abilities to 'see' were passed on to her at the moment of death. Furthermore, Nanna knew she was the 'one who was able and had to do what she (Nanna's grandmother) did so far'.

Nanna was not sure if she would follow a classic shamanic path. Around the time her grandmother died, she started seeing images when her eyes were closed. Later a shamanic teacher she met told her she should do more. A short time later Nanna learned about Franco's workshop on astroshamanism at Findhorn. That was her first shamanic workshop, and she said she brought great fear about what would surface. Though some of her experiences were emotionally challenging, she said they were helpful. Nanna planned to attend another workshop with Franco.

Tessa from England, in her fifties – Astroshamanism Workshop Participant

Born and raised in Kilkenny, Ireland, Tessa told me that she began seeing what others could not see when she was a child – something her mother said was a sin. However, at that time a wolf came to her as a spiritual ally, and has been with her ever since. She wouldn't have called that a shamanic experience at the time, but now she sees that working with spiritual allies, or helpers, for her own growth and/or for others is an essential part of shamanism.

Tessa said her first official exposure to shamanism was in February of 2003, when she attended a weekend introductory shamanic workshop with Franco and found it to be the most powerful experience she had ever had. Because of that, she wanted to know more, which is why she came to this week-long workshop. Tessa was not sure what her shamanic future would be, but she found that this workshop was very compatible with her spiritual practice.

Introducing the Seven Elements

What follows are responses from participants based on questions relating directly to each of the seven elements in the shamanic model. For each question I provide individual responses when they seem appropriate, and cluster the remaining responses to each question into separate summaries for the shamanic practitioners and for the community members. As you read the following accounts, observe how many of these experiences reveal characteristics of a paradigm shift and of the challenges embedded when one starts to 'see differently' the established norms of society – especially in matters related to religion and spirituality.

Shamanic Vocation and Initiation

Shamanic vocation and initiation can occur in ways that typically include heredity or a spontaneous call; illness and/or dreams; death and resurrection experiences; and/or the bestowal of spiritual allies or a possible power song.

Franco

Raised a Christian in Italy and later drawn to study yoga and astrology, Franco began to understand how apparently unrelated experiences throughout his early life were actually part of a long initiation and learning process for him. One of those early experiences had been the ability to 'go through' a door and leave his parents without their knowing it. When that happened, he had a strong sense of *déjà vu* – that this was not new or unusual for him.

While still a small boy, he also began to notice things that the adults either did not appear to see, or that they had decided should be only for adults, not children. Among the 'things' he saw were the *Bhi Jinah*, spiritual beings that were to become friends and allies for him throughout his life. At about four or five years of age, he spontaneously began playing games that involved spending time in a different world – one with twelve states, for which he drew maps to describe them. In these maps, his family's house became the world, and the various rooms in their house became towns or villages. The cosmology of this other world also developed its own mythology. There were even football teams with entire divisions. Each of the sectors in this world had a name, which Franco created as variations on family and environmental names he already knew. Though this was a creative way to integrate much of what he was learning in school, and it brought him great joy and ecstasy for many years, it was clear to Franco that this game was a fantasy.

Between sixteen and eighteen years of age, he began to question what he was doing, especially when he realized others did not share his enthusiasm about this game. As with many young people, this realization left him feeling inadequate when dealing with ordinary reality, and he decided to destroy the maps. At age eighteen, he experienced a very powerful response to reading a book by Alan Watts, which then awoke something else within him. A short time later, he spent eight years exploring what he calls 'the dark side' – namely, the 'provisional order' that keeps ordinary reality alive and separate from non-ordinary reality. All of these experiences from childhood into adulthood joined together to form a shamanic initiation for Franco. Among the challenges he continually experienced was his ability to see power, and our multidimensional selves, while having to accept that others often say they have not had those experiences and do not see what he has seen.

Stephen

During one his visits to where Peggy Dylan was living and working in France, Stephen experienced what he described as a 'fire initiation' through fire-walking. Having been faced with illness, relationship problems and general hard times prior to meeting Peggy, he found the initiation, along with the accompanying sweat lodge experience, most helpful and insightful. During it, he said, he felt as if love was both a space and a container for life. Afterwards, when his work in Glasgow was growing in a positive way, Stephen periodically telephoned Peggy to talk and reflect on his life.

He continued his spiritual work with her and then, at her invitation, trained as a teacher with her. During this time, which also coincided with a series of shamanic dreams, Stephen began learning about shamanism in a very conscious and personal way.

However, initiation experiences for Stephen had begun with recurring dreams he had as a teen. In these he would see a large fire burning in the forest and then stand back, observing people who were dancing ecstatically around the fire. While watching, some of them would call him to come forward and join them. He also started to see teachers. At some point after he had awoken and was looking through a book, he would recognize some of the photos in the book as being people from his dreams. Shamanic dreams he experienced at some later point revealed spiritual allies who came to help and warn him about fierce energy that potentially could kill him. Once when he was seriously ill in hospital and in a state of 'twilight consciousness', he actually experienced what he called the 'bardo of death' (from the *Tibetan Book of the Dead*). During this time, he travelled through a tunnel of darkness into a circle of teachers who were surrounded by love and light. In this near-death experience, Stephen realized he could die, but his teacher Peggy was there and urged him to go back. He chose to return and discovered afterwards that while he had been having this experience, an ulcer in his stomach had burst and he needed immediate medical attention. Finally, he said another initiation occurred with a bankruptcy and the ending of a romantic relationship. The bankruptcy left him feeling judged by others, and the end of the relationship instilled grief and loss.

Cláudia

At intervals of about five years throughout her life, Cláudia said, she experienced numerous life initiations, or crises. One of these was to unlearn and heal some of the unhealthy and unhelpful thought patterns and memories that she had developed during her Christian upbringing. Another was affirming her ability as an intuitive channel, and opening up 'her heart and life to Spirit in Divine and Unconditional Love, allowing what it is that her soul, in its profound and eternal wisdom, has chosen and more than that, what Spirit has chosen for her' (Edinburgh, 2004a: 12). To do so, Cláudia said, she needed to deal with her own fears about being a medium or a shamanic practitioner. Though those fears are not as strong now, she said she still has to address them, especially as she develops new shamanic ways that integrate the ancient traditions of her youth with new shamanic learning and practices for life today.

Mark

During his second year at university, Mark described a series of three nights in which the bedroom of the flat where he stayed was icy cold, and he would awake to see a pair of eyes. On the third night he saw, standing two or three feet from the bed, a lady in Victorian dress with long brown hair. She looked at him for a while, then turned and walked through the wall. The next day he went to the local bookshop to learn about spirits. Because he also began to sense that large wolves were following him, Mark started collecting feathers as power objects. He told of meeting with a friend living in the next room who suffered from manic depression. When Mark spontaneously put his hands on his friend's heart and head, a powerful jolt of healing passed through to the friend. However, Mark had not prepared himself for that, and the experience left him understanding the need for ritual cleansing and purification when doing healing work.

At twenty-five Mark remembers walking down Dundee high street feeling an 'awesome connection to all life' – a sense of bliss and ecstasy that washed over him for two or three minutes. After that he started meditation and chanting, but his spiritual experiences scared him, and he started drinking and taking drugs to lessen their intensity. Finally, when sober, he decided to face his own shadow self. Having read *Black Elk* and other Native American literature at university, he started writing his own spiritual poetry, and bought some chanting and drumming tapes. Soon after this, he remembers raising his hands to the sky and connecting the sky to the earth in a Cheyenne way. For him God then became the Great Spirit, and his shamanic work began in a 'proper' way.

When he was thirty-two, he had what he called a series of three initiation dreams. In the first one he witnessed a spiritual marriage of two beings not of this world. They each received an oak leaf crown, and Mark interpreted this as the divine union within himself. In the second dream, angelic energies put a cloak of golden light around his shoulders and said, 'Your job now is to bring people home – back to God. Release everything.' The third dream found him flying in the sky over a group of female shamans in an American Indian tribe in the USA, pulled down by a kind of magnetic beam, and finally placed over a symbol drawn in the sand, where he sat as the shamans chanted. Mark intuitively knew that the tribe and the symbol were Navaho.

At age thirty-four, he began attending shamanic workshops with Franco. He also described Jesus entering his body to open his heart, and Mary coming to bring him purity and clarity. Another of his experiences occurred in response to questions he had about shamanism and the angelic path. He awoke one night to a voice that said, 'You're to be a solar shaman. You know everything already. Put it into practice.' He knew he was to channel 'the masculine, active energy of Great Spirit' (Edinburgh, 2004a: 11).

Alistair

During one of his shamanic journeys after the original class with John Matthews, Alistair experienced a 'spontaneous initiation', in which the Celtic goddess Cerridwen ladled inspiration into his hand and gave him moss agates. These he keeps in his 'crane medicine bag' (the carrier used as a shaman's toolkit), along with other sacred objects. Alistair said he was initiated by the spirits for his Ovate grade, and again for his Druid grade. At these initiations, he described being acutely aware of the presence of crow, water and sun, and of Iolo Morgannwg, who was an eighteenth-century Unitarian and a Druid.

Preben

Preben clearly identified initiation experiences that began at age nine when he was walking home from a Scout meeting at about 7 p.m. on a dark winter's night. Suddenly he sensed a presence watching him from the sky. He looked up and saw strange lights that appeared to be part of an 'invisible' object – invisible because though he saw the object itself, he could also see 'through' the object to the stars beyond it. Later in the week he discovered that others in the village had seen it, too. That experience was followed by some disturbing dreams that ended around age twelve, leaving him feeling protected at last.

The next initiatory experience came at age thirteen, when he began having visionary dreams that revealed information he initially thought was about the future, or precognitive, but later decided was about some of his past lives. In one case, when he saw a television programme about some people in France, he recognized the area and the associated feelings as having been in his earlier dream.

A third significant initiation was at age fifteen, when he and his family travelled to Apple Island in Denmark. While on the way, he started feeling 'weird' and afraid – so much so that by the time they reached the house where they were to stay, Preben was shaking. When the children went to their assigned room, he recognized it as the room where in a dream he had died. For the three nights the family remained there, Preben was afraid he would die. He heard his own voice saying, 'What have they done to the place?' and experienced the scene surrounding him often shift into 'another time'.

Eventually he realized that in the remembered death he had been forty years old, and the bed was different. As a late teen he had read books about telepathy, and had joined with certain friends to test each other's telepathic abilities. One book, *Towards the Light*, combined Christian teaching with explanations of past lives and mediumship. Though the book provided some answers for Preben, it also raised more questions.

At age nineteen the sky opened one day, and a light appeared. Preben kneeled down in tears and saw in the opening a 'presence' that began talking to him and showing him his entire life up until his death. However, the presence told Preben he would not remember all of it, and for a number of years only snatches of the 'presence' experience came back to him. Nevertheless, he felt supported and held by 'spirit' – humbled by the experience, grateful to be alive and feeling quite empowered. That period marked a transition for Preben into what he called a multidimensional global consciousness in which we 'weave the web of wyrd' (destiny) as individuals and societies that have choices about how to live. It also led to his increased trust in the strong connection he has continued to feel with the beings who had started helping and advising him since he was seven.

Collette

Collette said she has had quite a few spiritual initiation experiences. The first she remembers was at age twelve. Though she had seen spirits before, this time the spirit was in the form of a woman standing in a bay window, staring at Collette, who learned later that the woman was named Alice, and she had been Collette's father's nurse in the Crimean War. At the time Collette had felt scared and overwhelmed due to the 'realness' of that experience. However, she said she realized later that the woman had 'come from a place of love'. From twelve to eighteen years of age, Collette said she fought the spirits and made negative choices about how to interpret them.

At age eighteen she moved to Australia to begin an adventure that she hoped would facilitate her own healing. Once there, the experience was much deeper and more intense than she had imagined. She then travelled to South Africa and spent a couple of years living through what she described as 'more destructive behaviours', though she eventually came 'back to herself' and returned to Scotland. In telling this part of her story, Collette said that what she loves about shamanism is that it encompasses the shadow. It recognizes that a person is not good or bad, but can utilize the theory of chaos and order to instigate change and growth.

Heleen

Recalling her first exposure to shamanic journeys and practices, Heleen described some of her experiences during the workshop as meaningful and at times powerful. Perhaps because they are so new, she has not actually called them 'initiation experiences', though hindsight may lead her to view them in that way. She said the consciousness (including her intentions) that she brought involved a longing for experience.

Jonathan, Susan and Nanna

Though some of their spiritual experiences were powerful, they were not sure these experiences could be called initiations.

Tessa

Though she did not call it an initiation experience, Tessa described how about eight years prior to this interview, she fell down the stairs and knew she would die. However, in the midst of her fall, a presence of some kind, which Tessa called an angel, actually turned her over while she was in the air and laid her on the stairs. Then there was a bump, and she sensed the angel hovering in the air above her. Obviously, Tessa survived the fall.

Shamanic Cosmology

Shamanic cosmology initially refers to the distinction between ordinary and non-ordinary reality, but then further divides non-ordinary reality, or the spirit realms, into an overall geography that includes the upper, lower and middle worlds. These non-ordinary realms are generally accessed from an ordinary-reality starting point on earth. These points are often associated cross-culturally with the *axis mundi*, the tree of life, because that image seems to portray the connection existing between all the 'worlds'.

Franco

With Franco's background in astrology, non-ordinary reality is what he calls the Sacred Circle – something with a structure that includes sectors, energies and archetypes that help all beings eventually come to awareness of ultimate unity. In this 'transitional' structure there are physical, mental and spiritual levels. Also within it are a vertical axis that reflects the higher, lower and middle worlds, and a horizontal axis that contains the four major directions of east, south, west and north. The structure possesses twelve sectors, which are the signs of the zodiac. This entire cosmology is described in Franco's book, *Epic of the Sacred Cone* (Santoro, 2000). Franco says he can travel to any part of the Sacred Circle to learn something important about life. He believes that each part of the Sacred Circle represents a way that leads to the Centre and is also an emanation from the Centre, since there are no true separations. As a shamanic practitioner, astrologer and spiritual explorer, Franco sees how all these dimensions fit together, and he easily travels within these realms.

Cláudia, Stephen, Mark, Alistair and Preben

For Cláudia, non-ordinary reality feels like a meditative state helping her connect with her feelings and be supported; she said she does not focus on the different 'worlds'. However, Stephen, Mark, Alistair and Preben all described travelling to the upper, lower and middle worlds during their journeys. Stephen said he finds animals and nature in the lower world and the goddess in the upper world. Mark talked about meeting geometric shapes, beings, and awareness of feelings and thoughts in the upper world; creatures and mythological figures in the lower world; and a 'glow around reality' in the middle world. Alistair said non-ordinary reality seemed much like ordinary reality to him. Preben described seeing the 'big picture of the cosmos', including the Star Nations, in the upper world; links to parallel existences, not past lives, in the middle world; and, like Alistair, something like ordinary reality in the lower world.

Community Members

Susan was the only one to describe travelling to upper and lower realms. Collette, Heleen, Jonathan, Nanna and Tessa were able to journey under Franco's direction. However, they did not make specific distinctions between realms, or worlds. Heleen responded by telling me about one of her journeys, and Jonathan explained that he is not visual, but gathers information through intuition and other senses.

Shamanic Soul Flight/Journeying

Shamanic soul flight, or journeying, refers to the ecstatic experience of travelling into the non-ordinary realms of the spirit world and then returning to ordinary reality. The one journeying generally ascends or descends, though middle world journeys involve travel into the spiritual dimensions of what appears to be ordinary reality. On these focused and interactive journeys, one meets and works with spiritual allies who function as partners with the journeyer in the provision of healing and/or information.

Franco

Franco journeys to all the realms he describes in his cosmology of the Sacred Cone, and in this process he works with a variety of spiritual allies. Though he talks about the journey and teaches people about the importance of holding a clear intention prior to and throughout the journey, his best description of the method itself is in his book, *Astroshamanism, Book 1* (Santoro, 2003a: 66–78). There he not only discusses intention, but also draws upon the work of Michael Harner for a specific methodology of journeying.

Stephen, Cláudia, Mark, Alistair and Preben

Stephen, Cláudia, Mark, Alistair and Preben each described meeting their spiritual allies, and feeling their strength, support and guidance for living their lives and doing their healing work. Cláudia said that journeying helps her connect with an intuitive way of knowing.

Community Members

Collette, Heleen, Nanna, Susan and Tessa all described some form of meeting and communicating with spiritual allies during a shamanic journey. Because Jonathan integrates his experiences through senses other than the visual ones, his experience of a journey was more like a meditation, and did not easily fit into the journey format. Like Cláudia, Collette found that journeying helped her tap into her intuitive abilities. Heleen said she did not see anything, but felt a hand on her shoulder – something she interpreted as the hand of God helping her explore this new spiritual process.

Shamanic Consciousness

Rhythmic music, drumming, rattling, chanting and dancing are typical ways of achieving a shamanic state of consciousness that facilitates the shamanic journey into non-ordinary reality. Other ways of assisting this process include the use of costumes, and fasting.

Shamanic Practitioners

All of the practitioners use drums, rattles, bells and other rhythmic instruments; ritual, ritual clothing and ritual objects; music, song or chant; dance; and incense or sage. Franco also uses drawing, meditation, silence, gibberish, physical movement, body postures and elements of nature (e.g. earth, air, water, fire). Stephen says whistling and 'being in nature' help him, and Mark describes 'stilling his mind' and breathing as helpful. Cláudia, Mark and Preben referred to invoking the spirits and/or calling on the 'spirits of the directions' as being particularly useful.

Community Members

All of the community members described being helped into a shamanic state of consciousness by using drumming, rattling or some kind of music. Collette said that sage, and stating a clear intention, helped her. Nanna and Tessa mentioned dancing, though Nanna added the presence of water and air at the seaside, and Tessa included using colours, aromatherapy and massage. Jonathan and Susan both said 'breath work' and relaxation helped them – with Susan adding that she often relaxed in that way by taking a bath with candles nearby.

Shamanic Spiritual Allies

Spiritual allies in a shamanic context are experienced in a number of ways by humans who work with them. These allies form protective and supportive partnerships – becoming sources of power and guides to information and healing. They generally appear in human, animal and plant form; and in some cases, they unite with their human partners in a kind of spiritual marriage.

Franco

Franco tends to draw upon the spiritual energy of the Sacred Cone – the overall cosmology that connects the non-ordinary reality worlds – when he works shamanically. For him, that includes all spiritual guides, which are inter-connected and part of the whole anyway. When he works with groups, he calls upon whatever images make sense, are relevant, and help people access their spiritual support. Because of his own Christian background he sometimes uses saints, especially the Madonna. Due to his understanding of astrology he calls upon the planets, the sun and the moon. Furthermore, his experience with the *Epic of the Sacred Cone* prompts him to call upon the Bhi Jinah, beings who populate the empty spaces and help keep whatever exists together.

Stephen

Stephen's spiritual helpers have come to him in various ways. Some initially appeared in his early dreams as the teachers. During his fire initiation, he met a goddess on the hill. At one point he felt the wind as an ally rocking him back and forth on the mountain. In his shamanic dreams he met the 'spirit of tiger', who also shifted shapes between tiger and Jim Morrison, one of Stephen's teenage idols who had seen himself as a shaman. During his near-death experience, Stephen said, he sat with the circle of teachers who loved and advised him on his decision about life and death. With these non-ordinary reality spiritual allies, Stephen not only receives healing and guidance for his own life, but he partners with them in offering healing service to others. Stephen also calls upon teachers in ordinary reality. Not only does he value Peggy Dylan's teaching gifts, but he has also worked with various other shamans, especially from South America.

Cláudia

Cláudia's week-long shamanic experience in Scotland was particularly powerful, because at that time her great-great-grandmother, a native Brazilian medicine woman who could not practise her medicine while she was married to an orthodox Catholic white man, came to her in the 'sweat lodge ceremony'. Cláudia said her grandmother had come 'to remind me of who I am, where I come from, my gifts, my roots, my medicine' (Gonçalves: 13). In addition to the non-ordinary reality support of that grandmother, Cláudia acknowledged the ordinary reality spiritual guidance and support of Morning Star, a native Mexican/Apache ceremonial leader and medicine pipe carrier who was conducting the ceremony and the work during that week. She works with her spiritual helpers, or guides, partly by calling on them for help. Cláudia said she feels their presence in her body, and they speak to her through her feelings, which are central in her way of working intuitively and shamanically. In addition to several power animals who help her, Cláudia works with Yemanja, a traditional Brazilian queen and 'Goddess of the Sea', and with the Black Madonna, known in Brazil as the Black Goddess. The nature of the problem or issue determines which guide(s) will come to help. As she learns to embody these spiritual allies, Cláudia says, she makes different sounds and chants, which are incorporated into her work. These are the sounds and chants of her spiritual allies.

Mark

From the time Mark was small he started seeing auras, lights and spirit forms, and he began hearing spirit voices, which brought important messages to him. Mark unites with the spirit of an ally in order to more fully access the qualities it possesses to help him. Besides wolf, other spiritual allies Mark said he works with include angelic beings of light; a Native American 'brother', who helps him with healing; a Chinese man, who helps him with physical and emotional health and well-being; god and goddess energies, which promote a unified integration of both male and female gifts; Hopi guides; angelic helpers, who help him clarify his path; and two shamans – one Aboriginal and one Peruvian – who help him with his own spiritual development.

Alistair and Preben

Alistair and Preben said they experience connections with spiritual allies in various forms that include elements, trees, plants, animals, ancestors and guides. Deities and fairies also help Alistair, and beings from the Star Nations figure prominently for Preben.

Collette

Her first awareness of 'spirit' was as the wind, which talked to her and comforted her like a soul mate. Though it was not quite tangible, Collette said she has felt spirit in her self and in creation. She also described what she called a 'guide system' of deep feelings that often manifest as a quiet voice within, or as her intuition. She said she longed to understand this inner awareness, learn to work with it more fully, and see its connection to shamanism.

Susan

Susan described how for a few years she felt the support and love of a female spiritual guide who told her that she didn't have to struggle. When she would ask the guide a question, the guide would paraphrase the question, and Susan instantly knew the answer. Eventually the guide left, and Susan felt abandoned. However, she also sensed that this guide left because Susan had been relying on her too much and needed to move on. Susan also knew there would be other guides to help her. Though she didn't call that an initiation experience, it was an experience that propelled her into the next phase of her spiritual growth. Susan described experiencing the essence, not form, of an ancestor spirit named Agnes, a rabbit, and a female gorilla, who all revealed themselves as spiritual allies for her. She also said that a divine presence guides her own spirit and functions as a protective presence in her life.

Heleen, Jonathan, Nanna and Tessa

Heleen's primary sense of a spiritual ally is a presence she thinks might be God, who seems to be supporting her in these experiences. Jonathan said he experiences only a sense of guidance – a sense of being. His insights are more direct and don't seem to come from individual beings. One of Nanna's primary spiritual allies is her grandmother, though she has also discovered the help of 'owl'. Both help by giving her messages about how she should proceed in her life. Tessa feels supported, guided and protected by many, including 'wolf', the 'angelic presence' who helped her on the stairs, Kwan Yin, who helps in Tessa's healing practice, a Native American grandmother who came to her during a healing session, and a High Star Being.

Shamanic Soul Healing

As soul doctors, shamanic practitioners work on the soul level to help people in their healing process. Some of the classic methods of soul healing include: divining for important information; power animal retrieval; soul retrieval; extraction; helping people prepare for death; and performing psychopomp work for those who have died.

Franco

Franco has experienced spiritual healing himself and has helped others in that process. For him, the most important thing in healing is to create a relationship with what the illness represents – as in the Pythagorean tradition. He strives for luminosity out of darkness, and refers to the temples of Apollo and to underground caves where those seeking healing would go through a stage of darkness, then face the difficult reality that their illness had helped them deny, and finally experience the authentic light of integrating those first two steps of darkness and confronting reality. Though Franco can use the shamanic method of extraction, he does not consider that as part of his tradition, because it perpetuates the illusion of separation and fragmentation.

Cláudia, Stephen, Mark, Alistair and Preben

All of the practitioners said they have experienced their own shamanic healing, in addition to helping others to heal. Stephen said his major experiences of personal shamanic healing have often occurred during his periods of initiation. For Cláudia, personal healing included facing and releasing her fears about opening up to the shamanic path and beginning her more focused shamanic training. She also said she does soul retrievals for people. Alistair referred to helping with extraction work, and Preben said he uses a variety of healing methods with people who come to him.

Community Members

In response to this question, Collette, Heleen, Jonathan, Susan, Nanna and Tessa all described experiences of personal healing. As people just learning about shamanism, it was not surprising that none of them described shamanic healing they had offered to others. Collette had gone to Cláudia for shamanic healing from depression. Jonathan found healing while walking in the woods at the Findhorn Foundation, and Tessa had experienced a soul retrieval. Susan said she found healing primarily through the insights she had gained at the workshop, while Nanna described the guidance and protection of her spiritual allies as a healing experience.

Community Support

Included in the concept of community support are aspects of a shamanic system in which members of the community somehow acknowledge that the call they recognize has come to a potential shamanic practitioner; support the work of that person by encouraging continued training and seeking spiritual assistance from the identified person; and monitor the effectiveness of the shamanic services that are provided. This may happen in different ways, depending upon the nature, size and location of the community.

Shamanic Practitioners

Franco said that community reflects the inter-relatedness and interdependence of all life. His worldview is that all is one, which by definition draws people to each other in mutual support for their individual work of releasing any sense of separation, and discovering connections with each other. Stephen's perspective was that community allows people to share the spiritual path – supporting and teaching each other, acknowledging and affirming diverse gifts, and collaborating with love and care. He described the presence of mentors and teachers as bringing into focus a lineage of passing on the traditions that have existed for many centuries.

Cláudia said she sees community as a gathering point for those who heal and those who seek healing, and she discussed the importance of 'embracing' people with a kind of healing group energy. Likewise, Mark described community as a network of kindred spirits – a family that needs and wants to function as a healthy society. He explained that when we have forgotten that connection or feel separated, ordeals and initiations can help us remember, and awaken to, our fundamental unity.

Community within a contemporary shamanic tradition is still developing for Alistair, though his spiritual history reflects an ongoing desire for and affiliation with spiritual communities. His attempts to balance individual spiritual practice with spiritual service and relationships within society are reflected in his varied religious experiences in Ireland, England, the USA and Scotland. For Preben, community is central. He said it reminds us of how important it is to know who we are, connect with the land, and help each other learn how to be record-keepers for the earth in passing on the wisdom we inherit and discover ourselves. For him, true community embodies the whole circle of life in the universe and reflects the Yggdrasil, the Norse World Tree, with all its diversity.

Community Members

The role of community in shamanism was something most of the community members had not thought about. Collette, Heleen and Nanna said that the spirituality they had been exposed to was more individually oriented, though they were open to something different. Jonathan thought community could be valuable as a support for people who are searching spiritually. Susan and Tessa stressed the importance of community in any spiritual process, though they were just learning about how that might happen within a shamanic tradition.

Overall Observations and Themes

Regarding shamanic characteristics, all of the participants worked with spiritual allies of one form or another, used various methods to achieve a shamanic state of consciousness, and had experienced at least one form of shamanic journeying. The practitioners described their initiation experiences, and discussed healing both as recipient and in the role of healer. They also emphasized the importance of community. Most of the community members were beginning to learn about a shamanic cosmology and different types of shamanic healing, but many of them were unsure about whether they had experienced a shamanic initiation.

From the perspective of a religion/spirituality paradigm, all participants were open to and interacted with beings or presences they encountered in an unseen dimension they called 'spiritual'. Interacting with that dimension brought experiences most of them did not understand at first – in part, because those experiences did not match the prevailing cultural paradigm of rational thought and bounded religious dogma. Many also developed an intuitive sense that all life was related and of value. This intuition moved beyond the concept of kinship and inter-relatedness into a 'felt sense' of its reality in their lives. For some, facing and accepting those 'different ways of seeing', in addition to living with the associated implications, formed an essential component in their shamanic initiations. Furthermore, they knew not only that their lives and the world in general were in the midst of massive change, but also that they had chosen spiritual growth and service as the way to move through that transformative process.

Chapter Seven

Applying Hervieu-Léger's Analytical Model of Religion to Reveal a Lineage of Spirituality, Not Belief, in the Shamanic Chain of Memory

Introduction

Now that we have an initial understanding of how the participants I interviewed, especially the shamanic practitioners, see the world from a perspective of kinship and inter-relatedness, it is time to deepen that understanding by asking specifically how that shamanic worldview relates to religion, spirituality, and the shifting relationship between those two phenomena. The following interviews centred around discovering whether the participants' shamanic traditions and practices fitted Hervieu-Léger's model of 'religion as a chain of memory'. However, they actually revealed much more than that. In the responses and stories shared below, we can observe and learn how this new paradigm of spirituality and religion is being lived in the daily lives of these participants.

Structured like the previous chapter, this one begins with an overview of the key components in Hervieu-Léger's model, and a listing of the questions asked during the interviews. What comes next are the responses participants gave to the first three questions, which explored their perspectives on religion and spirituality, and identified any religious or spiritual heritage dating back to earlier in their lives. This is followed by a presentation of the remaining interview information, which is organized as categories reflecting the five key headings in the Hervieu-Léger model. As in Chapter Six, this one ends with a brief statement of overall observations and themes, which are incorporated into part of the analysis found in Chapter Eight.

Overview of Hervieu-Léger Model

One way to capture the essence of what Hervieu-Léger spent an entire book describing is to say that 'religion as a chain of memory' refers to a community of people who, by invoking a tradition, or parts of a tradition, and by consciously joining with others who have gone before them in that invocation, experience that entire process as the legitimizing authority for the way they believe. Though many factors contributed to the development of her definition, several of which will be addressed in the analysis, I have chosen five components that form the core of her model. These components are: forming community; understanding tradition; invoking a tradition; determining legitimate authority; and believing.

Interview Questions

Below are the questions that guided the religion/spirituality portion of the interviews:

1. How do you define religion?
2. How are religion and spirituality related, or not related, for you? Please describe.
3. Do you have a spiritual or religious heritage, or tradition, from your childhood or earlier adult life? If so, please describe it.
4. If you do, how does that background affect and/or interact with your spiritual, or religious, life today?
5. How does community fit, or not fit, into your experience of religion and/ or spirituality?
6. In your shamanic practice, who or what do you invoke, or call upon, when you work shamanically?
7. How do you determine that what you are learning or practising, from a spiritual or religious perspective, is legitimate and authoritative?
8. Please describe how the way you believe today is like, or different from, how you believed in the past.
9. Do you call upon traditions other than shamanic ones? If so, which ones and why?

Religion and Spirituality as Defined by Interviewees

What follows are responses to the first three questions about religion and spirituality. Due to the nature of the questions, I did not see the need to separate the responses of the shamanic practitioners from those of the community members.

Franco

For Franco, religion is an agreement among people about the nature of reality, the desire to share that reality and a decision to explore other realities. It allows a person to enter another reality and utilize various rituals as containers for moving between realities. Though Franco did not formally define spirituality, the descriptions he has used for his work reflect an understanding of spirituality as the process of awakening to the unity, or oneness, of all life. He said religion and spirituality initially worked together, but sometimes when people changed their beliefs or understandings of reality, caretakers of the original agreements (religion, as understood by Franco) did not allow for changes in those agreements. That kind of dilemma has often prompted those whose beliefs and perceptions have shifted to create among themselves new agreements about what rules, guides and beliefs to employ, though the new agreements have not always been perceived as carrying legitimate religious authority. In effect, they have often been excluded from being considered religions. Franco considers the shamanic tradition a 'public performance' of a shamanic worldview, not an expression of a binding agreement with rules, guides and beliefs. For him, shamanic traditions can respond to whatever is relevant and makes sense to those present.

Stephen

Stephen said that religion started with love, but developed a hierarchy to teach people. However, in the process, documenting religious experience took precedence, and religion became mechanical. Spirituality for him is an internal gift in which one connects with the 'beloved essence of life', with the 'life force'. In that sense, spirituality remains alive and vibrant, while religion easily loses its vitality.

Cláudia

Cláudia said that religion was a structure in which people had to follow rules. To the question about whether religion and spirituality were related, she emphatically said, 'No!' This remark was quickly followed by a statement about how often it was important to break the rules of religion for the sake of spirituality, especially when one is following the shamanic path.

Mark

Mark defined religion as 'beliefs'. He said it not only connotes an 'ordered system of beliefs which promote a moral structure to explore the universe', but it implies a supernatural or higher power. Spirituality to Mark is an 'experiential moment of self-realization where one achieves a self-actualized peak that may or may not relate to a god'. Based on that, it appears spirituality for Mark does not require specific beliefs or the existence of a particular supernatural being, but allows experiences of moving beyond the self into something more. He said that religion is didactic, while spirituality is the experiential component; however, he urges others to find out for themselves the relationship between the two concepts.

Alistair

Religion to Alistair should be spirituality as expressed in faith and beliefs. The essence of this spirituality for him is spiritual practice, which he sees as expressed only through religion. In effect, religion and spirituality are intimately related, with religion being the outward expression of an inner experience fostered primarily through spiritual practice.

Preben

Religion to Preben is knowledge passed down about something that at one point reflected 'present' spiritual experience, but over time has become dusty tradition reflecting second-hand communication. It is too political and dogmatic in that it holds on to ideas that don't flow with nature. According to Preben, spirituality is in-the-moment guidance that emerges from direct individual experience of 'spirit'. For him it provides more space than religion does to roam and be real.

Collette

Religion for Collette is a cultural construct that is organized as a set of beliefs in a structured environment. Spirituality to her is much the same as religion. Religion and spirituality share boundaries that can be crossed.

Heleen

Heleen said religion was tradition, though there are different traditions. To her religion can be everything – 'what you are used to, so different for everyone'. Spirituality for Heleen has to do with feeling. Actually, she thinks religion and spirituality belong together; otherwise religion would be very dry. It would be like taking a book, reading it, and 'that's it' – no thinking, reflecting, or incorporating ideas in a meaningful way.

Jonathan

To Jonathan, religion is oneness with God, though he did further distinguish organized religion as a structure manifesting that oneness. Christianity, Buddhism and other religions join together for Jonathan as examples of how 'all paths lead to the One'. He did not distinguish between religion and spirituality.

Susan

Susan said that religion is a 'set of rules' that is tight, judgemental, focused on sin, and designed to tell people how to get to God without thinking for themselves. She described it as a 'trap', and said that organized religion is not on her horizon any more – in great part because church hierarchy tends to say 'you're less than', rather than 'more than'; it displays an attitude that they know best; and their expectation is for people to follow blindly and do what they're told to do. For Susan, spirituality is her connection with the divine, with the universe, with God. It is that personal relationship with God that she thinks religious authorities discourage, because if people developed their relationship with God on their own, religious authorities would be out of a job and not in control.

Nanna

Nanna said religion must have started out as something natural, but it became adoration – something separate from what is natural. Spirituality for her is a feeling; it is the purest interpretation of being free to use and be with your intuition. She said religion and spirituality used to be together, the same, but over time they separated from each other. To her, spirituality is a 'higher' thing – something felt with all senses. She also said she does not want to give it a three-dimensional form; that is not the way she wants to look at it.

Tessa

Though she did not formally define religion, for Tessa it seems to be a somewhat formal 'way' of helping people relate to the divine. However, for her religion is too narrow to contain enough ways to access God or the divine. It is 'OK' for some people, but she needs more and is still searching. From what Tessa said, her understanding of spirituality appears to refer more to the actual relationship with what she called the 'divine essence', or 'universal love'. As such, religion could play a part in supporting someone's spirituality.

Introducing the Five Components in Hervieu-Léger's Model

What now follows are participant responses based on questions relating directly to specific components in the model of religion as a chain of memory. As with the shamanic interview responses in Chapter Six, for each question I provide individual responses when they seem appropriate, and cluster other responses to each question into summaries. As before, when reading the following accounts, please reflect on how many of these comments provide valuable insights into the religion/spirituality paradigm shift that is the subject of this book.

Community

As a critical contextual component in the Hervieu-Léger model, it is important to determine the role, function and importance of community in the lives of those who participate in shamanic work. Because community is an element in the shamanic model, the summary responses below include only comments that expand upon what was presented about community in Chapter Six.

All Participants

The role of community for Franco is to facilitate individual growth and development within the Sacred Circle. It does so by supporting personal spiritual work, and also by sharing in community ritual dramas that stimulate spiritual awareness and growth. Stephen said that community allows people of different backgrounds with diverse gifts to affirm each other, to nurture and encourage individual and personal development work. Cláudia senses a growing importance in the ability of group energy to heal, and she hopes the Centre can provide more of that kind of experience. Mark said that while a degree of detachment is sometimes needed within a community, its function is to clarify perspective and serve the whole, not to foster alienation.

Community is important to Alistair, because for him it offers support and encouragement for a spiritual or religious path. In his search for community, Alistair has not always found all he was seeking, but his disappointment has often impelled him to help create communities that foster spiritual growth both individually and collectively. Preben places great importance on community as a central way to help people remain connected to all life, and part of the universe. In the initial interview Collette had not thought much about community, but in a follow-up conversation a year later, she said community was 'imperative'. Based on her understanding that the term 'sacred' describes a way to 'feel together' in relationship to God, community does a play a part in Heleen's experience of religion and/or spirituality; community is now what she has started to call 'the sacred'.

As an alternative to attending church, as she used to do, Susan said she discovered friends who had experienced similar processes with the church, and decided to join together in supporting each other as they explored educational and meditation options at a local centre. Eventually, they started meeting regularly in a space owned by one of her friends. There they began conducting rituals of protection or healing, and celebrating seasonal festivals, birthdays, or other life events. They also went out into 'nature' for meditation, weekends of renewal, and times around a central fire. For Susan, her circle of friends are now her spiritual community.

Though community had not seemed particularly important to her, Nanna said she had come to realize that many of her meaningful spiritual experiences have occurred in a context with others from both ordinary and non-ordinary reality – a different, but important, perspective on community.

For Tessa, community remains important in her healing practice and spiritual training and growth.

Understanding Tradition

The role of religious tradition, with its ability to remain consistent yet adapt to the cultural and spiritual needs of a given generation or era, is something of great relevance in contemporary society. What follows shows that many traditions are being adapted by those who were interviewed.

Franco

Franco grew up with a Christian heritage, and he also learned about yoga, shamanism and astrology. Though he does not let himself be confined by self-imposed limitations in any of these traditions, he draws upon them freely because he sees how they all eventually lead to ultimate unity. What has helped him connect with this unity is the central energy of the Sacred Cone, which for him provides a model or structure that gathers chaotic, fragmented energy into a matrix with neutral containers and a common language. The matrix facilitates understanding and the wisdom of unity. He sees how the Sacred Cone allows individuals to map where they are in their lives, and then create changes that help them more clearly take a road of inner experience towards the centre of unity. Franco said he also sees core shamanism as being this same kind of matrix, with empty spaces that allow and encourage a spiritual progress towards unity.

Stephen

Stephen's religious heritage from childhood is Catholic, which he says offered no power to people, and lacked joy and laughter. In contrast to that kind of rigid attempt to control life experiences, his parents allowed him opportunities for failure, freedom, and trust something he said he appreciates. His spiritual life today includes empowerment of himself and others, and it is filled with laughter and joy. As a result, today he takes responsibility for making decisions about his spiritual growth and development. Furthermore, he helps others do the same.

Cláudia

Although her religious upbringing was Catholic, Cláudia considers the indigenous spiritual cultures of Brazil and Africa, which provided important dimensions in her spiritual formation, to be her real spiritual heritage. She said she went through a time of rebellion against the dogmas and rules promoted by the Catholic Church. However, today she finds herself befriending Jesus as a figure outside the Church 'box' as an avatar, a shaman and a guide. She said she also feels close to the Black Madonna and to Nossa Senhora Aparecida, the patron saint of Brazil, who is also known as the goddess of miracles, and who is as important for the Catholic Church in Brazil as she is in spiritual centres all over that country. Cláudia's spiritual experience with 'Power Plant' is through the Santo Daime Community of the Amazon in Brazil. She said Santo Daime is also known as the Spirit of Ayuasca, or the Blood of Christ. According to Cláudia, many Catholic saints have parallels in indigenous Brazilian cultures. She said she wants to embrace the whole of humankind and help any people she can help – regardless of their background or heritage.

Mark

Mark grew up as a member of the Church of Scotland, but as a teenager explored Taoist philosophy, Zen and the I-Ching. Later he studied Native American, Peruvian and Aboriginal spiritualities and traditions, including shamanism. As an adult, Mark has integrated many dimensions of his religious and spiritual heritage. He said he draws upon the help of Jesus and Mary from his Christian background; Native American, Aboriginal and Peruvian guides from his shamanic training; and Eastern philosophy and meditative practice from his Taoist study. In addition, he honours the intuitive healing abilities that he discovered he possessed as a child.

Alistair

When Alistair was about eleven, he remembers feeling a strong closeness to his ancestors, especially when standing near two dolmens in his hometown. That same year his grandfather died, and Alistair spontaneously enacted a druid-style memorial service for him in the woods. At age thirteen, Alistair was 'born again' and began having ecstatic experiences that continued over the next five years. During those years he participated in Pentecostal, charismatic, evangelical and High Church Anglican services that supported and nurtured his mystical experiences. At age eighteen he went to England, where he became a Church of England youth worker, then he lived in an Anglican Benedictine community from age twenty to twenty-two. Alistair found monastic life there strict and contemplative rather than focused on community, so he left.

Though he did not cut his links with the Anglican Church, he began to move towards the Spiritualists and the Quakers. At one point he moved towards becoming a Spiritualist medium. During this period he also remembers participating with others in a pagan ceremony at Stonehenge. Eventually he moved to the USA, where he lived for two-and-a-half years as a Shaker brother in a community of eight people. They retained a spiritualist, ecstatic, charismatic orientation which incorporated a natural closeness to the spirit world, especially with spirits of the departed. There they lived in natural woodland, making black ash baskets as part of fulfilling what they called 'hands to work and hearts to God'. Because Alistair wanted more intellectual stimulation and learning, he left that community and moved to Edinburgh in October of 1998, where he began an MA in Divinity and became part of the Anglican Chaplaincy at the University of Edinburgh. His study of Christian theology led him to believe that the gospels were not entirely 'historical', and that a feminist theology was lacking. As a result, his wrote his dissertation on the subject of 'the Divine Feminine in Shaker Theology'.

At the same time, he realized he had had enough of conventional religion, and felt drawn towards paganism. While working on his MA, Alistair began druidic training through a correspondence course. He has continued druidic training and practice, served as minister at a Unitarian church in Glasgow, and was ordained a priest in the last few years.

Preben

Baptized and confirmed as a Christian in Denmark, Preben had a religious heritage connected to Protestant Christianity in general, rather than to a specific church. His parents were open-minded, but Preben found Christianity annoying and wanted to learn more about 'native' people. His early intuitive connections to animals, other people and their thoughts, and to the spirit beings who started visiting him as early as age four, led him to determine that life held more wonder and breadth than what was taught in conventional Christianity. Furthermore, his developing healing abilities exposed him to healers with a spiritual worldview that seemed different from a Christian one. Preben started exploring other spiritual perspectives at an early age, and his life today seems to be a natural outcome of his continuous spiritual development.

Collette

Though she does not claim a specific religious heritage, because of her parents' healing work she participated several times in functions at the Foundation of Spiritual Healers. Collette said that her religious, or spiritual, heritage is quite compatible with her spiritual life today.

Heleen

As a child Heleen was exposed to what she called a kind of 'global Christianity' in which there was no priest, and men and women were separated, though together, in church. There was singing, and most of the churchgoers were baptized as adults. However, Heleen said she rebelled against church traditions, especially the church's pleas for money from younger children. She had connections with another church too, though she decided not to get married at either, choosing instead the Town Hall, with a theologian as the 'minister'. Later her son and daughter were baptized, but church was not part of their lives. When asked how this background interacted with her spiritual or religious life today, Heleen again talked about the term 'sacred'. Determining what is sacred, for Heleen, depends on the occasion, the environment and the people. Her various experiences have led to her current understanding that the sacred can be a way of having fun; a way for people to 'feel together' in relationship with God.

Jonathan

As a child Jonathan was exposed more to Christianity than to other religious or spiritual paths. He sees no conflict between the Christian path and what he understands as shamanism.

Susan

The Free Church in Scotland and the Presbyterian Church in New Zealand were her religious homes for thirty-five years. She took her children to church, read the Bible, and taught Sunday School for most of that time. However, she eventually realized that she felt 'used and abused' by the church's attitudes, especially towards the Maori and towards homosexuals. She also felt 'betrayed' by the church when her father was ill. Susan said her faith in God has never been stronger than now, but that she is on a different road – one that gives her more freedom and support for her spiritual growth. She said she still values the energy of church buildings and music, but she no longer tolerates church communities of people who do not think, want to be told what to do, and then hypocritically do what they are told, not what they believe, because 'It's the thing to do.'

Nanna

Nanna started out as a Roman Catholic in Italy, but said she lost her spirituality, as a feeling, when she went to school at age four. Though her grandmother prepared her for her first Communion at age seven, her grandmother never went to church, but stayed at home to work. Likewise her grandfather did not go to church. Nanna thinks Jesus was a shaman and that the Bible has some good guidelines – perhaps some truth and wisdom – but that most of it was invented by human beings. In her current spiritual practice she incorporates elements such as ritual, candles, flowers, water and statues, from her Catholic heritage. However, she uses them with flexibility and in ways that have evolved and seem natural to her. Otherwise, she does not seem concerned about potential conflicts between her current spiritual practice and her Catholic background.

Tessa

Though raised Irish Catholic, Tessa is not active in the church structure in part due to her experiences related to her divorce and remarriage, a condition not allowed by the church. In spite of this she loves some of the rituals, the candles and the incense, and she occasionally takes part in a service.

Currently she see herself as being 'all or none' regarding religion because for her each religion, or 'way', may have something of value when connecting with the divine. She remembers her mother's warning that seeing what others don't see – as in shamanic practice – is a sin, yet she possesses the gift of 'sight' from her Celtic father, who also 'saw'. Tessa herself finds no conflict between her spiritual healing practice – which to her is much like shamanic healing – and her Catholic heritage.

Invoking Tradition

The process of invoking a tradition or parts of a tradition is central to Hervieu-Léger's model of 'religion as a chain of memory'.

Franco

When he works shamanically, Franco invokes the central energy of the Sacred Cone and all the spiritual guides who facilitate movement, learning and healing within the levels, worlds, directions and sectors of the Sacred Cone. He calls upon numerous traditions other than shamanism, especially astrology and Christianity, because they are part of his heritage and learning. They also 'work' and make sense to him. Additionally, he has incorporated into his astroshamanic work aspects of ancient pre-Christian mystery religions, paganism, and Gnostic and Christian shamanism.

Stephen

Stephen invokes the presence, guidance and support of various spiritual allies when he works shamanically. He also invokes a lineage of knowledge that has been passed down through various shamanic teachers he works with in ordinary reality. Some of these masters and teachers include Peggy Dylan, Peruvian shaman Dr Pio, New Mexican shaman Emaho, South American shaman Don Alexandro, North American shaman Sandra Ingerman, and other mentors and elders. In addition, Stephen calls upon traditions from Buddhism, fire-walking and stargazing, which he integrates into his shamanic work.

Cláudia

When Cláudia works shamanically, she invokes her spiritual allies. Some allies come for protection while others assist, depending upon the need.

Cláudia allows them to speak to her through her body, particularly in the way she feels when she is asking for their guidance and help. She invokes traditions other than the shamanic, including some from her childhood. One is *umbanda*, which came from Africa. Another is *Mesablanca*, meaning 'white table seance', which is a way of channelling the spirits of light. Other traditions she invokes are *candomble*, which originated in Africa, and Afro-Brazilian Capoeira, which is very common in Brazil. As a result of both Cláudia and Mark's backgrounds, the Shamanic Centre has offered Afro-Brazilian Capoeira, West African drumming, guided meditations, healing circles, art and creativity experiences, Celtic Druidic traditions, Native American teachings and practices, and 'working with the angels'. To Clàudia and Mark, these traditions offer a variety of ways for expressing a fundamental shamanic perspective of looking at life in relationship with the world, and with the spirits of non-ordinary reality.

Mark

Regarding who or what he invokes when he works shamanically, Mark said he is not comfortable with stating or defining exactly what should be done. He supports each person's right to identify what feels right and to call on whatever ally may be needed to help – in part because that is how he himself works. The process of invoking spiritual help may be a constant, but the ways in which that is done, or the identity of the allies called upon, may differ according to the circumstances. Mark has discovered that certain spiritual allies help with specific issues. He calls upon the angelic realms, personal guides, the 'Great Spirit' and animal guides, and says he 'isn't attached to the traditions from which they come'. He 'feels Spirit communicates in ways that we can all understand: a line from a song, poetry, movies, nature, thoughts, and above all, experience'.

Alistair

In his shamanic practice Alistair invokes many of his spiritual allies. One of the ways he determines which allies to invoke, or which issues to explore when he follows his weekly shamanic journey, is to use the Celtic Shaman's Pack, which was created by John Matthews. Working with these cards helps him discern guidance and direction that is offered to him. Alistair often does divinations and extractions for people who ask him for shamanic help. Regarding other traditions, Alistair draws upon and integrates many that have been part of his life over the years. For him, each tradition has something to offer, especially when it can help with his current work.

Preben

In his shamanic practice, Preben tunes into what is going on with the person who has come to him in an attempt to clarify any presenting issues, discern any natural cycles, and arrive at an intuitive sense of where the person is spiritually in relation to the healing request. He then asks 'spirit' for guidance and works with whichever spiritual allies present themselves to help with healing – calling upon a variety of traditions. However, they all seem to have a shamanic dimension in that they involve relationships with spiritual beings who help with information and healing that bring about an increased sense of kinship and oneness.

Collette, Heleen, Jonathan, Susan, Nanna and Tessa

When Collette does shamanic practice she invokes spirits that will help, and trusts that the appropriate one(s) will assist her in her own life or in helping others – regardless of what tradition(s) they may represent. Regarding traditions or memories, Heleen said she does not consciously call upon them. Ritual for her is present and 'goes along with all the things you do'. With reference to shamanism's compatibility with other spiritual traditions, she said that since everything God created is good, all ways of developing spiritually are good.

Jonathan invokes guidance, but hasn't necessarily experienced that guidance as coming from an ally in a specific form. His actions have demonstrated that he calls upon those spiritual traditions that both his faith and his instinct guide him to explore, and to utilize as tools along his spiritual path.

When Susan works shamanically she calls upon spiritual allies, or guides, and traditions that speak to her life and support individual discernment and choice in growing a relationship with God. In her spiritual practice, Nanna invokes 'the universe', not one person. She referred to the Buddha in saying that the universe is there with no tradition, no building, and no donations expected. Regarding access to traditions other than shamanism, Nanna calls on what works, but finds particular support in Buddhism, which to her represents places she has been where there is good energy. When she works shamanically, or in her healing practice, she invokes many of her spiritual allies or guides, and calls upon various spiritual traditions that help in her spiritual growth and development. Though numerous, they include energy balancing, magnified healing essence, light work and the invocation of specific spiritual allies.

Determining Legitimate Authority

A critical factor in societal decisions about what is credible and acceptable is the perception of what confers legitimate authority – who has authority, and why.

Franco, Stephen and Cláudia

For Franco, legitimacy and authority derive from his worldview that all is one and that we can learn something positive and life-giving from all experiences. The need for a legitimizing authority outside one's own experience would be for Franco an expression of the fragmented energy which he strives to heal and bring into wholeness.

'Love and blessing' provide the legitimizing authority for Stephen when he is determining what is authentic on his path of spiritual growth. Furthermore, he said he knows intuitively when he is practising the internal spiritual discipline necessary for surrendering to that life force of 'love and blessing'. He trusts and believes that the universe will nurture and take care of him when he presents a pure intention. As he learned from Sandra Ingerman, intention and trust are essential.

Cláudia said her legitimizing authority comes from 'spirit'. She feels the spiritual presence(s) in her body, and knows when her ego is working for control and when she is tapping into spiritual guidance. That spiritual authority is new, different, free, and refrains from judging others harshly. Though in the beginning she needed to rely more on what others told her was legitimate, now she continues learning to know and trust her self and 'the spirits' for that legitimacy.

Mark, Alistair and Preben

When asked how he knows his guidance is legitimate and authoritative, Mark said he feels several sensations. They include a feeling of enthusiasm, a tingling in his body, an inner shift of emotions, and the appearance of spiritual colours. He also experiences a peaceful assurance that his work is appropriate and will not hurt anybody. He said his intention is always love, which he considers to be the energy that heals.

Alistair said he knows something is authoritative when it contains truth, if it works to help himself or others, and when he discovers supporting evidence emerging through 'synchronicity'.

Preben determines whether what he is learning and doing spiritually is legitimate and authoritative by letting go of ego, continuing to learn from 'spirit', and not allowing others to dictate what he believes must come from 'spirit'. He attempts to step away from trying to control a situation, and to let 'spirit' work. Experience has helped him know what brings truth (e.g. his vision, reflections, and travelling dreams), because they have a quality he recognizes as valuable. In them he can sense a strange confidence and a security that comes from being held by 'spirit'. He 'knows' when he's letting words flow because they are beyond regular consciousness, and they reflect his having learned to be a 'hollow bone' for 'spirit'.

Collette, Heleen and Jonathan

Collette 'looks inside', accepts herself as she is, and trusts her own intuitive guidance, truth and experience when determining what is legitimate and authoritative in her shamanic practice.

Heleen, asked how she knows her spiritual practice is legitimate and authoritative, said she experiences a lot of miracles, and that when she is open to recognize the signs, it makes her happy. In her words, 'It makes you strong in difficult situations. God, take me in your hands.'

Jonathan said his legitimizing authority was his strong belief in utilizing both his faith and his instinct – also, his feelings or emotions and his intellect. As an example, he described how drawing upon that combination of personal resources and experience has allowed him to disagree with those who say that Christianity is the only true religion, or with a vicar friend of his who has criticized transcendental meditation.

Susan, Nanna and Tessa

Susan said that the core of her, which connects with the divine, is her legitimate authority. Furthermore, she surrounds herself with people she trusts – those who help her discern her path, but know that the final choices are hers. She said she tries to be sensible, practical and grounded, and she is careful about those with whom she shares her 'precious experiences' or 'spiritual treasures'.

Nanna herself is the legitimizing authority for what she believes. When asked how she knows she is aligned with the universe, she said that when she communicates with other human beings and experiences a feeling that something good comes out, the 'ball starts rolling'; she then feels good and gives out good energy. That is how she knows whether or not she is in alignment with the universe.

   Tessa's legitimizing authority for her spiritual perspectives and choices is her own experience. She 'just knows', and nurtures her relationship with the 'divine essence', or God. Not only does she incorporate a number of traditional spiritual exercises into her daily spiritual practice, but she also remains in communication with other spiritual healers and teachers who help and support her discerning process.

Believing

How one believes, and what it means to believe, are challenging questions that relate directly to Hervieu-Léger's definition.

Franco

Growing up, Franco learned to believe that he was living in a fantasy world, but that everyone else was grounded in reality. That reality was spelled out in rules and maxims that had been externalized, and were believed to be objectively true. However, his own experiences, along with his lifelong passion for learning and inner growth, led him to understand beliefs as strategies that can change if they are based on experience and 'work' or make sense. He described beliefs as agreements about the way the world is, though they can and do change as our perceptions and experiences interact with and influence the continued validity of those agreements. In effect, believing has become for him a process of growing, expanding and transforming his worldview as that worldview is regularly informed by his life experiences.

Stephen

Today Stephen believes in ways that are both similar to and different from his past. His legitimizing authority is something he determines internally, rather than him accepting an external authority. At the same time, he invokes the lineages of knowledge passed on to him by various respected teachers, and he calls upon his spiritual allies for guidance and protection. As a younger person, he was not as confident as he is now about how to work with his spiritual experiences.

Cláudia and Mark

How Cláudia believes today relates to the process of relationship, rather than to an acceptance or rejection of religious rules. She now has more confidence in, and support for, finding ways of integrating and incorporating the varied spiritual dimensions of her background. In effect, she 'believes' in the beneficial help of spiritual allies to help her 'know' through her own intuition and body; in contrast, she does not 'believe' in a set of constructs, or rules, that outline and dictate what she should think spiritually.

Mark's way of believing today is different from earlier in his life, in that he does not doubt himself as much. He told me he realizes he is not alone, and that the love of people and life is the basis of who he is. He said, 'We are all manifestations of the divine.' His way of believing is the same in that he remains 'irreverent and humorous' – laughing a lot, and not being too serious in the face of adversity.

Alistair and Preben

The way Alistair believes today is somewhat different from before in that he is now more practical. What counts for him is healing, wholeness, good health and happiness. Today he feels freer to be himself, in part because he feels more fully affirmed as a worthwhile human being. One of the ways Preben believes differently today is in his shift from looking at 'past lives' to looking at 'parallel lives'. Another is in recognizing the difference between what needs to be built, using the element of fire to create and nurture, and what needs to be learned, using the 'heart energy of unconditional oneness' which is mostly found in wise elders.

Collette, Heleen and Jonathan

Collette's way of believing today is different from the past in that she trusts herself more and honours her own path, rather than placing her total trust in something external. Feedback from a trusted community helps, but she believes she alone has ultimate accountability for her own life.

Heleen said that the word 'believe' is not definitive, and can be applied in different ways. For example, one can say, 'I believe it will rain today.' However, she equates believing rather with feeling an inner power, and with knowing something from deep within. She thinks 'you have to feel it,' and should not judge other people and their religions, or try to pressure another person into believing something you believe.

Though he did not explain how his way of believing is different today from when he was younger, Jonathan's exploration of transcendental meditation and shamanism as an adult seems to reflect an openness to new learning and to processes, or tools, that help people reach points of spiritual growth. This is consistent with his earlier statement about all paths leading to one.

Susan

A key way in which Susan believes differently today than she did in the past is her sense of self-trust and self-confidence regarding her own personal and spiritual growth, her acceptance of a growth and change process that includes exploring doubt, and her realization that she is 'blessed'. She said she no longer believes that churches, or anybody else for that matter, have the only right interpretations of the Bible, since the Bible contains passages that support almost anything a person wants to claim no matter how contradictory. Regarding evil, she thinks evil is created and materialized only when someone gives it energy and life. Furthermore, people are still able to shine light on that kind of darkness.

Nanna and Tessa

The way Nanna believes today is different from how she believed in the past, primarily in the growing confidence she has in her own relationship with the universe. Tessa currently has a view of religious expression that has expanded from that of her youth. She now believes in, and accesses, whatever she discovers from different religious traditions that helps or supports her relationship with the divine.

Overall Observations and Themes

Regarding Hervieu-Léger's model of religion, participants very clearly stated that the legitimizing authority for the way they believe is their own inner knowing based especially on their relationship with what they often call 'spirit', or 'guidance'. They described having little or no conflict between their early religious background and the ways they believe today. Furthermore, they said they find great support and encouragement from the variety of multi-cultural and multi-spiritual traditions they access on their path of spiritual growth. Though many spoke of invoking various traditions, and of feeling connected to many who are not physically present, their invocations do not focus on sets of beliefs, but on spiritual allies and traditions that reflect ways of believing and living. Community is something growing in importance for them, but they are still exploring what that means and how to make it happen over time.

From the perspective of detecting elements in a new paradigm of spirituality and religion, the shift towards inter-relatedness and transformational growth described in the last chapter, this process is now manifest in the ways world spiritual traditions are incorporated into the lives of these participants. When one's worldview has expanded to become global or universal, and all life in that universe is part of a unified whole, then choosing and integrating perceived 'best practice' from a variety of global traditions makes perfect sense. It is not 'pick and mix' on a superficial level, but a conscious choice on a deeper level to move towards integration within a global society. This does not mean that issues of appropriation can be ignored. However, the context and intent are not necessarily political. They can be motivated by respect, and by the perceived need to bypass the power struggles currently hindering many contemporary religious institutions.

Chapter Eight

Patterns, Conclusions and Resulting Issues

Introduction

The search to describe a new paradigm of spirituality and religion has guided our path through working definitions of religion, spirituality, paradigms and shamanism; critical factors driving transformational cultural change; key components in Hervieu-Léger's model of religion; cross-cultural elements of shamanism; and profiles of, and interviews with, people involved in contemporary shamanic practice in Scotland. The purpose of this chapter is to tie these varied strands together in a way that reveals patterns, conclusions and issues that are relevant to our understanding of the new paradigm of religion and spirituality.

Because shamanic practitioners and people in their communities are the ones who provided the stories and experiences for my field research, the first strand is an analysis of the relationship between their shamanic practices and my model of cross-cultural shamanism. The next one is an analysis of correlation between their work and Hervieu-Léger's model of religion as a chain of memory. The last strand is assessing the impact those I interviewed may have experienced from critical factors effecting the transformation of religion. Each analysis ends with what I consider to be the significance of the findings. The chapter ends with a summary of how these similar, yet diverse, approaches form a coherent picture of the new spirituality and religion paradigm.

Comparing Elements from the Model of Cross-Cultural Shamanism

Overview

The model of cross-cultural shamanism contains the following elements, which are analysed in the sections presented below: vocation and initiation; cosmology; soul flight/journeying; consciousness; spiritual allies; soul healing; and community support.

Significance of the Results

The research presented in this book provides evidence that all seven elements in the model of cross-cultural shamanism are present, but what difference does that make? First of all, the model of core shamanism presented in Chapter Four arose primarily from scholarly research into traditional, indigenous shamanism, not from an extensive study of neo-shamanisms. Also, 'core shamanism' as a concept came from Michael Harner, the anthropologist who coined that term after living and working with indigenous shamanic cultures. Chapter One briefly addressed contemporary forms of shamanism, but scholar Robert Wallis noted that academic research into that area has been minimal. The fact that the core elements found cross-culturally in traditional, indigenous shamanic cultures are also present in the shamanic work of the contemporary practitioners in this study tells us that there is a fundamental similarity between traditional shamanism and these particular expressions of neo-shamanism in Scotland. That similarity comes initially in a shamanic worldview that embodies ways of perceiving reality, and of interacting with this perceived reality, that can be found underlying diverse and unique cultural expressions throughout the world. Essential in this worldview is the perception of a kinship system of inter-relatedness that exists now, has done so 'from the beginning', and is often represented by the symbol of the World Tree or the Tree of Life (Drury: 38–9). Furthermore, those who perceive this kinship system as real actually maintain and hold the memory of a 'wholeness paradigm' – of how on both micro and macro levels, all life forms are intrinsically valued, relate to each other, and can work in harmony. Those remembering the 'wholeness paradigm' understand illness as separation, alienation and fragmentation; and they work on a soul level to heal those divisions by remembering and releasing barriers of alienation, and by restoring connections with the self, society, other life forms in the environment and all life in the universe. That is why shamanic initiations have often involved the initiate in experiences of feeling separate from their communities due to seeing life differently; wrestling with their non-ordinary reality visions and demands; and coming to terms with how they can relate to their new spiritual allies as they rejoin their communities, and offer themselves and their gifts in service to a fragmented society that, at best, only partially understands and appreciates them.

Those interviewed in this study came to their shamanic calling through experiences that prompted them to learn more in order to understand what had happened to them. Though some of them eventually read accounts of shamans and shamanic ways, the reading usually came later. During the interviews and participant observation sessions, none of the practitioners referred to core shamanism. In other words, learning about traditional shamanism was what helped them understand their experiences, and core shamanism as a concept was not something they articulated or talked about wanting to integrate. Though Cláudia is currently offering a class on 'core shamanism', when I briefly mentioned the idea of core shamanic elements to her during one of our initial discussions in 2003, she responded by explicitly stating that she did not want to exclude people by setting up rigid parameters declaring who was 'in' and who was 'out' as a shamanic practitioner. In other words, the elements of core shamanism were seen among the contemporary practitioners from a more inductive perspective, rather than from their having made conscious attempts to reflect a particular model. In fact, I did not tell them my questions were based on a model. At the same time, individual shamanic elements, such as working with spiritual allies or practising soul healing, may well have been learned from other practitioners and/or from books that together helped these participants to conceptualize and understand their experiences. Indeed, they have been influenced, helped and taught by others throughout their training, but that training did not entail learning the configuration of elements presented in the model provided in Chapter Four.

These results also affirm a growing recognition among researchers, described more fully in Chapter Two, that traditions reflecting a worldview with fundamental values and principles able to survive the 'test of time' are ones that can change their external forms to meet cultural needs – without compromising their underlying sense of integrity in purpose and vision. In fact, that is exactly how they survive. As cultures change, these traditions adapt to human needs by creating new expressions of coherence and meaning out of an emerging cultural context (Halbwachs: 40; Hervieu-Léger, 2000: 87). Another way this happens is by looking beyond the historical reality of a tradition to discover the symbolic reality and recover the memory that it sustained (Nora: xvii).

Many of the elements represented in this shamanism model are also found in various parts of Western society. Using music, drumming or dance (trance or other types) to achieve a state of consciousness that facilitates praying and/or accessing other ways of knowing is characteristic of, but not exclusive to, shamanism. Likewise, communicating with spiritual allies for help, support, protection and information is not limited to shamanism. People from various religious traditions for millennia have called upon saints, angels, prophets, goddesses, gods and mythic figures – all spiritual beings perceived to be in the non-ordinary realms. Many of the 'alternative spiritualities' contain elements that could be labelled shamanic. However, just as certain processes can have therapeutic results without constituting a system of therapy, having a few elements that are shamanic does not constitute a system of shamanism. What distinguishes shamanic practice in this study is the way in which all of the shamanic elements from the model come together to form a unique system that is called shamanism, not something else.

The difficult issue of 'community' in contemporary shamanic circles tells us as much about the overarching paradigm of Western society as it does about the shamanic practitioners and those who work with them. As discussed in Chapter Four, over several centuries many traditional shamanic communities within the Western world have been attacked, oppressed and marginalized almost to the point of extinction. Many of them have survived by quietly holding on to fragments of tradition and to memories of a worldview that had sustained them and their ancestors over time. One example of that is the Oglala Sioux holy man Black Elk, who prophesied about a day when the 'sacred hoop' of oneness would be restored around the Tree of Life (Black Elk, 2000). Throughout Europe during the Inquisition, many of the people executed as witches were women and men who 'saw' what others could not see, worked with spiritual allies, and healed on a soul level (Ankarloo, 1993; Briggs, 1998; Ginzburg, 1991). Their way of life was not understood or sanctioned by those in authority, and they paid for that with their lives. Though the Reformation brought needed changes in some areas, it prompted both Protestant and Catholic church leaders to narrowly define, and thus dictate, what was acceptable thinking, belief and behaviour; and that did not usually include a shamanic worldview.

In Scotland and other parts of Europe, 'those claiming to heal outside the context of the Church must have got their powers from the Devil'; as a result, they were often severely punished or killed as witches (Larner: 9). Though shamanic healing and witchcraft may have had similarities, research to date does not substantiate their being the same. The Enlightenment focus on reason, combined with an intense suspicion of intuition, or of anything that could not be empirically validated by the acknowledged five senses, only intensified that mindset. Belonging to a 'public' shamanic community of any kind was dangerous. Though there is no documented evidence to date of a seamless historical thread of shamanic practice in Scotland, Trevarthen, cited in Chapter Four, has provided some evidence of shamanism playing a role in Celtic religion from around 500 BCE to 500 CE, and of a shamanic worldview being present in certain aspects of early Celtic culture (Trevarthen, 2003). Building upon that, some of the tales gathered by ethnologists and stored in the archives of the School of Scottish Studies at the University of Edinburgh have been shown to contain shamanic elements listed in the model of shamanism used in this study

(Burgess, 2002). The 'tradition bearers' who told those tales may have made no conscious connection with shamanism. However, Bowman has addressed the issue of how vernacular religion, with its 'belief stories', has often provided informal modes of transmitting and maintaining the unofficial belief traditions of a given community (Bowman: 84–5).

The power of traditional religions and governments to exclude and marginalize those with a shamanic type of worldview has direct relevance to the fragmented state of shamanic communities today. Contemporary shamanic practitioners have often had to face their 'different' way of seeing without the guidance of traditional shamans or the benefit of living in shamanic communities. At the same time, the emergence of alternative spiritualities within the last thirty years has also opened up new ways of finding teachers and of forming other types of community support for their work. What we see in this study is a network of practitioners that are both learning shamanic ways from each other, and also seeking training from other shamans in various cultures. This type of small-group networking among contemporary 'spiritual seekers' is very well described throughout Sutcliffe's book *Children of the New Age* (Sutcliffe, 2003).

On a very practical level, such 'spiritual seekers' are also facing the challenge of finding spaces where they can do their healing work and gather as a shamanic community – in whatever form. As a result, those who have invested financially in the creation of centres where shamanic work occurs have the added challenge of handling the business end of their work. Because of their not living in a traditional indigenous society that has developed ways of supporting their shamans, and not being affiliated with an institutional religion that understands or supports their work, they must either have some kind of independent income or earn enough money to pay for both business and personal living expenses. As with most other people, they also face decisions related to setting boundaries that balance work and personal life, developing shamanic and business skills, and facilitating the human relations element of working with groups and co-workers. Carrette's concern about people who commercialize religion in the name of spirituality does not apply to these practitioners (Carrette, 2005).

Though all of the traditional shamanic elements are present in the work of the practitioners in this study, they also reflect some of the contemporary forms of shamanism briefly addressed in Chapter Four and more fully studied in Wallis's book on neo-shamanisms (Wallis, 2003). As noted in both places, the position of neo-shamans in the eyes of certain indigenous shamanic societies has come under growing scrutiny. As a result, most neo-shamanic practitioners will very likely be faced at some time with having to address the question of appropriation. However, Cláudia, one of the practitioners, was born and raised in Brazil, where she grew up learning various aspects of indigenous Brazilian shamanism, along with other types of spirituality that were a natural part of her living environment. Some of the other practitioners have been studying with traditional shamans who have taken them in as apprentices in one way or another. Because a number of these practitioners draw upon their own native shamanic traditions and/or continue to learn from indigenous shamans in the ways just described, the issue of appropriation may not figure as prominently in the challenges they ultimately face.

Finally, from a global perspective, the diverse cultural backgrounds of those in this study reflect a variety of spiritual practices that are grounded in the core elements of traditional shamanism, which claims an existence over centuries, if not longer. This cross-cultural nature of shamanism, and its history of longevity, reflect continuity across cultures and from the past into the present. Furthermore, practitioners in this study see themselves as serving not just individuals and local communities, but all life on the planet and in the universe. Their commitment to a kinship system is all-inclusive. Because of this, the very presence of shamanic communities like those in this study brings the larger society face to face with another example of the need to address effectively the diversity and plurality of religious perspectives that exist outside the institutional faith traditions and religions, but also reflect a growing spirituality that is emerging as part of a global consciousness.

Correlating Components from Hervieu-Léger's Model of Religion as a Chain of Memory

Overview

The key components from Hervieu-Léger's model that are used in this analysis include: community; understanding tradition; invoking tradition; determining legitimate authority; and believing.

Significance of the Results

The research data related to the Hervieu-Léger definition of religion provides evidence that while the shamanic practitioners may possibly fit most of the components in this model, they invoke a chain of memory and embrace a way of believing that together more accurately reflect a parallel core lineage of spirituality, not religion. Theirs is a paradigm of experience and relationship with all life, which they see inter-related with Spirit, and their interactions with various chains of belief from specific traditions occur in order to support and develop those kinship relationships. It is a lineage that does not involve passing on a set of beliefs from a tradition, or even a mixture of traditions, that can be evaluated, accepted and handed down even if the community itself has claimed legitimate authority over such traditions. This lineage of spirituality complements the lineage of belief contained in this model of religion, but its priority is to keep alive the relationships and experiences that prompted the formation of religion and religious beliefs in the first place. Indeed, religion and spirituality are best seen as intertwined, though the role of religion is seen as supporting, guiding and serving the relationships inherent in spirituality, rather than as controlling or stifling them.

The fact that this research data tends to match religion and spirituality, resulting in some degree of confusion, points to the perceived tension that currently exists between the two concepts as realities in people's lives. It also highlights the dual role of a shaman as one whose vocation is to bridge ordinary and non-ordinary reality. Unlike a pure mystic who can remain 'lost' in a personal experience of mystical oneness, the shaman is called to bring together what is perceived to be the physical and non-physical worlds – all for the benefit, ultimate well-being, and healing of the people and other life forms served by the shaman. That perceived call to a dual role, and the shamanic experience of an overarching kinship paradigm, provide insights into why the field data found considerable correspondence with both the model of religion and the lineage of spirituality.

Regarding the model itself, this study has shown that Hervieu-Léger provides a quality analytical tool that has supported a rich and credible investigation of contemporary shamanic practice existing in three parts of Scotland. Her desire for a working definition of religion, which could move scholarship out of the trap of tying religion exclusively to institutional forms, has proved to be quite valuable. A carefully chosen component in that process was to exclude 'the sacred' as a part of her model. By doing that, she created a contained, yet open, way to study a group of people involved in a system of shamanism functioning outside the parameters of institutional religion, but intimately related to what its practitioners perceive to be 'the sacred'.

Some aspects of her model that caused confusion in this analysis, and might benefit from further clarification, include the nature of belief, believing and a chain of belief – especially when compared to a paradigm; the relationship between belief and tradition; and a fuller explanation about why an appeal to a cloud of witnesses adhering to a chain of belief is needed as a legitimizing authority. Also, the significant insights Hervieu-Léger gained about her model occurred when she was studying a neo-rural intentional spiritual community. It would be helpful to know what those community members thought had given them a legitimizing authority. Was it due to the external validation, or did that validation only increase their existing commitment?

Beyond testing Hervieu-Léger's model of religion, the significance of these results lies in a number of other areas. First, there was an overwhelming need for participants to reclaim their voices and choices, related to what most of them called their spirituality; this points to a newly found freedom, with societal support, to think as adults in an area that for centuries has been powerfully controlled by the Christian church in Western society. In its early emergence, the need to explore options, and to develop trust and confidence in one's own way of intuiting and perceiving 'truth' − initially without having to commit to any one tradition − reflects the urgency of this development, and its involvement in the relativism of post-modern thought. However, as witnessed especially with the practitioners in this study, once the freedom of choice was fully experienced, and exposure to new spiritual practices brought what they experienced as a 'resonance of the heart', they began to coalesce around a paradigm, or set of beliefs about the world, that reflected their own inner spiritual experiences. In the process, they met others of like mind and affiliated with networks of 'kindred spirits' who shared similar perspectives.

This raises two important issues: distinguishing between belief and believing, and identifying the difference between a set of beliefs that form a 'chain of belief', and a set of beliefs that form a paradigm. Regarding the former, when the content of belief emerges out of the experience of a person or people, it becomes something the believer 'holds dear' and tries to share with others who might understand. When that is possible, the sharing, reinforcing and 'holding dear' together through stories, rituals, questioning and exploring form an interactive process of believing that takes place in an environment of collective support for continuing to seek a commonly perceived truth about the meaning and coherence of life. In this way, 'dearly held' belief systems are internalized and serve to inform, guide and occasionally modify attitude and behaviour, rather than to externally and arbitrarily control, stifle or eliminate motivation for holding the beliefs, or for collectively supporting each other in the believing process. The beliefs of participants in this study prompted them to incorporate spiritual practices that required discipline, and helped them live what they hoped would be better lives both personally and as contributors to society-at-large. Their freedom to address religious or spiritual issues as capable adults who seek guidance, but retain personal responsibility for their choices, was what mattered to them. The latter issue about sets of beliefs related to tradition, and sets of belief that form a paradigm have already been addressed in earlier sections. It is mentioned here, because detecting the subtle difference between the two is important. Also, Hervieu-Léger specifically said that her focus was on chains of belief, not worldviews.

Another area of significance is how to define community. During this post-modern time when 'traditional' communities have fragmented or changed, and many people have started recognizing the relativity of what they had been taught was stable or unchangeable in their religion, they have also begun experimenting with various forms of community – whether groups, colonies, networks or collectives (Sutcliffe, 2003). In the process they have also attempted to retrieve what they considered to be lost fragments of traditions that had been destroyed, or hidden from them for a variety of reasons. The search for these traditions, coupled with the explorations of community, provide important aspects of learning how religion and religious forms change and transform. To restrict our definitions of community by using inflexible rather than flexible parameters, in ways that exclude marginalized people from our study, would be a grave loss. In her Occasional Paper on the role of scholars of religion when addressing the issue of 'community', scholar Kim Knott warned those who study 'the religious' not to become 'trapped into an acceptance of the pre-given categories of "community" and "religion" and thus into their reification and manipulation' (Knott: 80–1). Also concerned about a wider vision of community is sociologist John Urry, whose article on 'Mobility and Proximity' explores the 'socialities involved in occasional co-presence, imagined co-presence and virtual co-presence' (Urry: 256) and the importance of 'intermittent co-presence' (Urry: 264).

An additional issue worthy of attention is one discussed by Hervieu-Léger and other scholars: the self-focus of those in 'alternative spiritualities'. Participants in this study, particularly those learning to do shamanic journeys, regularly raised the question of how to know the difference between when their experiences were mere creations of what they wanted for themselves, and when those experiences were ways of learning how to consider the greater good of self and others. What became clear was that most participants, especially the practitioners, spoke about wanting to heal and grow personally as part of the process of becoming better able to help and serve others. This desire to distinguish between spiritual guidance and self-focused 'wish fulfilment' parallels some of the findings in The Kendal Project, described more fully in Chapter Three. In that context, Paul Heelas and Linda Woodhead wrote that 'those active in subjective well-being culture are by no means unfamiliar with "the we of me"' (Heelas, 2005: 100).

In other words, the concern about self is often part of developing the capacity to help others appropriately.

Finally, the pluralism and diversity discussed in the shamanic analysis and present in this one, too, are indications of a shift society is in the process of making into a global consciousness similar to the kinship paradigm invoked by the shamanic practitioners in this study. Recognizing the interconnected nature of this multi-faceted planet, and discovering ways to identify common values while addressing the differences, are large-scale challenges facing society. In this small study, we have had a glimpse of how a small network of people in Scotland have attempted to address that issue.

Assessing Critical Factors Effecting the Transformation of Religion and Culture

Chapter Two identifies and briefly examines a number of critical factors that have emerged as major influences effecting the transformation of religion and culture. Three of those factors – tradition, determining legitimate authority, and believing – have been analysed in some detail as part of addressing the Hervieu-Léger model of religion. The remaining eight factors are: social and cultural change; secularization; changing religious forms; personal and collective memory; consciousness; faith and belief; developmental theory; and the patriarchal paradigm. They are presented below in a format that identifies the key aspects of each factor, describes their influence on the findings of this study, and points out the significance of that influence.

Social and Cultural Change

Participants in this study exemplified a response to the social and cultural changes of modernity and post-modernity that matches the theories of change discussed in Chapter Two. They described many of their experiences as having propelled them into an awareness of global interdependence with all life, and a multi-layered identity that is inclusive – from self through all life in the universe. Furthermore, their forms of neo-shamanism have revealed a cross-cultural underpinning of elements that have also been identified in indigenous shamanic societies. The global interdependence and kinship perspective most of them described had a 'whole-systems change' way of seeing the bigger picture. However, they arrived at that 'way of seeing' through experience, rather than from theory. Though many spoke about challenges that at times have thwarted them, they also described how they have survived and prospered through these experiences by discovering and focusing on the possibilities for growth and new learning.

Secularization

Most participants indicated that they value many of the underlying tenets, rituals, stories and figures from various religious and spiritual traditions, but that they are not willing to constrict their own spiritual growth when those traditions create inflexible parameters, or display intolerance for questioning or for diverse personal experience. Regarding Sutcliffe's claim that secularization is really about the existence of a 'post-Christian' environment, the attitudes of people in this study tend to support his contention. Participants have drawn upon a number of elements from their Christian backgrounds for their spiritual practice, but they have not assumed those elements must be expressed only in ways designated by the institutions. However, rather than creating parallel institutions, they have opted for a variety of community forms to help them come together in ways which meet their needs for connection with others who share a similar commitment to, and interest in, spiritual growth. What remains to be seen is if and how they will maintain and sustain those new forms. Because these shamanic practitioners have a commitment to serve others through their work, they are likely to seek creative ways of sustaining shamanic communities. At the same time, a long-term commitment of that nature is difficult to maintain during times of intense change.

The significance of these findings lies in the perspective, or worldview, assumed by the participants. For most of them, the decline of religion and the associated relativism, diversity and pluralism have together created for individuals a perceived freedom to embark on a path of personal and spiritual growth that is enhanced and deepened by those very factors. Whatever crises may have accompanied – and may still accompany – the breakdown of familiar religious forms, coping with that process for these people has been part of an ongoing initiation into a new spiritual consciousness, the development of self-confidence, and the discovery of new ways to form community. In fact, the deconstruction of religious power structures has allowed them to focus on some of the inherent and underlying meanings that originally had given rise to those religious forms.

Changing Religious Forms

Building on the above discussion is the next critical factor, which addresses the fact that religion has been moving from its place of primacy as a holder of universal cosmology towards a kind of psychological support for individuals in relative isolation. This globalization of religion, which Luckmann described in Chapter Two as resulting in 'privatized religion', also reminds us that historically during periods of major religious change, spirituality has emerged and sought new forms – in part by re-focusing on the initial experiences that gave rise to the religion in the first place. Many of the new forms are described by Barker, who was also cited in Chapter Two for her pioneering work on new religious movements.

This research highlights a number of ways in which shamanism has found contemporary forms of expression. Not only have these participants come from eight different countries – bringing their own cultural traditions and perspectives – but also they have shared rituals and ceremonies created by combining many of these multi-cultural perspectives, in order to do their shamanic work. The significance of this lies in the ways these participants have demonstrated how a system of shamanism can itself change and adapt many of its forms – both cross-culturally and across long periods of time – without essentially altering its core components as a system. Furthermore, the shamanic system has done so without creating institutions that must be maintained by inbuilt structures of power and control – the apparent norm in organized Western religions. Their willingness to work with flexible parameters and guidelines, rather than rigid definitions, may be another component in their 'success'. If those concerned with the perceived demise of religion in the West would analyse the history of neoshamanic growth, they may gain some helpful insights into coping with religious change.

Personal and Collective Memory

Memory is critically important to the process of transmitting cultural and religious traditions, along with their underlying codes of meaning. Unfortunately, modernity has hastened the fragmentation, and in some cases the repression, of many of those memories, which are our primary sources for linking the past with the present. The fast pace of contemporary life, the ways in which disputes over heresy and orthodoxy have been addressed historically, and the ongoing resolution of conflicts between dogmatic tradition and lived mystical remembrance, have all contributed to the existence of missing, mutating and metaphorical memories. Some fragmented memories have found 'homes' in folklore and in attempts to revise personal and collective genealogies in order to maintain the symbolic meanings of places, historical events and cultural myths. However, the question of power or control over the 'legitimacy' of memory remains a contested issue in many religious arenas.

People participating in this research project are inheritors of these situations, and they too have struggled to remember and to access traditions that might support and enhance their spiritual growth. Their comments about religion and spirituality show how they have had to face discrepancies that have periodically arisen when their own personal experiences have been at odds with religious teachings, doctrines or practices. These practitioners represent the mystical line of 'lived remembrance' – those who challenge the pure legitimate authority of the dogmatic traditions – though most of them have also continued to draw upon spiritual, or religious, practices from these various religious traditions. One of the shamanic memories they have retained is the process of partnering with spiritual allies for protection, guidance, and assistance in healing.

In some cases, participants have accessed memories and traditions in a manner that resembles Nora's description of metaphorical memory. In other words, they have recovered a symbolic meaning of underlying cultural myth that allows them to be living representations of the past in the present. For example, their approaches to soul healing still centre around restoring wholeness to individuals, communities and the environment, but the causes of fragmentation or alienation are understood in different ways in today's society; therefore, some of these practitioners' contemporary healing practices tend to vary. Likewise, the sense of kinship with all life – part of a long-term shamanic worldview – takes on a new dimension when enhanced by current knowledge of global inter-cultural connections, and by recent scientific information about life in the universe. All of the shamanic practitioners and most of the community members have incorporated into their conscious personal identity the roles they play as citizens and as stewards of the planet and the universe.

The significance of these findings is that participants, especially the practitioners, have learned ways of remembering that form special links between the past and the present. Regardless of the fragmentation, they have been able to tap into a core of shamanic elements that are also shared cross-culturally with indigenous societies, even though their expressions of those elements are often different. Overall, they have kept alive the worldview of kinship and relationship with all life – not letting that memory or viewpoint slip from consciousness. In the midst of widespread alienation throughout contemporary society, knowing and learning from people who retain the memory of oneness in their daily is a gratifying endeavour.

Consciousness

A significant factor in these findings is identifying ways in which people 'awaken' to a sense of being part of something larger. Understanding how to see themselves in a global framework, without losing their identities as individuals or as members of specific cultures, is one of the major challenges facing people in contemporary societies. Those in this study showed us how they maintain identity on several levels that are complementary, not antagonistic. This has not excluded challenges, differences, or conflicts requiring attention and resolution. However, the shifts in consciousness that led them to work with spiritual allies for personal healing have also brought many of them an expanded sense of how they can contribute to healing on larger social and global scales. In a world filled with dualism and polarities that at times seem insurmountable, many of these participants have described ways in which they have come to see the world holistically, and in the process have discovered a sense of peace.

Faith and Belief

Findings in this area show how participants have focused quite clearly on the importance of relationships with what they call 'spirit' and with their perceived spiritual allies. Reflecting the previously discussed meanings of belief and faith, they have incorporated spiritual practices designed to help nurture and grow relationships with their spiritual helpers. If asked to choose between an external set of codes or concepts and what they experience as real in their relationship with 'spirit', the answer is clear: the relationship takes priority. In addition, that commitment to relationship extends to other people and life forms. However, they seemed quite realistic in their descriptions of the time and attention required to maintain relationships with spiritual allies, and to live in a way that reflects a worldview of inter-relatedness. Several spoke about the importance of striving to live according to those intentions, even though at times they have felt unable to do so adequately.

The significance of this finding is in its alignment with many of the factors already presented, and with the notion that relationship is at the core of participants' experiences within the spiritual realms and with other beings. This is not a new development in the history of religion and spirituality. It is rooted in earlier ways of maintaining a relational commitment to fundamental values that support and surround the experiences being cherished and remembered.

Developmental Theory

Inherent in this factor are the issues of culture, identity and gender within lifespan theories, cognitive development, moral decision-making, faith development, the dynamics of moving and growing through the various stages contained in these theories, and where one positions the locus of control or authority. Relevant to this topic is how these theories can provide psychological insight into the ways people move through and cope with cultural change, especially the turbulent challenges of religious change in contemporary society.

By virtue of their global paradigm and their attention to the values and principles underlying various religious traditions, participants in this study appear to reflect Piaget's 'dialectic and synthetic' functions at the formal operational level; Kohlberg's 'principled understanding of fairness' and in some cases 'loyalty to being' processes of moral decision-making for males; Gilligan's 'standard of relationship and care' in moral decision-making for women; Fowler's 'conjunctive' and in some cases 'universalizing' stages in faith development; and Slee's additional pattern of 'alienation', 'awakening' and 'relationality' in the faith development of women. At least in the areas of shamanism and spirituality, all our participants seem to have moved beyond the early 'formal operational', 'law and order', 'individuative-reflective', and 'alienation' stages in which life and its challenges are to be handled in a black-and-white manner with fixed rules, rigid boundaries, and clear statements of good and bad/right and wrong.

Most of these participants have been protective of their efforts to establish and maintain quality relationships with all life, and many spoke of a freedom they felt in finding their own voices through their shamanic work. For the practitioners in particular, their work as ones who create bridges between the ordinary and non-ordinary worlds through their teaching and healing has found resonance with the ways in which people are known, within the developmental theories mentioned above, to move from one stage to another. The fear generally prompted by the relativism accompanying stage changes is best addressed by meeting those who have already moved through the turmoil of change, and reached the next stage of understanding and insight. In that way, these shamanic practitioners regularly help people to work through the fears of growth and its associated changes.

Of what significance is this information? First of all, these participants appear to have successfully moved through some difficult periods of relativism and emerged with considerable clarity about values and principles that underlie religious rules, laws and sets of beliefs. Second, it also appears that many in the world today, including religious leaders, may be abstract thinkers, but the paradigms that guide their moral decision-making processes often reflect early operational thinking, and an attachment to laws and dualisms that leave little or no room for diversity and pluralism. From the standpoint of developmental theory, their fears about the relativism of post-modernity are part of the turmoil inherent in having the opportunity to move to a 'principle-centred' and/or 'relational' way of making moral decisions. However, without communities of 'kindred spirits' who have already moved to the principle-centred, relational perspective and are willing or able to offer support and encouragement for the necessary 'surrender', those experiencing the stress of relativism may allow themselves to be propelled with great force back into their law-and-order comfort zone – often with a fundamentalist zeal for concrete, rigid boundaries that are perceived to provide a sense of security and protection.

Finally, the presence of these participants, who have followed various paths in moving to a principle-centred, relational perspective, shows that the transition is possible. Indeed, in a world that requires a global perspective for its survival, religious and governmental leaders will be ill-equipped to function effectively if they do not internalize a more global, principle-centred and relational way of dealing with difference, value, and meaning.

The Patriarchal Paradigm

Related to the struggle of learning to grow through change and diversity with values and principles as guides and signposts, which can potentially lead to new expressions of religious laws and rules, is an overall paradigm of patriarchy that has been present in Western society for millennia. Presented more fully in Chapter Two, this paradigm has several important aspects. Furthermore, the unconscious internalization of this paradigm by both men and women has often prevented the development of a new paradigm that better serves all of humanity.

Of particular importance for contemporary society is recognizing that this internalized and institutionalized patriarchal paradigm feeds and maintains a mindset that does not understand difference without assuming inherent inequality, and requiring that one perspective be 'the best'. On a societal scale, it has a parallel with the cognitive and psychological stages of concrete, dualistic thinking, and moral decision-making. These stages assume an external locus of control that prompts fearful adherence to law and order, and a vision of relativism as something evil, rather than as a potential source of growth into a new way of thinking and viewing the world. It also frames efforts that involve the other 'inferior' functions named above as insufficient and unworkable, because the 'either/or' perspective obscures the option of drawing upon a variety of functions. It is significant that in a patriarchal paradigm the experience of women, who approach moral decision-making and faith from the perspective of relationality and the common good, is not considered of value.

The participants did not appear to reflect elements in a patriarchal paradigm, though certain features seemed to reflect the larger society. From a gender perspective, five of the six practitioners were male, and five of the six participants were female. During the participant observation sessions, several men were present, but most of the participants were women. Practitioners were primarily in their thirties, and the ages of participants spanned several decades. Based on these facts, one might initially wonder if the predominance of males as practitioners and of females as participants actually represents an internalized patriarchal perspective. Practically speaking, those who are drawn to this work come from cultures with patriarchal dimensions. However, the ways in which these shamanic practitioners and their community members have perceived the world and worked together have fallen more in line with a non-patriarchal model. I did not detect competition among the different practitioners, though its presence on some scale would not be unusual – especially when they must support themselves financially through their work.

All the participants appeared to assume an inner locus of control for determining steps for personal growth, though 'listening to spirit' and/or guidance from spiritual allies is considered part of the shamanic process. Following that, the legitimizing authority for all participants was either self or their relationship with their own spiritual guidance. That relationship has been part of a larger kinship system of relationships with all life, which in turn has called for collaboration, empowerment, inclusion, honouring experience and feeling, respecting nature, attending to spirituality, peacefully resolving conflict, and creating supportive networks of people with similar perspectives. In these ways the participants have clearly reflected a way of functioning that is not patriarchal.

Significance of the Findings

One of the consistent themes in the literature describing the contemporary transformation of religion has been the gradual shift in consciousness towards a global perspective and a global spirituality. Worldwide communication systems provide regular reminders that the earth can no longer function as if all societies were separate and totally independent of each other. At the same time, cultural differences that were previously unknown or not discussed must now be addressed and resolved. Though many other societies may also operate in a patriarchal paradigm, the West has certainly done so for millennia. Because of that, the relativism, pluralism and diversity that have ushered in the deconstruction of institutions and ways of living that were familiar, have caused extreme anxiety, concern and fear about whether anything can rise from the remnants of what seems to be dissolving in our midst. Add to that the fragmentation of memory and tradition, the fast pace of modern life in the West, and the fact that increasing numbers of people are becoming better educated, embracing an inner locus of control that prompts them to 'think for themselves' rather than just assume the legitimizing authority of patriarchal institutions, and it is easy to see why many observers wonder how all this conflict will be resolved successfully.

Conclusion

This study reveals how three sets of contemporary shamanic practitioners and their communities in Scotland have somehow shifted their consciousness into a global awareness of inter-relatedness; tapped into traditions and memories that contain what they perceive to be fundamental values and principles that had been original catalysts for the development of those traditions; and embraced a system of shamanism that actually reflects core elements found cross-culturally in many indigenous shamanic societies, yet recognizes the validity of diverse expressions of those elements. From a developmental perspective, the individuals operate primarily from a place of relationality and principle-centred decision-making that can experience global spirituality. These participants have claimed a worldwide spirituality that sees a role for religion if it functions as guide and servant, not master and judge. They also exemplify a type of serial 'seekership' – one in which people follow a plurality of paths that may include shamanism, but not to the exclusion of all else. The new paradigm of spirituality and religion reflects this quality of openness to diversity and change.

Chapter Nine

Seeing Differently – A New Paradigm of Spirituality and Religion

Owning My Own Perspective

As this book comes to a conclusion, I am compelled to remind myself and the reader that the ways I have approached, observed, listened, understood, interpreted and written about what I have learned flow through the filters formed by my life experiences. Of course, I have worked hard to be open, objective, academically rigorous, and focused in ways that honour both cognitive and intuitive approaches to gathering and integrating new information. However, I still see the world from a developmental perspective, and I also understand what it is like to have a sudden 'a-ha' moment that reveals a 'bigger picture' which I had previously been unable to see before me. Though I strive to hold a clear and positive vision of life with its many possibilities, I am conscious also of the potential for power struggles to emerge and create challenges. Finally, I think it is of great importance to hold a space for 'not knowing', and for discovering something new – even when doing so may challenge dearly held beliefs.

The New Paradigm of Spirituality and Religion

Shifting the Paradigm

Kuhn reminded us in Chapter One that paradigms 'work' until they increasingly falter in their ability to address problems in a helpful manner. At first, people following a particular paradigm just assume the 'faltering' is an anomaly, but when it continues they start looking for alternatives able to do a better job. However, the malfunction causes great stress for those facing such a dilemma.

Institutional religions are currently faltering in their ability to help people move through transformational change in meaningful ways. There are many reasons for this, some of which have been identified in this book.

However, the faltering continues, and in the process spirituality is beginning to emerge that has greater relevance than the institutional religions which for millennia, in Western culture, have operated with a patriarchal paradigm of 'power over'. Richard Roberts addresses this issue, and goes on to say that 'Unless and until religious traditions are judged in the light of their capacity to service primary human needs, they will remain both redundant or dangerous, or both' (Roberts: 204). In a similar vein, Matthew Fox says that 'when religion speaks only in the name of authority, rather than with the voice of compassion, its message becomes meaningless' (Fox, 2001: 332). From a historical perspective, theologian Karen Armstrong says we are in a second Axial Age. The first one, occurring from 800 to 200 BCE, brought the emergence of the great world religions as a response to the violence and suffering that prevailed in society. To her, this one has similar qualities, but its roots lie in the economic, social, political and intellectual revolutions that have resulted in 'an entirely different scientific and rational concept of the nature of truth'. Armstrong reflects on this, saying, 'We are – all of us – at one of those junctions in history when we are holding ourselves, our past, our future, and our integrity in the palms of our own hands. This is a moment when, if we allow that integrity to fall out, we might never recover it in the same way' (Armstrong: 36).

Describing the New Paradigm

What is the 'new paradigm' referred to throughout this book? The new paradigm of spirituality and religion, which became clearer to me as I interviewed the participants in the study, is a worldview that starts by shifting into a *global consciousness of inter-relatedness with all life*. Not unlike Matthew Fox's description of spirituality as compassion, this consciousness is a spiritual one, because it moves attention beyond the self to responsibility and care in all relationships. *Though religion can offer support and guidance to spiritual consciousness, it does not really control it.* In fact, religion more usually functions as the 'legitimate authority' for the doctrines and dogmas that describe original experiences and meaning. In a world of transformational change, successfully clinging to 'how things were' in the past is almost impossible. Drawing upon Halbwachs, when the lived memory of a spiritual experience has been translated into religious doctrines and dogmas that have then become distant from that experience, the mystics move in to recover meaning through direct experience. The shamanic practitioners I interviewed fulfilled that role by drawing upon, and passing on, their *lineage of spirituality*.

Another aspect of this new paradigm is understanding that *spirituality and religion, like notions of 'the sacred', are themselves transforming*, and can best be

described through working definitions that guide, and do not stifle, this process. Furthermore, those who embrace the lived experience of global consciousness often undergo an additional quantum leap into the assumption
of responsibility as *co-creators of emerging global spiritualities* that reflect relationships with the 'essence' of the planet – the *anima mundi*, or world soul.

Implications

The implications of this shift are significant. This global consciousness is
emerging among growing number of people, not just shamanic practitioners
in Scotland. In ways not previously experienced, many are claiming an
identity that begins with self and extends to include self within family, local
community, nation, hemisphere and the entire globe. Personal identities
are nested in expanding circles of connection, much like an individual musician can be a soloist, part of a small section within an orchestra, and a
member of the full orchestra, all at the same time. The person is the same,
but the identity subtly shifts and adjusts as the circles widen – without
detracting from the musician's fundamental ability or need to be a fine per-
former in each of those circles.

   Another implication of this shift is the challenge it poses to the existing
patriarchal paradigm. Because patriarchy functions through a hierarchy
based on essential inequality, people who have internalized that paradigm
perceive pluralism and diversity as enemies of 'traditional values'. For
them, 'traditional values' usually refer to rules, laws and assumed 'truths',
rather than to the values and principles underlying those more concrete
expressions.

   The growing presence and voice of women in spiritual arenas beyond religion also challenge the patriarchal paradigm. Closely related to that is the
gradual shift towards valuing some of the qualities typically considered by
Western societies as inherent in women, and therefore below the 'male
norm'. One such shift is the apportioning of credence and value to personal
experience and ways of knowing that are intuitive.

   Related to the above is a final theme, which centres on 'growing up' spiritually. Just as teenagers or young adults must trust that they have the qualities and skills needed to survive in the world, all people can benefit from
learning how to access the underlying spiritual and moral values and principles they need when faced with new, unexpected circumstances. This
includes, especially for women, knowing they can address issues of inclusiv-
ity, relationality and the 'greater good' when making moral decisions. This
requires an inner locus of control, but it could also be supported and encouraged by religious leaders who create opportunities for people to safely

question, doubt, search and explore within parameters that help them identify those values, principles and relationships that can serve as guides on the spiritual journey. Forming various types of community is an essential way of supporting these processes, and helping people learn the skills needed for working through differences and conflicts.

Co-creating the Future

Where do we go from here? Ideally, religion and spirituality form a helpful partnership that serves the well-being of society. However, unless religious leaders and people of influence address their fears about what will happen if or when they let go of power and control, history shows that they are condemning their religious traditions to extinction. Furthermore, marginalizing people who have searching questions, nagging doubts and challenging ideas primarily affirms the perception of such individuals that religion has no place for them. It also does not assist them in developing the skills of discernment and empowerment needed to live in this complex world.

I am reminded of the Lakota holy man Black Elk, who at the end of his life wondered why the marvellous vision he had experienced in his youth – one in which the tree of life was surrounded by a sacred hoop uniting all life – had not come to pass. Indeed, the Wounded Knee Massacre had taken place, and Black Elk could see only that the tree had withered, and the sacred hoop had been broken. However, even then Black Elk dared to hope that 'some little root of the sacred tree still lives', and to ask that 'it may leaf and bloom and fill with singing birds' – not for himself, but for his people (Black Elk: 210).

As Karen Armstrong has pointed out, our world is struggling with massive issues that our old paradigms about life, including spirituality and religion, are failing to handle adequately. Because of that, we are at a point of choice. I hope that this book has provided information and insights that will foster understanding and stimulate hope for creative problem-solving.

As in the first Axial Age, let us rise to the occasion and meet the challenges before us. I for one stand in hope with Black Elk that the tree of life will bloom again, and that the sacred hoop will be restored.

Bibliography

Ankarloo, B. and Henningsen, G. (1993), *Early Modern European Witchcraft – Centres and Peripheries*. Oxford: Oxford University Press.

Armstrong, K. (2005/2006), 'A new axial age', *What Is Enlightenment?* 31, December–February 2005/6, 346.

ASERVIC (2000), 'Spirituality – a white paper of the Association for Spiritual, Ethical, and Religious Values in Counseling'. Orlando: The American Counseling Association. www.aservic.org

Backman, L. and Hultkrantz, A. (1978), *Studies in Lapp Shamanism*. Stockholm, Sweden: Almquist and Wiksell International.

Baggett, J.P. (2001), 'Review: religion as a chain of memory', *Journal for the Scientific Study of Religion* 40(4): 779–80.

Barker, E. (1995), *New Religious Movements – A Practical Introduction*. London: HMSO.

Barrett, R. (1998), *Liberating the Corporate Soul – Building a Visionary Organization*. Oxford: Butterworth-Heinemann.

Barrett, R. (2006), *Building a Values-Driven Organization – A Whole System Approach to Cultural Transformation*. London: Elsevier.

Bates, B. (1983), *The Way of Wyrd – Tales of an Anglo-Saxon Sorcerer*. London: Arrow Books.

Bates, B. (1996), *The Wisdom of Wyrd*. London: Rider.

Beck, D. and Cowan, C. (1996), *Spiral Dynamics: Mastering Values, Leadership, and Change*. Oxford: Blackwell.

Beckford, J.A. and Luckmann, T. (eds) (1989), *The Changing Face of Religion*. London: Sage Publications.

Berger, P.L. (1973), *The Social Reality of Religion (The Sacred Canopy)*. London: Penguin Books.

Berger, P.L. (1999), 'The desecularization of the world: a global overview', in P.L. Berger (ed.), *The Desecularization of the World: Resurgent Religion and World Politics*. Washington, DC: Ethics and Public Policy Center, 1–18.

Black Elk (2000), *Black Elk Speaks – Being the Life Story of a Holy Man of the Oglala Sioux*. Lincoln: University of Nebraska Press.

Blacker, C. (1989), 'The seer as a healer in Japan', in H.R.E. Davidson (ed.), *The Seer in Celtic and Other Traditions*. Edinburgh: John Donald Publishers, 116–23.

Borg, M.J. (1995), *Meeting Jesus Again for the First Time*. New York: HarperSanFrancisco.

Bowman, M. (2000), 'More of the same? Christianity, vernacular religion and alternative spirituality in Glastonbury', in S. Sutcliffe and M. Bowman (eds), *Beyond New Age – Exploring Alternative Spirituality*. Edinburgh: Edinburgh University Press, 83–104.

Briggs, R. (1998), *Witches and Neighbours: The Social and Cultural Context of European Witchcraft*. London: Penguin Books.

Brown, C. (2005), 'Response to the book *The Spiritual Revolution*', in conference 'The Spiritual Revolution – Why Religion is Giving Way to Spirituality in Contemporary Britain'. University of Edinburgh: New College.

Brown, M.F. (1989), 'Dark side of the shaman', in J. Narby and F. Huxley (eds), *Shamans Through Time: 500 Years on the Path to Knowledge*. New York: Jeremy P. Tarcher/Putnam, 321.

Bruce, S. (2002), *God is Dead – Secularization in the West*. Oxford: Blackwell.

Burgess, M.C. (2002), 'Elements of shamanism in Scottish folklore'. MSc dissertation. Edinburgh: University of Edinburgh.

Cameron, G. (1997), 'Spiritual crisis in early Irish literature and later folklore'. MSc dissertation. Edinburgh: University of Edinburgh.

Carrette, J.R. (2005), *Selling Spirituality: The Silent Takeover of Religion*. London: Routledge.

Chittister, J.D. (1998), *Heart of Flesh – A Feminist Spirituality for Women and Men*. Cambridge: Eerdmans.

Choi, C. (2003), 'Artistry of urban Korean shamans', in G. Harvey (ed.), *Shamanism – A Reader*. London: Routledge, 170–85.

Coleman, S. and Collins, P. (eds) (2004), *Religion, Identity and Change. Religion and Theology in Interdisciplinary Perspectives Series*. Hants, England: Ashgate.

Connolly, P. (1997), 'A psychology of possession' (unpublished lecture). Lancaster, England: British Association for the Study of Religion.

Corbett, J. (1990), *Religion in America*. Englewood Cliffs, NJ: Prentice-Hall.

Corbetta, P. (2003), *Social Research Theory, Methods and Techniques*. London: Sage Publications.

Cox, J.L. (1998), *Rational Ancestors – Scientific Rationality and African Indigenous Religions*. Cardiff: Cardiff Academic Press.

Cox, J.L. (1999), 'Intuiting religion – a case for preliminary definitions', in J. Platvoet and A. Molendizk (eds), *Pragmatics of Defining Religion*. Boston: Brill, 84, 267–84.

Daniels, M. (2005), *Shadow, Self, Spirit – Essays in Transpersonal Psychology*. Exeter: Imprint-Academic.

Davie, G. (2000), *Religion in Modern Europe – A Memory Mutates*. Oxford: Oxford University Press.

Davie, G. (2002), 'From obligation to consumption: patterns of religion in Northern Europe at the start of the twenty-first century', paper presented at Bishops' Day Conference. The text can be accessed online at www.stalbans.anglican.org/daviepres.htm

Davis, W. (1995), 'Shamans as botanical researchers', in J. Narby and F. Huxley (eds), *Shamans Through Time: 500 Years on the Path to Knowledge*. New York: Jeremy P. Tarcher/Putnam, 286–90.

de Certeau, M. (1997), 'How is Christianity thinkable today?', in G. Ward (ed.), *The Post-modern God – A Theological Reader*. Oxford: Blackwell 142–58.

Desroche, H. (1973), *Jacob and the Angel – An Essay in Sociologies of Religion*. Amherst: University of Massachusetts Press.

Drury, N. (1996), *Shamanism*. Shaftesbury: Element.

Durkheim, E. (2001), *The Elementary Forms of Religious Life*. Oxford: Oxford University Press.

Edinburgh Shamanic Centre (2003), 'Calendar of events for September to December', in *The Edinburgh Shamanic Centre Initial Programme*.

Edinburgh Shamanic Centre (2004a), 'The shamanic workshop facilitators', in *The Edinburgh Shamanic Centre Primavera Programme 2004*, 1: 11–12.

Edinburgh Shamanic Centre (2004b), The Edinburgh Shamanic Centre Website, www.shamaniccentre.com, 2004.

Eliade, M. (1964), *Shamanism: Archaic Techniques of Ecstasy*. Princeton: Princeton University Press.

Fienup-Riordan, A. (1994), *Boundaries and Passages – Rule and Ritual in Yup'ik Eskimo Oral Tradition*. Norman, Oklahoma: University of Oklahoma Press.

Findhorn Foundation (2003), 'Welcome to the Findhorn Foundation' – leaflet, Findhorn Foundation.

Findhorn Foundation (2004), Findhorn Foundation Website – www.findhorn.org

Flanagan, K. (1996), 'Introduction', in K. Flanagan and P.C. Jupp (eds), *Post-modernity, Sociology and Religion*. London: Macmillan, 1–13.

Flanagan, K. (2004), 'Preface', in S. Coleman and P. Collins (eds), *Religion, Identity and Change – Perspectives on Global Transformations*. Hants, England: Ashgate, viii–xii.

Flood, G. (1999), *Beyond Phenomenology – Rethinking the Study of Religion*. London: Cassell.

Fontana, D. (1999), 'Eastern ideas and Western thought', in D. Lorimer, C. Clarke, J. Cosh, M. Payne and A. Mayne (eds), *Wider Horizons – Explorations in Science and Human Experience*. Leven, Fife, Scotland: The Scientific Medical Network, 193–9.

Fowler, J.W. (1995), *Stages of Faith – The Psychology of Human Development and the Quest for Meaning*. New York: HarperCollins Paperback.

Fowler, J.W. (1996), *Faithful Change – The Personal and Public Challenges of Post-modern Life*. Nashville, Tennessee: Abingdon Press.

Fox, M. (1999), *A Spirituality Named Compassion*. Rochester, Vermont: Inner Traditions International.

Fox, M. (2000), *Original Blessing: A Primer in Creation Spirituality*. New York: Jeremy Tarcher.

Fox, M. (2001), *One River, Many Wells – Wisdom Springing from Global Faiths*. Dublin: Gateway.

Geertz, A.W. (1992), *The Invention of Prophecy: Continuity and Meaning in Hopi Indian Religion*. Los Angeles: University of California Press.

Geertz, A.W. (1996), 'Contemporary problems in the study of native North American religions with special reference to the Hopis', *American Indian Quarterly*, Summer/Fall 20(3/4): 393–415.

Geertz, C. (1968), *Islam Observed – Religious Development in Morocco and Indonesia*. Chicago: The University of Chicago Press.

Geertz, C. (1973), *The Interpretation of Cultures – Selected Essays*. New York: Basic Books.

Geertz, C. (1973), 'Religion as a cultural system', in C. Geertz, *The Interpretation of Cultures: Selected Essays*. New York: Basic Books, 62–82.

Gerth, H.H. and Mills, C.W. (eds) (1948), *From Max Weber: Essays in Sociology*. London: Routledge & Kegan Paul.

Gilliat-Ray, S. (2001), 'Review: religion as a chain of memory', *Journal of Contemporary Religion* 16(1): 125–6.

Gilligan, C. (1993), *In A Different Voice: Psychological Theory and Women's Development*. Cambridge, Mass.: Harvard University Press.

Ginzburg, C. (1991), *Ecstasies – Deciphering the Witches' Sabbath*. London: Penguin Books.

Glass-Coffin, B. (1998), *The Gift of Life – Female Spirituality and Healing in Northern Peru*. Albuquerque: University of New Mexico Press.

Gonçalves, C. (2004), 'Thank you great-grandmother', *The Edinburgh Shamanic Centre Primavera Programme 2004*, 13.

Griffin, D.R. (2000), *Religion and Scientific Naturalism: Overcoming the Conflicts*. Albany, NY: State University of New York Press.

Halbwachs, M. (1992), *On Collective Memory*. Chicago: The University of Chicago Press.

Harner, M. (1990), *The Way of the Shaman*. New York: Harper & Row.

Harper, C.L. (1989), *Exploring Social Change*. New Jersey: Prentice Hall.

Harvey, G. (ed.) (2003), *Shamanism – A Reader*. London: Routledge.

Heelas, P. (1996), 'De-traditionalization of religion and self', in K. Flanagan and P.C. Jupp (eds), *Post-modernity, Sociology and Religion*. London: Macmillan, 64–82.

Heelas, P., Woodhead, L., Seel, B., Szerszynski, B., and Tusting, K., (eds) (2005), *The Spiritual Revolution – Why Religion is Giving Way to Spirituality*. Oxford: Blackwell.

Hegel, G.W.F. (1988), *L'Esprit du Christianisme et son destin*. Paris: Vrin.

Hervieu-Léger, D. (1999), 'Religion as memory', in J. Platvoet and A. Molendizk (eds), *Pragmatics of Defining Religion*. Boston: Brill, 73–92.

Hervieu-Léger, D. (2000), *Religion as a Chain of Memory*. Cambridge, UK: Polity Press.

Hodge, D. and Boddie, S. (2007), 'Social workers' personal spiritual characteristics and their conceptualizations of spirituality and religion: a mixed method study', *Journal of Religion and Spirituality in Social Work*, 26(1), 53–70.

Honko, L. (1969), 'Role-taking of the shaman', *Tenemos* 4, 26–55.

Hoppál, M. (1996), 'Shamanism in a post-modern age', *Folklore* 2 (electronic version), December 1996, 1–6.

Hoppál, M. (1997), 'Nature worship in Siberian shamanism' *Folklore* 4 (electronic version), June 1997, 1–11.

Hoppál, M. (2001), 'Cosmic symbolism in Siberian shamanhood', in J. Pentikäinen, H. Saressalo and C. Taksami, *Shamanhood Symbolism and Epic*. Budapest: Akadémaiai Kiadó.

Houston, J. (2000), *Jump Time – Shaping Your Future in a World of Radical Change*. New York: Jeremy P. Tarcher/Putnam.

Hultkrantz, A. (1973), 'A definition of shamanism', *Temenos: Studies in Comparative Religion*. Presentations by scholars in Denmark, Finland, Norway and Sweden, 20500 Turku 50, Finland (26): 25–37.

Hutton, R. (1999), *The Triumph of the Moon: A History of Modern Pagan Witchcraft*. Oxford: Oxford University Press.

Hutton, R. (2001), *Shamans – Siberian Spirituality and the Western Imagination*. London: Hambledon.

Hutton, R. (2003), *Witches, Druids, and King Arthur*. London: Hambledon.

Ingerman, S. (1991), *Soul Retrieval: Mending the Fragmented Self*. San Francisco: HarperSanFrancisco.

Ingerman, S. (1993), *Welcome Home: Following the Soul's Journey Home*. San Francisco: HarperSanFrancisco.

Ingerman, S. (2000), *Medicine for the Earth – How to Transform Personal and Environmental Toxins*. New York: Three Rivers Press.

IONS (2007), *The 2007 Shift Report – Evidence of a World Transforming*. Petaluma, Calif.: The Institute of Noetic Sciences. www.noetic.org

Jakobsen, M.D. (1999), *Shamanism: Traditional and Contemporary Approaches to the Mastery of Spirits and Healing*. Providence, RI: Berghahn Books.

Johnson, P.C. (2003), 'Shamanism from Ecuador to Chicago', in G. Harvey (ed.), *Shamanism – A Reader*. London: Routledge, 334–54.

Jung, C.G. (1967), *Alchemical Studies*. London: Routledge & Kegan Paul.

Kalweit, H. (1992), *Shamans, Healers, and Medicine Men*. Boston: Shambhala.

Kendall, L. (1987), *Shamans, Housewives, and Other Restless Spirits – Women in Korean Ritual Life*. Honolulu: University of Hawaii Press.

Kim, C. (2003), *Korean Shamanism – The Cultural Paradox*. Hants, England: Ashgate.

King, U. (1998a), 'Introduction', in U. King (ed.), *Faith and Praxis in a Postmodern Age*. London: Cassell, 1–14.

King, U. (1998b), 'Spirituality in a postmodern age: faith and praxis in new contexts', in U. King (ed.), *Faith and Praxis in a Postmodern Age*. London: Cassell, 94–112.

King, U. (2001), 'Introduction: spirituality, society and the millennium – wasteland, wilderness or new vision?', in U. King (ed.), *Spirituality and Society in the New Millennium*. Brighton: Sussex Academic Press, 284.

Knoblauch, H. (2001), 'Review: religion as a chain of memory', *Journal of Religion* 81(3): 527–8.

Knott, K. (2003), 'The sense and nonsense of "community"', in S.J. Sutcliffe (ed.), *Religion: Empirical Studies*. Hants, England: Ashgate, 67–89.

Kuhn, T. (1996), *The Structure of Scientific Revolutions* (third edn). London: University of Chicago Press.

Lancaster, B.L. (2004), *Approaches to Consciousness – The Marriage of Science and Mysticism*. Hants, England: Palgrave Macmillan.

Larner, C. (2000), *Enemies of God – The Witch-Hunt in Scotland*. Edinburgh: John Donald.

Laszlo, E. (1999), 'Consciousness-Creativity-Responsibility', in D. Lorimer, C. Clarke, J. Cosh, M. Payne and A. Mayne (eds), *Wider Horizons – Explorations in Science and Human Experience*. Leven, Fife, Scotland: The Scientific Medical Network, 323–7.

LeCompte, M.D. and Schensul, J.J. (1999), *Designing and Conducting Ethnographic Research*. London: AltaMira Press/Sage Publications.

Lendrick Lodge (2004a), Lendrick Lodge Holistic Centre (leaflet). Lendrick Lodge, Scotland.

Lendrick Lodge (2004b), Lendrick Lodge Spirit of Shamanism (leaflet). Lendrick Lodge, Scotland.

Lendrick Lodge (2004c), Lendrick Lodge Website – www.lendricklodge.com

Lévi-Strauss, C. (1949), 'Shamans as psychoanalysts', in J. Narby and F. Huxley (eds), *Shamans Through Time: 500 Years on the Path to Knowledge*. New York: Jeremy P. Tarcher/Putnam, 108–11.

Lévi-Strauss, C. (1962), 'Science and magic, two roads to knowledge', in J. Narby and F. Huxley (eds), *Shamans Through Time: 500 Years on the Path to Knowledge*. New York: Jeremy P. Tarcher/Putnam, 245–7.

Lewis, I.M. (1996), *Religion In Context*. Cambridge: Cambridge University Press.

Lewis, I.M. (2003), *Ecstatic Religion: A Study of Shamanism and Spirit Possession*. London: Routledge.

Lynch, G. (2007), *The New Spirituality – An Introduction to Progressive Belief in the Twenty-first Century*. London: I. B. Tauris.

Masterman, M. (1970), 'The nature of a paradigm', in I. Lakatos and A. Musgrave (eds), *Criticism and the Growth of Knowledge*. Cambridge: Cambridge University Press, 59–89.

McCutcheon, R.T. (ed.) (1999), *The Insider/Outsider Problem in the Study of Religion*. London: Cassell.

McCutcheon, R.T. (2005), 'Swapping stories in the classroom: the political implications of self-disclosure', electronic copy of lecture sent by author to M.C. Burgess. Tuscaloosa, Alabama, USA.

Merkur, D. (1985), 'Becoming half hidden: shamanism and initiation among the Inuit', *Stockholm Studies in Comparative Religion* 24: 305.

Narby, J. and Huxley, F. (eds) (2001), *Shamans Through Time: 500 Years on the Path to Knowledge*. New York: Jeremy P. Tarcher/Putnam.

Noel, D.C. (1999), *The Soul of Shamanism*. New York: Continuum.

Nora, P. (1996), *Realms of Memory – Rethinking the French Past*. New York: Columbia University Press.

Pearsall, J. (ed.) (2001), *The Concise Oxford Dictionary*. Oxford: Oxford University Press.

Pike, K.L. (1999), 'Etic and emic standpoints for the description of behaviour', in R.T. McCutcheon (ed.), *The Insider/Outsider Problem in the Study of Religion*. London: Cassell.

Potter, R.N. (2004), *Authentic Spirituality – The Direct Path to Consciousness*. St Paul: Llewellyn Publications.

Prozesky, M. (1984), *Religion and Ultimate Well-Being – An Explanatory Theory*. London: Macmillan.

Ravindra, R. (1999), 'Yoga and the future science of consciousness', in D. Lorimer, C. Clarke, J. Cosh, M. Payne and A. Mayne (eds), *Wider Horizons – Explorations in Science and Human Experience*. Leven, Fife, Scotland: The Scientific Medical Network, 186–92.

Roberts, R. (2002), *Religion, Theology and the Human Sciences*. Cambridge: Cambridge University Press.

Salisbury Centre (2003), *Autumn Programme*. Edinburgh: The Salisbury Centre, 48.

Salisbury Centre (2004), The Salisbury Centre website – www.salisburycentre.org

Santoro, F. (2000), *Introduzione agli aforismi provvisori della rete binaria del Sacro Cono*. Bologna: Sacred Cone Press.

Santoro, F. (2003a), *Astroshamanism, Book 1 – A Journey into the Inner Universe*. Forres, Scotland: Findhorn Press.

Santoro, F. (2003b), 'Calendar of events and workshops with Franco Santoro for Winter to Summer' (leaflet), Franco Santoro.

Santoro, F. (2004), Astroshamanism website – www.astroshamanism.org

Schensul, S.L., Schensul, J.J., and LeCompte, M.D. (1999), *Essential Ethnographic Methods*. London: AltaMira Press/Sage Publications.

Segal, R.A. (1986), 'The "De-sociologizing" of the sociology of religion', *The Scottish Journal of Religious Studies* VII, 1, Spring 1986, 5–28.

Senge, P.M. (1992), *The Fifth Discipline: the Art and Practice of the Learning Organization*. London: Century Business.

Shankar, S.S.R. (1982), The Art of Living Foundation. www.artofliving.org

Shaw, D.W. (2003), 'Reflections on Vatican II', personal notes of the author at New College Seminar, University of Edinburgh.

Shirokogoroff, S.M. (1935), *Psychomental Complex of the Tungus*. London: Kegan Paul.

Siikala, A-L. (1978), 'The rite technique of the Siberian shaman', in L. Honko, *FF Communications*. Helsinki: Academia Scientiarum Fennica, XCIII, 7–37.

Slee, N. (2004), *Women's Faith Development – Patterns and Processes*. Hants, England: Ashgate.

Smart, N. (1996), *Dimensions of the Sacred*. London: Fontana.

Smith, C.M. (1997), *Jung and Shamanism in Dialogue*. New York: Paulist Press.

Smith, L.T. (1999), *Decolonizing Methodologies*. London: Zed Books.

Smith, W.C. (1991), *The Meaning and End of Religion*. Minneapolis, Minn.: Fortress Press.

Smith, W.C. (1998), *Faith and Belief: The Difference Between Them*. Oxford: Oneworld Publications.

Stutley, M. (2003), *Shamanism – An Introduction*. London: Routledge.

Sutcliffe, S. (1997), 'Seekers, networks, and "new age"', *Scottish Journal of Religious Studies*, 18(2): 97–114.

Sutcliffe, S. (2000a), 'A colony of seekers: Findhorn in the 1990s', *Journal of Contemporary Religion*, 15(2): 215–31.

Sutcliffe, S. (2003), *Children of the New Age – A History of Spiritual Practices*. London: Routledge.

Sutcliffe, S. (2004), 'Unfinished business – devolving Scotland/devolving religion', in S. Coleman and P. Collins (eds), *Religion, Identity and Change*. Hants, England: Ashgate, 84–106.

Sutcliffe, S. and Bowman, M. (eds) (2000b), *Beyond New Age – Exploring Alternative Spirituality*. Edinburgh: Edinburgh University Press.

Tedlock, B. (2006), *The Woman in the Shaman's Body – Reclaiming the Feminine in Religion and Medicine*. London: Bantam Books.

Thevet, A. (1557), 'Ministers of the devil who learn about the secrets of nature', in P. Narby and F. Huxley (eds) (2001), *Shamans Through Time: 500 Years on the Path to Knowledge*. New York: Jeremy P. Tarcher/Putnam, 13–15.

Tice, L. (1976), The Pacific Institute website – www.thepacificinstitute.com

Trevarthen, G.A. (2003), 'Brightness of Brightness – Seeing Celtic Shamanism'. PhD thesis. Edinburgh: University of Edinburgh.

Tylor, E.B. (1871), 'Animism is the belief in spiritual beings', in J. Narby and F. Huxley (eds), *Shamans Through Time: 500 Years on the Path to Knowledge*. New York: Jeremy P. Tarcher/Putnam, 41–2.

Urry, J. (2002), 'Mobility and proximity', *Sociology* 36(2): 255–74.

Vitebsky, P. (2000), 'Shamanism', in G. Harvey, *Indigenous Religions – A Companion*. London: Routledge, 55–67.

Vitebsky, P. (2001), *The Shaman – Voyages of the Soul*. London: Duncan Baird Publishers.

Vitebsky, P. (2003), 'From cosmology to environmentalism', in G. Harvey (ed.), *Shamanism – A Reader*. London: Routledge, 276–98.

Wallis, R.J. (2003), *Shamanisms/neo-shamans – Ecstasy, Alternative Archaeologies and Contemporary Pagans*. London: Routledge.

Walsh, M.D. and Roger, N. (1990), *The Spirit of Shamanism*. Los Angeles: Jeremy P. Tarcher.

Ward, G. (ed.) (1997), *The Post-modern God – A Theological Reader*. Blackwell Readings in Modern Theology. Oxford: Blackwell.

WCFIA Publications (2000), 'Religion as a chain of memory', Harvard University, Cambridge, Mass., USA.

Weber, M. (1965), *The Sociology of Religion*. London: Methuen.

Whaling, F. (1995), 'Introduction', in R. Whaling (ed.), *Theory and Method in Religious Studies – Contemporary Approaches to the Study of Religion*. Berlin: Mouton de Gruyter.

Wightman, W.P.D. (1972), *Science in a Renaissance Society*. London: Hutchinson.

Wilber, K. (1999), 'An integral science of consciousness', in D. Lorimer, C. Clarke, J. Cosh, M. Payne and A. Mayne Leven (eds), *Wider Horizons – Explorations in Science and Human Experience*. Fife, Scotland: The Scientific Medical Network, 175–85.

Wilber, K. (2005), 'What is integral spirituality?' (first draft, June). Denver, Colorado: Integral Spiritual Center. www.integralinstitute.org

Woodhead, L. (2005), 'Shifts in church life – implications of the spiritual revolution', personal notes of M.C. Burgess from conference on 'The Spiritual Revolution – Why Religion is Giving Way to Spirituality' at New College, University of Edinburgh.

Yin, R.K. (1994), *Case Study Research Design and Methods*. London: Sage Publications.

Index